European Cinema

Also by Jill Forbes:

The Cinema in France: After the New Wave

Les Enfants du paradis

Contemporary France: Essays and Texts on Politics, Economics and Society
  (with Nick Hewlett)

French Cultural Studies (with Michael Kelly)

Also by Sarah Street:

British National Cinema

British Cinema in Documents

Cinema and State: The Film Industry and the British Government, 1927–84
  (with Margaret Dickinson)

Moving Performance: British Stage and Screen, 1890s–1920s (with Linda Fitzsimmons)

European Cinema

An Introduction

Jill Forbes and Sarah Street

palgrave

First published 2000 by
PALGRAVE
Houndmills, Basingstoke, Hampshire RG21 6X5 and
175 Fifth Avenue, New York, N. Y. 10010
Companies and representatives throughout the world

PALGRAVE is the new global academic imprint of St. Martin's Press LLC
Scholarly and Reference Division and Palgrave Publishers Ltd
(formerly Macmillan Press Ltd).

ISBN 0–333–75209–0 hardback
ISBN 0–333–75210–4 paperback

This book is printed on paper suitable for recycling and
made from fully managed and sustained forest sources.

A catalogue record for this book is available
from the British Library.

Library of Congress Cataloging-in-Publication Data

European cinema: an introduction/edited by Jill Forbes and Sarah Street.
      p.   cm.
   Includes bibliographical references and index.
   ISBN 0–333–75209–0—ISBN 0–333–75210–4 (pbk.)
   1. Motion pictures—Europe.   I. Forbes, Jill.   II. Street, Sarah.
PN1993.5.E8 E96 2000
791.43'094—dc21

                                                       00–031111

10   9   8   7   6   5   4   3   2   1
09 08 07 06 05 04 03 02 01 00

Printed and bound in Great Britain by
Creative Print & Design (Wales), Ebbw Vale

Contents

v

List of Illustrations

Acknowledgements

The authors gratefully acknowledge the support of the University of Bristol and of the Arts and Humanities Research Board in the preparation of this book. They have also benefited from the advice and help of many individuals and, in particular, Ross Chambers, Peter Evans, David Forgács, Jeremy Hicks, Jo Labanyi, Geoffrey Nowell-Smith, Keith Reader, Richard Taylor, and Ingrid Wassenaar. Special thanks are due to Michael Liversidge who, as Dean of the Faculty of Arts at Bristol, first encouraged the development of a course in European cinema and to the students whose comments and reactions did much to determine its final shape. We would also like to thank the following for permission to reproduce illustrations: Artificial Eye Ltd; the Bibliothèque du film (BIFI), Paris; the British Film Institute Stills, Posters and Designs Department; Igor Gnevashev; the Kobal Collection; Professor Richard Taylor.

Every effort has been made to trace all copyright holders, but if any have been inadvertently overlooked, the publishers will be pleased to make the necessary arrangements at the first opportunity.

Bristol and London

Introduction

This book was inspired by the attempts of its authors to design and teach an undergraduate course on European cinema. In so doing we were led to consider not just how European cinema might be defined but also how it might be studied, and we encountered the immediate difficulty that while there is a large, and growing, body of academic work in English devoted to national cinemas in Europe, there was until recently very little academic interest in questions of European cinema.

One of the reasons for this can be found in the way film studies have developed in the last twenty or even thirty years. Although the study of film as a cultural phenomenon – that is, outside the practice-related approach of art schools and film schools – is now well-established in Britain and the United States, it has been much slower to develop in continental Europe. Thus although there are several excellent textbooks which can be recommended to students wishing to be initiated into the academic study of films, such as those by Bordwell and Thompson, Cook, or Monaco, the case studies they use and the paradigms they establish almost always refer to Hollywood cinema which is considered the 'norm' or the 'classic'. In a different way this is also true of film theory, since it has almost always been tested in relation to Hollywood cinema whose characteristics it is, more often than not, designed to elucidate. A case in point might be Mulvey's celebrated and frequently reprinted essay 'Visual Pleasure and Narrative Cinema' which was explicitly conceived to account for the pleasurable experience of viewing 'classic' or 'mainstream' Hollywood cinema (Mulvey, 1975). The global reach of English-language publishing houses, together with the earlier institutionalisation of film studies in English-language territories, have compounded this emphasis. While 'film theory' has often relied on a range of sources, many not written in the English language, it is invariably when theoretical works are published in English translation that they begin to achieve an international impact and to inform film studies generally. For example, the success of Kracauer's *From Caligari to Hitler*, which in 1947 persuasively offered an analysis of German cinema that Anglo-Americans wished to read, overshadowed the same author's equally interesting – but less apparently politically relevant – work on French culture, not translated until 1995. Comparable observations might be made about the reputations of Christian Metz or more recently of Gilles Deleuze and, pre-eminently, of Russian-language writers, whose contribution to film theory has had a chequered history in the west and one which only recently began to be explored, in the path-breaking work of Taylor and Christie.

However, another tradition began to emerge in the 1990s. In the work of Sorlin in Paris, in that of Dyer and Vincendeau at Warwick and, above all, in the continuing investigations of Nowell-Smith and his collaborators, we can detect an urgent interest in questions of European cinema and an increasing dissatisfaction with the way film histories have been written in the past. Political developments such as the fall of the Berlin Wall, *glasnost* and *perestroika*, as well as the completion of the Single European Market and the creation of the European Union, have naturally had their part to play in this upsurge of interest. It was Mikhail Gorbachev who tellingly referred to the 'single European home', since when commentators have continued to explore the cultural implications of his remark. In their introduction to a selection of papers from a conference on popular European cinema, presciently held in 1989, two months before the breach of the Berlin Wall, Dyer and Vincendeau wrote: 'Europe has never appeared a more contested notion, as the European Community seeks to engineer a new economic and political (and cultural?) unity into place, and as the nature and allegiances of eastern Europe change daily as we write (summer 1991)' (Dyer and Vincendeau, 2).

From 1992 the effects of a European Union policy for the media began to be seen, on European film production and, although less clearly, on film distribution. At the same time the increasingly global nature of the media industries, of which cinema is now a small part, gave rise to a counter-interest in the heritage of the past, a heritage whose specificities, it is sometimes feared, are rapidly being submerged or effaced. The funds the European Union allocates to research and conservation, spectacularly evident at the time of the celebration of the centenary of cinema in 1995/6, have already enhanced our knowledge of European cinema and will certainly continue to do so in the future. As archives are opened and films are restored, and as new technologies make previously little-known films more readily and widely available, our critical assumptions and our canons will require revision. For the present, however, there remain immense historiographical lacunae in the study of the first century of European cinema.

The contents and organisation of this book require some explanation. Part I is an introductory survey which attempts to place European cinema in its economic and political context and to raise questions relating to its ideology, aesthetics and style. The intention is to introduce students to areas of debate and to suggest ways in which they can explore such topics further. There are major difficulties in attempting to survey the economy of European cinema which were raised by Thomas Guback, as long ago as 1969, in his fascinating account of the international film industry. He wrote:

> On the elementary question of foreign films coming into a country several standards exist. One nation may state this in terms of total meters of

exposed film imported. Another nation may decide to tabulate the number of pictures that have actually gone through the customs office. A third may base its measure on the number submitted to censorship. And a fourth may count the business licenses issued which permit films to be exhibited. (Guback, 37)

Not only are statistics collected differently according to the territory, they are also, frequently, massaged for political and economic purposes. From 1992, uniform statistics on the economics of film-making and film distribution within the European Union have, in theory, been collected and are published, but for earlier periods comparative work, except of a very broad-brush kind, is virtually non-existent. Kristin Thompson's meticulous and groundbreaking study of American cinema in the pre-Second World War world film market attempted to 'lay the groundwork for further, more detailed studies' (Thompson, x) but to date these have not been forthcoming. As we have found in attempting to describe the economics of European cinema, the available information depends on the questions which have been asked, most of which relate to Hollywood in Europe. The account we present here is therefore distilled from existing sources. Its broad outlines are, we hope, accurate, but there is an urgent need for the detail to be filled out with further research of a comparative kind.

If the economics of European cinema are difficult to study, what of its politics? Here film scholars are at the mercy of events which have had a direct impact on their approach to their subject. The Russian Revolution and the rise of totalitarian dictatorships precipitated movements of film personnel across Europe, and ultimately, in many cases, to Hollywood, to the greater benefit of the American film industry. The censorship of Russian films in the west, and in the Soviet Union; the banning of American films from many European territories before and during the Second World War; the Cold War and the Iron Curtain, which for many years closed eastern archives to scholars and filtered the export of eastern-bloc films to the west; and the ruthlessness of the American film industry in dressing up its commercial policies as the triumph of democracy, all these factors have affected not only the interpretation of films that are released, but perhaps more important, whether films are released in the first place. As Taylor and Christie suggest, and as is discussed in this book, the marketing success of *The Battleship Potemkin* is an excellent illustration of the way in which the international availability of the output of an entire film industry can be determined by political considerations whose pertinence may have long since disappeared.

This is not merely a question of overt censorship, whose study has tended to fetishise the lost fragment, to the exclusion, as is suggested here, of much else that is interesting. The censorship and certification regimes, which exist in all countries, contribute to the creation of images which will be acceptable in national and international markets and which will conform to the picture each country desires to present to the outside world. An earlier and perhaps simplistic view of censorship under communism and fascism has given way, in more recent scholarship, to detailed national studies by Lindeperg, Taylor, Petley, and others, which have suggested that censorship was almost invariably more subtle, and more interesting, than had been supposed. Vasey has carried out groundbreaking work on this topic but although her book contains much that is of interest and relevance to European cinema it does not focus centrally on it, and primarily discusses Hollywood cinema and especially the 'Hays' Code'.

Censorship relates to questions of ideology, aesthetics and style, which are the subject of the last part of the Introduction. For example, the close involvement of the French and Italian governments, followed later by the German and Spanish, in subsidising and, as important, promoting a particular kind of art cinema has encouraged the development of critical narratives which seek to place the film production of a particular country or set of countries within recognised frameworks which can then be used to influence production. Thus French cinema is frequently placed within the framework 'new wave', Spanish cinema within 'surrealism', Italian cinema within 'neo-realism', and so on, all of which reinforce the notion that European cinema is art cinema. Alongside this kind of cinema, however, there exists, or existed, European popular cinema which was targeted at a small regional or national audience and did not fit into the preferred, and internationally recognised, critical canons. This cinema is not well known because it is defined, to use Jeancolas's term, by being 'unexportable' (in Dyer and Vincendeau, 141). Although, today, it has largely been replaced by television, this does not mean that European popular cinema or the structures which produced it do not merit study.

Studios, genres, and stars are generally considered to have been the constitutive elements of the 'Hollywood system', the source of its industrial efficiency, economies of scale, and capacity to produce for the mass market. However, before the Second World War, and to some extent after it as well, studios also made a major contribution to the cinema in Europe. Scholars have certainly examined individual studios such as Albatros, Éclair, Gainsborough or Ealing, or indeed, the Soviet Film Factory, but the work of synthesising this knowledge and identifying the specific contribution of film studios in Europe has only just begun. Similarly, little has been published on the role of film stars in Europe, or on the development of specific genres and their function in European cinema.

The existence of European studios, genres and stars brings into focus the central question which this book raises but naturally does not answer: What, if any, are the common features of European cinema? Whatever the policy developments within the European Union, a European cinema cannot be brought into being by fiat, and in any case the Union is not co-terminous with Europe. Is European cinema a collection of national cinemas, some more vibrant and successful than others? Is it increasingly characterised by featureless co-productions, 'europuddings', in which the composition of an international cast list and a choice of international locations is determined by the relative significance of each country's financial input? Is it now influenced, primarily, by Hollywood's vision – or fantasy – of Europe, just as in the past it offered the occasion for the *mise-en-scène* of European fantasies of the American myth, and by the narrative structures preferred in Hollywood which are often inimical to other, national traditions? How has gender been represented and does the more open narrative often favoured in European cinema allow for more mobile conceptions than elsewhere? Is it, as Nowell-Smith suggests, wedded to realism, 'a commodity deeply rooted in European culture' but, in his view, inimical to a successful cinema which must '[reconnect] with the everyday mythologies of fear and desire' (Nowell-Smith and Ricci, 13)? And what of European audiences, about whom there are many statistics but remarkably few studies? The essays which follow are intended to engage with these questions, and to raise others, rather than to provide answers.

Part II consists of a series of 'case studies', free-standing analyses of individual films (two from each of six major European film-producing countries) together with a filmography and suggestions for further reading. The studies are intended to exemplify some of the salient features of particular national cinemas and European film styles as well as to offer points of cross-national comparison relating to the questions outlined above. Thus they can be read separately by students interested in a particular director's work or a particular national cinema, but they also provide the material for aesthetic and thematic comparisons across European national boundaries.

We have adopted a definition of 'Europe' which encompasses both Britain and Russia since the film production of these two countries is important for our purposes – Britain because it shares a language with the United States and because its film industry has, perhaps, been more intimately connected with Hollywood than that of any other European country; Russia because the post-*glasnost* rediscovery of Russian cinema has altered, and will continue to alter, our perception of cinema and of film history. It may well be objected that by not including films from Scandinavian countries, from the Czech Republic, from Hungary, from Poland, from Portugal or, indeed, from Ireland, we have distorted the picture of European cinema. It might also be objected that the present volume does little to disturb what Dyer and Vincendeau described as the 'high white tradition' (2), even though some of the most fascinating modern cinema is made in territories which are former European colonies and/or by ethnic or immigrant groupings within Europe. We can only plead lack of space in extenuation.

Our choice is not canonical; it is not intended to celebrate 'great' films or 'masterpieces of European cinema'. Instead, it has been guided by a number of practical considerations and critical needs. On the practical side we have attempted to choose films that will appeal to student audiences, that will be stimulating to viewers who do not necessarily have a highly developed knowledge of the cinema, and that will offer a range of critical points of entry. We also wished to achieve a reasonable chronological spread so as to include films from the silent era (*The Battleship Potemkin, The Lodger*) as well as films made within the last decade (*La haine, Trainspotting*). And we considered it essential that the films chosen should be readily available in sub-titled versions – a criterion which, of course, massively restricts the possibilities as far as concerns the film output of many countries, particularly Russia.

Beyond these practical considerations, it is intended that the case studies will illustrate ways in which themes such as modernism and the avant-garde, gender, reception, heritage, performance, narrative or language, are differently inflected in different national cinemas but can be illuminated by cross-national comparison. To take the most recent works first, *La haine* and *Trainspotting* share characteristics which we recognise as postmodern: both are firmly rooted in their local contexts but both are also designed to appeal to international audiences through their playful use of visual styles derived from television, their use of popular, internationally recognised music, and in their manipulation of elements of western youth culture. However, the treatment of race relations, of the aspirations of young people, and of space, also permits fascinating comparisons between *La haine* and *Das Versprechen*, even though each film apparently engages with very local cultural concerns. Again, despite their differences of style and subject-matter, *La règle du jeu, Ossessione, Viridiana* and *Das Versprechen* all deal with the Second World War and its legacy: none of them is a 'war film' in the traditional sense since none involves a *mise-en-scène* of the events of the war, but all attempt to confront the ideological issues arising from it. It is perhaps hardly surprising that such a major conflict should have been frequently represented in European cinema but it is interesting that the theme should persist in Europe throughout the twentieth century and should give rise to such a variety of treatments. By the same token, these films stage the confrontation between traditional ideologies and modernisation, which is a constant theme of European cinema. This is already evident in *The Battleship Potemkin*, frequently cited as an example of modernism, but can also be seen in *The Lodger*, whose less well known modernism is made explicit by a juxtaposition with *Potemkin*. Similarly, *Alice in den Städten* and *Good Morning Babilonia* explicitly examine the often fraught but always productive relationship between European cinema and Hollywood, which is less overt but none the less present in *La haine, Das Versprechen* and *Ossessione*. Though this relationship is seen through different national prisms, it also becomes a metaphor for the processes of modernisation and for the acute sense of cultural loss that such processes often generated, suggesting that ambivalence in the face of modernisation is a defining European experience and one which the cinema was particularly capable of documenting. By contrast, *Carmen* and *The Barber of Siberia* illustrate the opposite trend, namely a desire and even an obligation to celebrate the national heritage, even to the point where it becomes stereotypical, and to treat cinema as a privileged medium in which to debate questions of national culture.

Such categorisations can never be definitive and readers of more than one case study will detect other points of comparison which are constants in film studies and especially in the study of European cinema. Thus Birgit Beumers explores the relationship between the use of montage and the narration of history in *The Battleship Potemkin*, while Sarah Street considers the way reference to expressionism inflects the depiction of gender in *The Lodger*. Jill Forbes shows how a literary and cultural tradition is worked into a political critique in *La règle du jeu* and how its impact has increased over the years, while Derek Duncan considers the way an American source was controversially adapted in *Ossessione* to provide a critique of fascism through the subversion of gender relations. Annella McDermott suggests how *Viridiana* uses the iconography and thematics of Catholicism and surrealism to expose the oppressive nature of Franco's Spain and to plead for the country's reintegration into the European mainstream, while in *Das Versprechen* Stuart Taberner discovers similar artistic and intellectual ambiguities in the reintegration of the two Germanies in the 1990s. In examining the extraordinary intertextuality of *Alice in den Städten* and of *Good Morning Babilonia* Stuart Taberner and Derek Duncan raise questions about European film culture in a context made ever more pertinent by globalisation. One response, explored by Annella McDermott in *Carmen* and Birgit Beumers in *The Barber of Siberia*, is the deliberate and flamboyant juxtaposition of the new with the old aesthetics, gender politics and nationalism. However, a different answer is provided by two recent European successes, *La haine* and *Trainspotting*, examined by Jill Forbes and Sarah Street. It is one which challenges the notion that 'realism' is a defining impetus of European cinema and which suggests that a more fluid and more hybrid aesthetic will be characteristic of Europe at the dawn of the twenty-first century.

References

Bordwell, David and Thompson, Kristin 1993: *Film Art*. New York: McGraw Hill.

Cook, Pam 1985: *The Cinema Book*. London: British Film Institute.

Dyer, Richard and Vincendeau, Ginette (eds) 1992: *Popular European Cinema*. London: Routledge.

Guback, Thomas 1969: *The International Film Industry*. Bloomington: Indiana University Press.

Kracauer, Siegfried 1947: *From Caligari to Hitler*. Princeton: Princeton University Press.

Kracauer, Siegfried 1995: *The Mass Ornament*. Translated by Thomas Levin. Cambridge, MA: Harvard University Press.

Lindeperg, Sylvie 1997: *Les Écrans de l'ombre*. Paris: CNRS Éditions.

Monaco, James 1981: *How to Read a Film*. New York: Oxford University Press.

Mulvey, Laura 1975: 'Visual Pleasure and Narrative Cinema'. In *Screen*, 16, 3, 6–18.

Nowell-Smith, Geoffrey (ed.) 1996: *The Oxford History of World Cinema*. Oxford: Oxford University Press.

Nowell-Smith, Geoffrey and Ricci, Steven (eds) 1998: *Hollywood & Europe*. London: British Film Institute.

Petley, Julian 1979: *Capital and Culture: German Cinema, 1933–45*. London: British Film Institute.

Sorlin, Pierre 1991: *European Cinemas, European Societies*. London: Routledge.

Taylor, Richard 1998: *Film Propaganda: Soviet Russia and Nazi Germany*. London: I. B. Tauris.

Taylor, Richard and Christie, Ian 1988: *The Film Factory*. London: Routledge & Kegan Paul.

Thompson, Kristin 1985: *Exporting Entertainment: America in the World Film Market, 1907–34*. London: British Film Institute.

Vasey, Ruth 1997: *The World According to Hollywood*. Exeter: Exeter University Press.

Part I

European Cinema: An Overview

1

Economics and Politics

In the space of a century, the cinema has grown from a curiosity exhibited in the fairgrounds of western Europe and America to be part of a multi-billion-dollar business. In the early years, cinema was dominated by buccaneering capitalists like Charles Pathé; today it is an integral part of a global electronics industry which is likely to expand massively in the twenty-first century, with feature films making up a 'significant element' alongside sports programming and news gathering, and playing 'a leading role in the growth of fresh ancillary and new technology-driven markets' (Finney, 1). In this introduction we seek to trace the means by which cinema in Europe gradually became a vital component of the culture industries and, in the process, acquired a symbolic function in Europe's fight to protect itself against economic and cultural domination by the United States.

The First World War and After

Until 1914 the French film industry was the most important in the world, and its closest competitors were the industries of Italy and Denmark. It was founded on the success of the Lumière Brothers' *cinématographe*, which was publicly demonstrated for the first time in Paris in December 1895, and on the brilliant inventiveness of the theatre impresario Georges Méliès, whose Star Film Company built a world-wide empire with offices in London, Barcelona, Berlin and New York. However, it was the business genius of the gramophone manufacturer Charles Pathé which transformed the cinema in France from a series of small-scale, craft-based operations into a large, vertically and horizontally integrated company. Pathé's company manufactured film, built studios, set up processing laboratories and created subsidiaries abroad, and it owned the means of production, distribution and exhibition (Sadoul, 2: 221). Pathé expanded rapidly outside France, opening offices across Europe, including Russia, as well as in the United States and the Far East. One reason for its success was that the film business was extraordinarily profitable in the early years. According to the historian Georges Sadoul, the entire production of the Vincennes Studio for the year 1905 was amortised in 12 days, and in a situation where most films were less than 300 metres long it was enough to sell 20 copies for the initial outlay to be recouped (Sadoul, 2: 225, 235). However, although the French and Italian film businesses were the most dynamic in Europe before the First World War, they operated in societies that were still very rural, with the result that continuous film exhibition was limited to a few large towns and cities. Thus both these film industries relied on exports for their profits and their largest market was the United States, where, in the decade preceding the First World War, only about one-third of the films screened were American (Nowell-Smith, 1996, 24).

The First World War dramatically altered this state of affairs. The war mobilised personnel, diverted natural resources and industrial capacity, and disrupted patterns of trade. It consolidated the position of the United States as an exporting nation since, even before the US entered the war in 1917, the Allies turned to the US to import munitions and foodstuffs. It also helped the US and Japan to supplant Britain as a major shipping power since the British merchant fleet was mobilised for the war effort. Even European countries like Sweden, which remained neutral, or which were engaged in a civil war, like Russia, did not escape the impact of the hostilities.

By 1914, films had become an important element of world trade and were naturally affected too. During the first two years of hostilities the Americans exported fewer films to Europe, but by 1916 American sales were increasing in Italy, France, Spain and, above all, in Britain where, by this time, only 9 per cent of films screened were domestically produced and American films represented between 75 per cent and 90 per cent of those exhibited (Thompson, 67). Likewise in France, domestic productions had accounted for about 80 per cent of films screened before the war, but this figure had dropped to about 37 per cent by 1917, with approximately 30 per cent of the remainder being taken by American films. In Italy, the domestic industry had competed successfully against the Americans both at home and abroad but this was less and less the case by the end of the war, while in non-combatant Spain the Americans had captured almost 50 per cent of the domestic market by 1918 (Thompson, 91). Not surprisingly, the export manager of one American film company wrote of 'cashing in on Europe's war' and of 'invading' European and world markets (Thompson, 50).

However, the war was not the only factor which dented the economic strength of the film industries in Britain, France and Italy. In Britain the production of films had only really been buoyant in the early years of the century and the quality of British films was often poor or imitative of American products. Because London was still the financial and trading centre for a large Empire and because the British merchant navy still dominated the seas, London very quickly became the centre for processing American films and for re-exporting them across the world, not just to the British Empire but to other countries too. Film negatives would be shipped to London, positive prints would be struck in British laboratories, and agents would take advantage of British trading expertise and facilities to ship American films to the Far East, Australasia and, indeed, to Latin America. By 1910, hiring out films was proving much more lucrative than making them as far as the British were concerned, and it is from these pre-war imperial arrangements that the British tradition of providing technical facilities for American productions can be dated.

In France, where pre-war American films had been seen primarily in large towns, it was not just a decline in film production which allowed the Americans to export more, but also a change in the content and quality of the films themselves. The serial, which was Pathé's showcase product, became far less popular while the new feature films which came from America during 1915 and 1916 proved extremely successful (Thompson, 89). At the same time as the Americans were making significant inroads into the French market for the first time, French producers were losing their share of foreign markets. Pathé, Gaumont and Éclair had all set up production facilities in the US. The latter two were not part of the American motion picture producers' cartel and found operating in the American market difficult as a result. Pathé, however, was initially very successful but, from 1913 onwards, transformed itself into a distribution rather than a production company in America, a miscalculation which meant it lost its early advantage (Thompson, 59). French producers also lost considerable ground world-wide, especially in Latin America and the Far East from where much of their profit derived. The same is true of Italy whose small domestic market had been boosted by profits from Spain and especially Latin America, which had allowed the Italian industry to invest in expensive, longer than average spectaculars, with elaborate sets and large numbers of extras, the best known of which are Enrico Guazzoni's *Quo vadis?* (1913) and Giovanni Pastrone's *Cabiria* (1914). Until 1915 or 1916 such productions successfully rivalled American films, in Italy and America as well as farther afield, and stimulated many imitations.

Perhaps the war would not have enabled the Americans to compete successfully in Europe if the change in the style and content of American films had not been matched by significant changes in the structure and organisation of the American industry. The creation of the cartel known as the Motion Picture Patents Company (MPPC) in 1908 had ended undercutting and patents wars and had created a relatively stable oligopoly, reinforced by the end of the initial period of frenetic technological experimentation. It also tended to favour domestic production, and although it included the largest foreign companies, it tended to freeze out foreign competition (Nowell-Smith, 1996, 25). After the MPPC was declared illegal in 1915, the American industry, which had relocated to Hollywood, began to organise itself into vertically integrated conglomerates which controlled all stages of the production and sales process and which competed not through price and patent wars, as before, but through product differentiation based on named stars, who were used as marketing devices. The teens were thus the period when the 'Hollywood system' was established, a system based on 'a division of labour, maximum exploitation of resources, and the canons of beautiful cinematography' (Thompson, 89). The Americans were thus organised like a big business whereas the European industries, with the exception of Pathé, remained small and craft-based.

In this way, the First World War enabled the US to establish a world-wide hegemony in exporting films, which was helped by standards of quality and reliability that created international benchmarks for production. This reduced the European (and especially French) presence in America and increased the American penetration of Europe, especially in Britain, France and Italy. However, it should not be forgotten that this process did not take place throughout Europe, as is sometimes assumed. In Russia, where in any case relatively few American films were seen by the very scattered population, currency devaluation and transport difficulties meant that American films lost ground during the war. Then came the Revolution of 1917 and the Civil War, followed by a trade blockade of the Soviet Union by the western powers which was not lifted until 1921. This not only cut off imports of foreign films but also led to an acute shortage of film stock which stifled national film production. At the same time, Lenin declared film to be 'the most important art' and attempted to encourage domestic production and exhibition. Meanwhile in Germany, an Allied blockade and a ban on supplying films to Germany (lest the nitrate used in film production could be diverted for military purposes) meant that the German film industry had to supply its domestic market. It was consolidated by the creation of the partly nationalised Universumfilm Aktiengesellschaft (UFA) holding company in 1917, a move which was to have an immense impact on the European film industries and which was to enable the German film industry, alone, to present a significant challenge to Hollywood in the aftermath of the First World War.

The 'Silent Salesman'

The War demonstrated the potential for the use of cinema in information and propaganda and it also consolidated the belief in the broader, indirect, economic significance of the cinema. The magazine *Collier's Weekly* wrote in 1918: '[T]he American moving picture is...familiarising South America and Africa, Asia and Europe with American habits and customs. It is showing American clothes and furniture, automobiles and homes. And it is subtly but surely creating a desire for these American-made articles' (quoted in Thompson, 121–2). Indeed, the idea that 'trade follows the film' came to replace the earlier imperialist notion that 'trade follows the flag'. This was reinforced by social changes which occurred partly as a result of the war, especially in the position of women who, symbolically, gained the vote in Britain and America and who, throughout the west, were the prime targets of the consumer boom that took place in the 1920s. This was not lost on most European film-producing countries, which attempted to protect their film and other industries by using import quotas to fight Hollywood domination. The Soviet Union, however, adopted a different and, as we shall see, arguably more effective approach to the American domination of the world film industry.

Protecting the domestic market was led by Germany. In 1916 an embargo was imposed on inessential imports, which continued beyond the armistice until 1920. Then, in 1921, Germany introduced the first of a series of quota measures designed to limit film imports, based initially on a fixed percentage of footage and from 1925 on a proportional basis which stipulated that one foreign feature film could be imported for every German feature film distributed. In theory, this should have limited the number of foreign films in distribution in Germany to 50 per cent. In practice the figure seems to have been slightly lower, perhaps because, until 1923, hyper-inflation meant that German distributors could not afford to buy foreign films. Throughout the silent period, Germany managed to supply much more of its domestic market than did other European countries. In 1927, the quota was again altered to the so-called 'Kontingent' system under which imports were based on an estimate of the 'needs' of the market, and this remained in force throughout the Nazi period (Thompson, 211–12).

The German example was imitated more or less effectively in other European film-producing countries. Britain introduced a quota in 1927 which stipulated that 7.5 per cent of films handled by British renters (distributors) and 5 per cent shown by British exhibitors must be British films; both quotas to rise gradually to 20 per cent by 1936. The measure was only partially successful since although it led to an increase in the number of British films screened, it also stimulated the production of what were known as 'quota quickies', that is poor quality films made in Britain, by foreign and often American companies, in order to fulfil the requirements of the quota. But it nevertheless protected the industry to some extent and the British film industry recovered from its weak position in the 1920s as British films – even some 'quickies' – became more popular. In 1927, Italy attempted to impose a rule that 10 per cent of screen time should be devoted to Italian films, although the measure could not be enforced for lack of domestic product, while France imposed a highly ambitious quota of seven French films for one foreign film, with import licences granted only on the basis of French film exports, and which resulted in a temporary American boycott of the French market (Thompson, 121).

The economic impact of these measures is difficult to assess. It appears incontestable that import restrictions limited – more or less, depending on the territory – the number of American films imported into Europe (Thompson, 127). This in turn confirmed the treatment of films as a commodity to be exported like any other and underlined the extent to which Hollywood movie production had become big business. Indeed, in 1926, the American Congress voted funds to support a 'Motion Picture Section' within the Department of Commerce's Bureau of Foreign and Domestic Commerce. At the same time the American government supported the film boycott of France for fear that strict quotas for film imports might set a precedent for the imposition of quotas on other American products. On the other hand, the number of films exported to a given country does not necessarily equate with box office receipts within that country, and those are much more difficult to assess. Furthermore, by reducing the number of American imports, it has been suggested that European governments rendered a service to the Hollywood exporters, who, as a result, enhanced the quality of their product and increased profitability: '[f]ewer movies not only meant a better return per picture but also assisted the American industry by boosting the prestige of the Hollywood product' (Vasey, 89).

The Soviet approach was, interestingly, to use imported films to help the USSR's own industry recover from the effects of war and revolution, a system that was not generally adopted in western Europe until after the Second World War. The film industry was partially nationalised in 1919 and in 1922 was concentrated and centralised into the organisation Goskino. Part of the impetus for this was to control scarce resources. Most cameras were imported but spare parts were unavailable because of the trade blockade. Film production slumped and many cinemas closed for lack of anything to exhibit. From 1922 onwards Lenin therefore ordered the importing of foreign films into the USSR but under an arrangement which provided, first, that imported films should be exhibited alongside Soviet educational and propaganda shorts – this was the so-called 'Leninist film proportion' – and secondly, that revenues from exhibiting foreign films should be ploughed back into Soviet film production. This meant that by the mid-1920s, 85 per cent of films in the Soviet market came from abroad, and many of these were American. At the same time, Soviet production rose from a meagre 13 feature films in 1923 to 109 by 1928, suggesting that the policy had been rather successful (Kepley, 65, 77).

Pan European Cooperation

The other line of European defence, especially in the 1920s, was to develop cooperation through the 'Film Europe' movement, which some commentators have considered a precursor of today's European Union policies. The impetus came initially from Germany, and the reasons are understandable. In the period after the First World War, Germany probably had the most dynamic film industry in Europe. As we have seen, its domestic market was protected. Hyper-inflation meant that until the currency was stabilised in 1923, imported films were prohibitively expensive, and in 1917, with state backing, much of the film industry had been concentrated into the UFA holding company which brought together the government film propaganda unit and a variety of small production companies. UFA also owned offices, laboratories, film equipment and processing plant, cinemas, and new, purpose-built studios at Babelsberg. UFA was further strengthened by taking over another large production company, DECLA, in 1921, and the conglomerate was backed both by the Deutsche Bank and by the electrical and chemical industries. The involvement of finance and industry in film production illustrates a new attitude towards the significance of the cinema, and more broadly the culture industries, in the 1920s, and in this the Germans led the way.

However, a further important reason for the Germans to preach cooperation was that the war had made European audiences xenophobic. In France, for example, it was considered highly unpatriotic to appreciate German culture or to buy German goods. Thus if UFA was to export, it had to win over foreign viewers and it was helped by the international success of Lubitsch's *Madame du Barry* (1919), the subject-matter of which was 'French', and of Wiene's *Das Kabinett des Dr Caligari* (*The Cabinet of Dr Caligari*, 1919), produced by DECLA, which inaugurated the expressionist style that came to be considered distinctive of German cinema in the 1920s. Indeed, Elsaesser has suggested that the expressionist masterpieces, which include celebrated films such as Fritz Lang's *Der müde Tod* (*Destiny*, 1921) and *Metropolis* (1926), or F. W. Murnau's *Der letzte Mann* (*The Last Laugh*, 1924), were deliberately encouraged as a means of distinguishing German film production from that of Hollywood and of recruiting the middle-class and intellectual audience abroad to support German films (Elsaesser, in Nowell-Smith, 1996, 144).

Shortly after becoming overall head of UFA, Erich Pommer declared in an interview in a French film magazine: 'It is necessary to create "European Films" which will no longer be French, English, Italian or German films; entirely "continental" films, expanding out into all Europe and amortising their enormous costs, can be produced easily' (quoted in Thompson, 113), and he did so in order to promote his new distribution agreement with one of the major French film distributors, the Établissements Aubert (Thompson, 112). Similar agreements followed: in 1926 the Alliance cinématographique européenne provided further outlets for UFA films in France; in October 1926 a joint Russian–German production and distribution company, DERUFA, was created which, before it went bankrupt in 1929, had imported into Germany Barnet's *Devushka s korobkoi* (*The Girl with a Hat Box*, 1927), Pudovkin's *Konets Sankt Peterburga* (*The End of St Petersburg*, 1927), and Eisenstein's *Staroe i novoe* (*Old and New/The General Line*, 1929) (Thompson, 116); in 1927 UFA signed an agreement with Gaumont-British, and in June 1928 UFA and the Italian state company LUCE agreed to distribute each other's films.

One of the weaknesses of Pommer's proposals was that they were confined to distribution and exhibition. They were not sufficient to prevent the financial difficulties which struck UFA in 1925 and which enabled the Americans to buy a share of the company, effectively circumventing distribution restrictions. However, another German company, Westi Films, concluded an agreement with Pathé in December 1924 and its owner suggested collaboration on the production of expensive and artistically meritorious European films via a European 'syndicate' of the major European film-producing companies (Danilowicz, 54–6), and indeed the company invested in arguably the most spectacular European film of the 1920s, Abel Gance's *Napoléon* (1927).

At the same time, proposals for European cooperation were not entirely self-interested. The League of Nations, founded in 1919 to promote international peace and understanding, agreed to make cinema one of its areas of concern and convened a congress which took place in Paris in September–October 1926 (Thompson, 111). It was attended by many of the leading film-makers of the day, it served to publicise the possibility of cooperation, and it passed resolutions that films should avoid inflammatory, racist or nationalistic material and should promote understanding between peoples. One example of such a cooperative approach was G. W. Pabst's film *Kameradschaft* (*Comradeship*, 1931), a Franco-German co-production, set in a mining town on the Franco-German border, which depicts French and German miners working together to rescue people after an accident in the mine. Yet, ironically, it appears that Pabst shot two endings, one of which shows this ideal cooperation continuing, the other which shows the border re-established under ground after the mine is reopened – alternatives which were, perhaps, symbolic of the uncertainty many felt about putting pan European cooperation into practice.

Technology and the Birth of the 'Culture Industries'

The advent of sound cinema further underlined cinema's role as a showcase for and locomotive of new technologies and the participation of big business in film production. It also, initially, provided the means for further economic protectionism in Europe. The first successful American sound film, Alan Crosland's *The Jazz Singer* (1927), reached Europe in 1928–9 and immediately revitalised interest in sound technology, precipitating a turf war in Europe. Huge sums of money were at stake for film producers, for those who owned the patents of the sound processes and for those who supplied the equipment to wire the cinemas. Once again, Germany led the way with the creation, in 1929, of a cartel called Tobis-Klangfilm, which had been formed by the merger of two powerful companies, the former including Swiss and Dutch venture capital, the latter significantly bringing together two large German electrical companies, AEG and Siemens. Tobis-Klangfilm, in a series of successful lawsuits, prevented Western Electric, the holder of the main series of American sound patents, from operating in Europe until July 1930 when an agreement was reached on an international cartel which essentially divided the European market between the two systems, one German-controlled, the other American-controlled.

The advent of sound in Europe temporarily arrested American domination of the European film industries – a moratorium which lasted until dubbing techniques had been perfected, or, more important, accepted by non-English-speaking audiences, around 1932. It also helped to consolidate German investment in other European markets, especially in France where Tobis built its own studio. On the American side, sound accelerated the standardisation of the product, which was no longer exported 'semi-finished', as well as its cultural specificity. And it also marked the moment, as the Germans realised, when the audio and visual industries came together for their mutual benefit and cinema became a significant element in the expansion of electrical conglomerates. Finally, sound posed questions, as perhaps the silent cinema had never done, about 'national cinema' and put an end to embryonic European cooperation.

Censorship and Propaganda

All European countries had various systems of censorship, either directly controlled by the state, or via systems of self-regulation which were instituted by the film industries with tacit approval from their governments. These were frequently instituted under the guise of safety regulations, but then extended to content control. In any examination of European cinema it is important to consider the extent to which censorship influenced film content in the direction of promoting specific, officially sanctioned 'national' images. As Richard Maltby explains, censorship is 'a practice of power, a form of surveillance over the ideas, images, and representations circulating in a particular culture' (quoted in Nowell-Smith, 1996, 235). The existence of censorship had different effects in different periods: in wartime or dictatorship, for example, it was more acute and focused than in peacetime. It is without question, however, that whatever the period, it exercised a significant constraint on what could be shown. Once these strictures became accepted by film-makers as facts of life they inhibited them from broaching delicate or forbidden subjects in their films. While there are many cases of film-makers managing to get around the letter of censorship laws by including subtle yet risqué material, for example, the celebrated sexual scene (which would not have been apparent in the script) in Alfred Hitchcock's *The Thirty-Nine Steps* (1935) when Madeleine Carroll and Robert Donat are handcuffed together, the overall impact of regulatory systems acted as a force which contributed to the shape of a particular country's film production. And, by exercising control over film imports, European countries could, via censorship, regulate images from abroad which were deemed to be 'unsuitable', or which were set up as objectionable in comparison with indigenous films. They could also, and frequently did, use dubbing to excise politically or morally unacceptable references from films.

The British system of censorship was founded in 1912 when the film industry established the British Board of Film Censors (BBFC), a body which received government approval. The Board had no statutory power but its rulings tended to be accepted by local authorities, who could ban films as an extension of their control over saftey regulations in cinemas. The Board proceeded to classify films under categories including sex and politics, and in the 1930s required film producers to send them scripts so that time and money would not be wasted on films which were unlikely to satisfy the censors. This system was fairly strict and served to exclude films which were considered to be 'dangerous' in political terms, including imports from the USSR so that Eisenstein's *Bronenosets Potemkin* (*The Battleship Potemkin*, 1926) was banned from 1926 to

1954. Films such as *Potemkin* were seen in Britain, but only by members of film societies, which were allowed to show banned films because of their status as private (and expensive) clubs, and this meant that they were viewed only by a minority of the intelligentsia. Films which broached contentious subjects like unemployment in the 1930s were not allowed to be produced, a famous case being the filming of Walter Greenwood's novel *Love on the Dole*, which could only be made after the outbreak of the Second World War when unemployment was no longer a politically sensitive issue. In the 1930s, as Jeffrey Richards has shown, censorship in Britain bolstered the National Government, reinforced its political ideology of 'consensus' and helped to defend the status quo (Richards, 89–107). Direct state involvement was not necessary since the film industry colluded with a system which purported to be independent yet at the same time could be subject to official influence since the President of the BBFC had to be approved by the Home Secretary.

In France the Ministry of the Interior established a Commission in 1916 which issued visas to films that were deemed to be acceptable for exhibition. As in Britain, the localities also had power to ban films, and films made in the USSR received particularly harsh treatment. By contrast, censorship in Germany, during the Weimar period, became more liberal and encouraged the importing of films from the USSR as a political move to forge closer relations between the two countries. Consequently, *The Battleship Potemkin* was a huge success with working-class audiences in Berlin, more so than with audiences in the Soviet Union. Much of its status as a classic of silent cinema rests on its reputation as a 'banned' film which was nevertheless seen by key groups of critics and admirers, and on the enthusiasm with which it was received by the European intelligentsia. Its success in Germany, however, is interesting because it provides evidence for the film as an accessible and *popular* film amongst the audiences for whom it was intended. In this instance, therefore, censorship had a direct impact on the critical reception and popular memory of what became probably the USSR's most famous film in the west.

The rise of the totalitarian regimes had the most dramatic impact on the established norms of censorship regulation in Germany, Italy, Spain and the USSR. The Nazi regime was intent on controlling cinema and it excluded films made in other countries, primarily Hollywood, which competed with German films in the ideological sphere. In Italy the cinema was subject to similar strictures, although Mussolini was less successful than Hitler in completely banning foreign films. The Catholic Church also exerted a conservative influence over film content, as it did in Spain where censorship was draconian, particularly after the Supreme Film Censorship Board was established in 1937 and proceeded to ban films made in the Catalan language and to require, from 1941, that foreign film imports were dubbed. The Church had its own body, the National Board of Classification of Spectacles, which pronounced on the suitability of film projects and raised objections according to its strict moral codes. In this sense both Spain's and Italy's censorship regulations sought to ensure that their respective film cultures were perceived both nationally and internationally as conservative and Catholic.

In Soviet Russia the Stalinist period was more draconian than the 1920s, when during the first part of the decade American films were exhibited and greeted with enthusiasm, particularly films by Buster Keaton, Charlie Chaplin, Douglas Fairbanks and Mary Pickford. Stalin's attempts to create an insular culture, based on the ideology of Socialist Realism, led to the USSR banning the entry of foreign films while at the same time protecting and encouraging the development of the Soviet film industry. Eisenstein's former assistant Grigori Alexandrov developed popular genres such as the musical, and the title sequence of one of his films even contained the lines 'Buster Keaton and Charlie Chaplin do not star in this film,' followed by a list of the Soviet actors who did. As in Germany, 'entertainment' and 'propaganda' went hand-in-hand and directors, including Eisenstein, who did not find favour with Boris Shumyatsky, the official in charge of Stalin's political cinema, were not allowed to make their projects. After *The Battleship Potemkin*, Eisenstein's films became more involved with 'intellectual montage' and even his celebrated classic *Oktiabr'* (*October*, 1928) was accused of being unintelligible to the masses. However, he was reinstated as a Soviet film-maker after Shumyatsky became a victim of Stalin's purges in 1938, and his contribution to the anti-fascist cause was *Aleksandr Nevskii* (*Alexander Nevsky*, 1938). In this case it was expedient for the state to use a film-maker who had proved that he could make films with overt propagandist intent in the 1920s.

During the Second World War these major methods of film censorship continued, and were reinforced by official concerns not just for morality but for national security and morale as well, and in the Axis powers imports of films from the United States and Britain were banned. In Italy, Visconti's *Ossessione* (1942), an adaptation of James M. Cain's novel *The Postman Always Rings Twice*, on its release, was severely criticised by the Fascist hierarchy and the Church who were concerned by its depiction of lust, murder and infidelity. Mussolini's censorship laws decreed that crime and immorality were not suitable screen subjects because they were supposed to have been eradicated by the Fascist regime. As a result, *Ossessione* was cut to under half its original length, given only a limited release in Italy, and all the original copies were destroyed. In Spain, censorship under Franco prevented the introduction of a Spanish branch of neo-realism despite attempts by film-makers such as Luis García Berlanga and Juan Antonio Bardem.

However, in the 1950s most European countries relaxed their censorship laws partly in response to a general trend of liberalisation and the need to support cinema in the face of competition from television. France, in particular, became much more liberal in its attitude towards the depiction of sexuality while in Britain the introduction of the 'X' certificate in 1951 permitted more sexually explicit films to be exhibited. On the other hand, France maintained political censorship until the 1970s, banning films such as Godard's *Le petit soldat*

(*Little Soldier*, 1963), Pontecorvo's *La Bataille d'Alger* (*The Battle of Algiers*, 1966), and even Yorkin's comedy *Start the Revolution Without Me* (1970). Censorship was not abolished in Spain until 1977 after decades during which directors had to make films which satisfied the censors but on occasion, as with the work of Carlos Saura, contained covert elements of critique. By utilising techniques such as allegory, ellipsis and subtle characterisation, Saura achieved a veiled critique of Francoism in films such as *Peppermint Frappé* (1967).

In 1986 *glasnost* liberated Soviet cinema from the straitjacket of totalitarian censorship, the most extreme case of which was, perhaps, Sergei Paradjanov's five years' hard labour for 'speculating in art' and for homosexuality. Paradjanov's *Nran Gouyne* (*The Colour of Pomegranates*, 1969) had been banned for its 'incorrect', surrealistic account of the life of the eighteenth-century poet Sayat Nova. A host of shelved and banned films were released including Alexander Askoldov's *Komissar* (*The Commissar*, 1967), finally completed in 1987, and Alexei Gherman's *Moi drug Ivan Lapshin* (*My Friend Ivan Lapshin*, 1984), and directors like Sergei Paradjanov and Andrei Tarkovsky, who had had their careers blocked in the 1970s, received international acclaim. As the western market economy has been reintroduced, however, American films have been greeted with enthusiasm while the Russian cinema continues to be vulnerable and unstable, dogged by different, but equally acute problems. As in Germany after the Second World War, it has been found that the legacy of dictatorship and censorship cannot be discarded overnight. A survey published in 1995 concluded that most European countries currently adopt a more lenient attitude towards censorship than twenty-five years ago, with the exception of Germany, which seeks to control neo-Nazism and to protect youth, and Britain, which seeks to censor domestic video.

The use of film as propaganda was an adjunct to censorship and can be seen as part of a dual system of forbidden and promoted images. Censorship was used to shape the perception of a country's national output in ways which were perceived by European governments as acceptable, or in accord with other elements of dominant conceptions of nationalist culture. It was generally accepted that film was an important means of national persuasion in times of national emergency; and while film propaganda had been a significant development in the 'total war' of 1914–18 it was the Second World War which accelerated its conscious use by European governments. In Germany, where the major film-production conglomerate was already nationalised, film was seen as a superb medium for the dissemination of Nazi ideas through newsreels and the spectacular documentaries devoted to the celebratory rallies the Nazis held in Nuremberg in 1933 and 1934, filmed by Leni Riefenstahl as *Sieg des Glaubens* (*Victory of Faith*, 1933) and *Triumph des Willens* (*Triumph of the Will*, 1935) and the profoundly anti-semitic *Der ewige Jude* (*The Eternal Jew*, 1940). A few films rewrote history from a Nazi perspective. *Titanic* (1943), for example, claimed that the famous liner sank because of British and Jewish aristocratic and capitalist agency despite the efforts of a heroic German officer to prevent collision with an iceberg, while *Aufruhr in Damaskus* (*Uproar in Damascus*, 1939) portrayed Lawrence of Arabia as an insurrectionist who incited Syrian rebellion against Germany in the First World War. But since Hollywood films were banned in Germany, Josef Goebbels, the Minister of Propaganda, considered that German feature films should mirror Hollywood entertainment values, and genres such as comedies, melodramas and musicals, and while they could in no way criticise the Nazi regime, most of them did not contain heavy-handed insertions of Nazi doctrines. For this reason, only one-sixth of the 1097 feature films made in Germany from 1933 to 1945 were subsequently banned in the post-war period by Allied censors because they could be construed as Nazi propaganda (Bordwell and Thompson, 308).

In Italy, the Fascists took a keen interest in the cinema. The LUCE (L'Unione cinematografica educativa) company was granted a monopoly of newsreel and documentary production and in 1926 it was decreed that every cinema programme had to include one of the four Mussolini-approved LUCE newsreels that were produced every week. Other measures to protect and promote the film industry included requiring films to be dubbed into Italian in Italy, a tax on dubbed films (levied from 1934 onwards), the creation of the Venice Film Festival (1934), a system of subsidies and prizes for 'high quality' films, and state funding for the new Cinecittà studios, which were opened by Mussolini in 1937. Thus by the end of the 1930s the state 'had a powerful distribution chain, a chain of first rate cinemas and a major production facility' (Wagstaff, 165–7). In 1938, the major American companies withdrew from the Italian market in protest against the monopoly on importing and distributing foreign films which was assigned to a state-run organisation, with the result that the Italian market was virtually closed to foreign imports and there was a concomitant increase in Italian film production. Popular cinema flourished, especially comedies and melodramas, but the facilities of Cinecittà also provided an important training ground for individuals who went on to become crucial figures in neo-realist cinema, including the directors Visconti and Rossellini, and de Sica who was originally a star actor. Similarly, in Spain popular genres like the *folklóricas* were used to glorify Spanish masculinity, and history was used as a blatant excuse to promote Francoism.

In the Soviet Union, the cinema operated within a command rather than a market economy and in the 1930s became a large, studio-based industry to which the state devoted considerable sums of money not just in Moscow and Leningrad but in the regions and outside Russia as well. Stalin's approach was to combine censorship with entertainment, while directors like Mikhail E. Chiaureli were used to inculcate the Stalinist 'cult of personality' in films such as *Velikoe zarevo* (*The Great Dawn*, 1938), *Kliatva* (*The Vow*, 1946) and *Padenie Berlina* (*The Fall of Berlin*, 1949). Despite censorship and Stalin's intimate involvement in film production, the 1930s and 1940s produced many film classics (whose value was ignored until very recently by film scholars) and Soviet citizens became enthusiastic movie-goers (Taylor and Christie, xix–xxi; Nowell-Smith, 1996, 640–1).

In occupied France a German company, Continental, absorbed the major Parisian film studios, took over many expropriated Jewish businesses, and produced French-language films, such as Henri Decoin's *Les inconnus dans la maison* (*Strangers in the House*, 1941). Censorship was circumvented by avoiding contemporary settings and subject-matter and by using the past, as with Marcel Carné's two wartime masterpieces *Les visiteurs du soir* (*The Devil's Own Envoy*, 1942) and *Les enfants du paradis* (*Children of Paradise*, 1945), to compose potentially allegorical narratives of tyranny and freedom. If anything, censorship was more severe in the immediate post-war period when supposedly collaborationist directors like Henri Clouzot were blacklisted, and when the scenarios of films were subject to pre-production vetting by a powerful committee of trade union representatives who had been active in the Resistance (Lindeperg, 145–67).

In Britain the Ministry of Information's propaganda directives urged documentaries and feature films to highlight what Britain was fighting for, how it was fighting the war, and the need for sacrifice at all levels if the war was to be won. A common strategy was to collapse class conflict into narratives which featured everybody 'pulling together': a united nation in the face of national emergency. Both *In Which We Serve* (1942) and *San Demetrio, London* (1943) used the device of a ship as a microcosm of society, loyalty to which united people from different class backgrounds. The home front was also considered to be an important arena for propaganda. *Millions Like Us* (1943) focused on a group of women who had been conscripted to work in a munitions factory, and *The Gentle Sex* (1943) on the training of women in the Auxiliary Territorial Service (ATS). Popular music-hall stars also contributed to maintaining home-front morale by making films which used comedy to communicate the same broad message that everyone must 'do their bit' in the fight against fascism. George Formby had been a popular star in the 1930s and his wartime films included *Let George Do It* (1940), in which a concert performer is mistaken for a British intelligence agent and becomes a hero when he passes a vital message which facilitates the destruction of a Geman U-boat.

The Second World War was therefore a key period when most European governments exerted a considerable degree of control over film production, and even when the war had ended all the Allies continued to see cinema as a key ideological weapon. The Psychological Warfare Branch (PWB) of the American army arrived in Italy and Germany bearing American documentary and feature films. In Berlin, the occupying forces vied with each other to re-open or rebuild cinemas in their respective zones (Bance, 153–68) and Allied funds went to assist the making of suitably anti-fascist films such as Rossellini's *Paisà* (1946), funded by American money, and Wolfgang Staudte's *Die Mörder sind unter uns* (*The Murderers are Among Us*, 1946), which was supported by the Russians. But as Vincendeau has pointed out, the war did not become 'the epic of modern Europe', largely because it affected the various European countries differently and they had to come to terms with their experience in different periods and in their own particular ways (Vincendeau, 1995, xv). France, for example, was unable to deal with the issue of collaboration until many years after the war, and post-war German cinema largely avoided its own recent history, while British films of the 1950s, like *The Dam Busters* (1954), tended to displace problems of masculine identity onto war subjects and generally adopted a less positive attitude towards heroism than in propaganda films made during the war.

To sum up, it would appear that while European governments tried to exercise control over film content via censorship and propaganda, this was not always successful in producing a monolithic and one-dimensional impression of a particular country's film culture. Censorship systems tended to be reactive – attempting to excise 'objectionable' images but operating in such a way that film-makers became unconsciously aware of their concerns, which could act as constraints on, or in some cases, as challenges to, their art. Propaganda, on the other hand, was more pro-active in seeking to perpetuate images which artic-ulated particular expressions of dominant ideology, whether they were fascist, socialist or consensual. The aim of both systems – formal and informal – was to create preferred expressions of national culture, expressions which invariably neglected other competing representations and ideologies.

Protectionism and Subsidy

After 1945, thanks to the experience of the war, state intervention in the European film industries was motivated by cultural as well as economic considerations. There is ample evidence that the Americans wished to dump films in the European markets, but they presented this as the promotion of democracy and freedom. American lobbyists shamelessly associated the triumph of democracy with the export of American movies: 'Whether one calls it propa-ganda or information, it is evident that as a result of World War II, the motion picture from this day must be regarded as an instrument of public policy as well as a great popular medium of entertainment', wrote the editor of *Film Daily* (quoted in Dickinson and Street, 176).

In Germany, after the collapse of the Nazi regime, the Hollywood film industry was able to 'hold the military government to ransom over the use of American films for education and propaganda purposes' (Elsaesser, 1989, 9) and ensure that the trading arrangements were extraordinarily advantageous to the US. In Italy, similarly, the American chairman of the film section of the Allied Commission declared that 'Italy, as a rural and former fascist country, did not need a film industry and should not be allowed to have one' (Nowell-Smith and Ricci, 6). But in other countries the Americans had a much less easy ride, largely because economic priorities lay elsewhere. Thus in Britain, film imports were associated with food shortages, leading one Member of Parliament, Robert Boothby, to use the graphic comparison of a choice between 'bacon' and 'Bogart' (Dickinson and Street, 180), while in France it was similarly acknowledged that it might be necessary to sacrifice the film industry 'in the higher interests of France' (Jeancolas, 17).

The Americans saw the end of the war as an opportunity to promote free trade which they wished to enshrine in the first General Agreement on Tariffs and Trade (GATT) concluded in 1947. The Europeans were much more ambivalent, as can be seen from the indirect treatment of the topic in films such as Rossellini's *Roma, città aperta* (*Rome, Open City*, 1945) or Cornelius's *Passport to Pimlico* (1949). Films were one of the Americans' major export commodities, the more so since a backlog of unexported movies had built up during the years of the war. The Motion Picture Association of America (MPPA) formed a subsidiary association devoted to questions of trade (the Motion Picture Export Association of America, MPEA) to lobby on behalf of American interests, primarily in Europe. But the cinema was of much greater significance in the American economy than it was in any of the European economies. For example, in 1947, dollar remittances from Britain to the US for films accounted for only 4 per cent of all dollar remittances, the major part being spent on foodstuffs and fuel (Dickinson and Street, 179).

European governments were aware of the popular desire to see American movies, of the need to provide leisure activities, and of the need to offer their people something to buy at a time of great austerity. They were concerned lest disputes over film imports would impede progress on discussion of aid for reconstruction. They were also urged on by powerful lobbies of exhibitors who were anxious for films to screen, since domestic film production had either collapsed, as in Germany, or was severely hampered by the shortage of raw materials. But they could not afford the outflow of dollars needed to import American films. Food rationing in Britain was stricter in the years following the war than it had been during the war. In Germany and Russia people were starving, and in the harsh winter of 1946–7 there was an acute shortage of fuel throughout Europe.

Gradually the arguments about the relative advantages and disadvantages of open and closed markets turned into a recognition of the need to subsidise film production in Europe. The measures put in place during the war to provide state support for the domestic film industries in countries such as France, Italy and Britain, survived in modified form and immediately after the war several European governments took steps to protect their industries against American competition. In August 1947 the British imposed a 75 per cent tax on the value of every foreign film. This led to a boycott of the British market by the MPEA, which was resolved by the Anglo-American Film Agreement of 1948 limiting the dollar remittances allowed to American companies but not the number of films which could be imported. It also encouraged American companies to spend their dollar earnings in Britain.

In France, where the market had been regulated until the war by the 1936 Marchandeau Agreement limiting the number of dubbed films imported (about 150 of which in any one year were American), a screen quota was instituted in

1946. This placed no restriction on the number of films that could be imported, but it obliged exhibitors to devote 4 weeks per trimester (or 16 weeks a year) to screening French films, increased to 5 weeks per trimester in 1948 (Jeancolas, 19).

In Italy the Andreotti Act of July 1949 instituted a system of taxing imports to support local production by means of the so-called 'dubbing certificate'. For each dubbed film imported, the distributor had to deposit a sum of money with the national Banca Nazionale di Lavoro, which was used to create a fund from which Italian producers could borrow at low interest. There was no restriction on the number of films imported, and exemption from the dubbing certificate could be acquired in return for export licences for Italian films (ironically, the Americans could not benefit from this since they had no restrictions on imports). In addition, a screen quota similar to that of France was imposed which was advantageous for film production in Italy.

In Germany and Spain circumstances were somewhat different. The Allies deliberately held back the growth of the German film industry while Americans secured a stranglehold on distribution so that there was little attempt to limit American imports (Elsaesser, 1989, 15). In Spain, imports of American films rose dramatically after the war and it was not until the mid-1950s that the government introduced the so-called 'Baremo', a term which refers to a complex points system by which distributors were allowed to distribute foreign films. Spain proposed to reduce American imports to a total of about 80 films and demanded in return that Spanish films should be distributed in the US, and this led to an American boycott of the Spanish market which lasted for nearly three years. The Baremo was extremely effective in limiting American imports into Spain and encouraging Spanish film production (Guback, 27–30).

After the financial crises of the late 1940s were resolved, western Europe embarked on a period of reconstruction, modernisation and economic growth which in most cases lasted until the first oil crisis of 1973. In societies like those of France, Italy and Spain, which were still very rural in 1945, large numbers of people left the countryside to work in towns. Mass secondary education was introduced in most countries, women were enfranchised and, in the 1960s, the 'baby boomers' of the post-war years came to maturity as a distinctive socio-economic generation. The profound social, economic and technological changes which resulted from the modernisation of the 1950s and 1960s had a significant impact on forms of culture, leisure and entertainment and on the tastes of European populations. Perhaps the most significant were those produced by the spread of car ownership and the rise of television. However, these changes were often opposed as passionately as they were welcomed and were frequently believed to represent an undesirable 'Americanisation' of Europe. In France and Italy, which both had electorally powerful Communist parties, the Cold War increased pressure on governments to resist 'Coca-Cola culture' and 'American imperialism' as embodied in Hollywood cinema.

Modernisation changed the relationship between European governments and European film industries. In the 1950s cinema attendances began to decline, more rapidly in some countries than in others, while television gradually replaced cinema as the mass medium of entertainment, again more rapidly in some countries than in others. Films continued to be produced for the mass domestic audience in all European countries, but they were not necessarily exported. At the same time, the audience that continued to go to the cinema became socially and generationally fragmented and this, in turn, altered the economic significance of the film industries in Europe.

Throughout the 1950s these changes translated into a spectrum of interventionist measures, some designed to encourage the production of more films, others to foster particular kinds of production. At one extreme, the British 'Eady Levy' on ticket sales returned the greatest amount of money to the producers of the biggest box-office successes, regardless of quality. At the other end of the spectrum was the series of measures developed in France which, in addition to 'automatic aid', of the Eady kind, gradually placed more and more emphasis on qualititative criteria for financial support. Thus in 1948 French producers were offered 'automatic aid' in return for accepting the newly agreed screen quota, which gave them a proportion of the box-office receipts from their films provided a new French film was produced, generating about 17 per cent of total investment in film production in the 1950s. However, in 1953 a proportion of the available subsidy was set aside specifically for projects which were 'French and of a kind to serve the cause of cinema or open new perspectives in the art of cinematography', and in 1959 a fund was created which provided interest-free loans to film-makers (*avances sur recettes*) granted on the basis of an outline or an idea, which was only repayable if the film earned a profit (Forbes, 5–6).

Alongside these various forms of subsidy were other measures designed to boost the supply side. Following the 'Film Europe' initiative of the 1920s, co-production agreements were seen as a means to secure large enough budgets and sufficient distribution guarantees to ensure international box-office success. The very fertile Franco-Italian agreement of 1949 took up an initiative which had begun in 1939 when Jean Renoir went to work in Italy, and had continued in the early years of the war when Italian money was invested in the Victorine Studios in Nice and Antonioni went to work in France. Both the Venice and Cannes film festivals (the former created in 1934, the latter in 1939 but relaunched after the war) became immensely significant as showcases for European films, as did the Forum of Young Cinema introduced at the Berlin Film Festival in 1970. Cannes, especially, became an extremely important meeting place for critical and commercial interests and for European attempts to sell films on the basis of their artistic quality. The films individual countries selected to represent their industries at such festivals were extremely influential in determining the image of a particular country's cinema and especially significant in fostering the notion that European cinema is 'art' cinema.

Modernisation and 'New Cinema'

The 1960s saw 'new cinema' flourishing almost everywhere in Europe. In the Soviet Union, Khrushchev's denunciation of Stalin's 'personality cult' at the 20th Communist Party Congress in 1956 led to a general cultural thaw, and, as far as cinema was concerned, to the release of many banned films, to a period of aesthetic experimentation and to massive investment in the cinema with production rising from ten films a year in the early 1950s to about a hundred in 1960. The west responded by awarding the Golden Palm at Cannes to Mikhail Kalatozov's *Letiat zhuravli* (*The Cranes are Flying*) in 1957 and the Golden Lion at Venice to Andrei Tarkovsky's *Ivanovo detstvo* (*Ivan's Childhood*) in 1962. In France, François Truffaut's *Les quatre cents coups* (*The 400 Blows*) won the Best Director prize at Cannes in 1959, inaugurating the 'nouvelle vague' (new wave) of young directors which included Godard, Chabrol, Rohmer and Rivette, who all made their first films at this time. Similarly, in Italy with Antonioni and Fellini, in Britain with Anderson, Richardson and Reisz, and in Spain with Carlos Saura there was an upsurge of 'new cinema' stimulated by young directors, technological innovation and aesthetic experimentation, in which state intervention sometimes, but not always, played a small but significant role.

However, critical success was not matched by success at the box office. Cinema attendances declined dramatically, especially in Britain and in Germany – in the latter they dropped from 800 million to 180 million at the beginning of the 1960s. In France, Italy, Spain and the Soviet Union, the decline was delayed until the 1970s, no doubt because television spread more slowly in those countries. Ticket sales halved in Italy in the latter part of the 1970s, falling from 514 million to 270 million, and continued to drop to a point below 100 million in the 1990s. In Spain, likewise, cinema audiences declined by two-thirds between 1971 (331 milllion tickets) and 1985 (101 million tickets), and in the Soviet Union they fell from 5 billion in the 1960s to 4 billion by the end of the 1970s. Even in France, where cinema audiences held up better than in any other country, the 1970s was a period of significant decline. This was accompanied in many countries by a production crisis. The British industry became so dependent on American investment that by 1969, 90 per cent of investment in British cinema came from the United States. In Italy in the 1960s, the industry was propped up by the production of comedies but entered a crisis when their popularity declined. In Germany, the loss of 75 per cent of the audience to television gave rise to the Oberhausen Manifesto of young German film-makers in 1962, which called for government intervention and was sympathetically received. From that point on it was recognised that cinema required state support in West Germany, even though debates raged about the amount and the kind of films supported. By the 1980s state intervention in the cinema had become overtly cultural rather than implicitly industrial and films were subsidised in the same way, although less generously, as other art forms such as theatre or opera. A similar process is evident in the policies advocated by Pilar Miro as Director-General of Cinema in Spain in the 1980s, where it was recognised that advance credits of up to 50 per cent of production costs would be needed to produce fewer, but higher-quality films (Jordan and Morgan-Tamosunas, 3).

Cinema and Television

From the 1960s onwards the scale of American investment in European cinema and the general decline in cinema attendances were rendering screen and import quotas irrelevant. The major preoccupation of film industries throughout the developed world was the loss of audience to television, and the relationship between these two media became the focus of state intervention.

In the 1950s and 1960s most European television was publicly funded and operated as a public service (Britain was exceptional in having a mixed public/private economy). Governments imposed strict quotas on the amount of foreign and foreign-language material which national television stations were allowed to screen, as well as regulating the proportions of each genre of programme. As audiences increasingly saw their films on television, so television and cinema operated in a climate of intense competition in the 1960s and 1970s. This evolved into one of necessary co-existence and cooperation in the 1980s and 1990s when television became the most important source of funding for European films.

Initially television's investment in cinema concentrated on radical or experimental films. In Germany, legislation enacted in the early 1970s permitted television to invest in cinema films, which led to the production of 74 films between 1974 and 1979. In France, similarly, the ban on television investing in cinema was lifted in 1979 and both the first and second channels became major players in cinema. Britain followed suit with the launch of Channel Four in 1982. Initially, investment favoured radical or experimental productions. Germany's second television channel, ZDF, adopted a 'philosophy of artistic patronage' with their series *Das kleine Fernsehspiel*, which financed such works as Hans-Jürgen Syberberg's *Ludwig – Requiem für einen jungfräulichen König (Ludwig – Requiem for a Virgin King*, 1972) and Theo Angelopoulos's *Alexander the Great* (1980) (Hartnoll and Porter, 12). In France, the Institut National de l'Audiovisuel, created in 1975, adopted a policy of funding experimental films by many of the most radical European film-makers between 1975 and 1979. By the 1980s, however, this period of experimental film production financed by television appeared to be over. Television finance for cinema films was increasingly devoted to mainstream film production, often of a kind which had to be able to be 'sold on the international market' (Hartnoll and Porter, 17), while in some cases television channels became instruments for the direct or indirect promotion of the interests of politicians. Thus in Italy in the late 1980s Silvio Berlusconi owned three large private televison networks through his company Fininvest, and a substantial share of the distribution company Penta Film, and this allowed him to use his media influence to promote his political campaigns and those of his party Forza Italia.

At the outset, television's contribution to the production of films for the cinema was an indirect form of public subsidy since European television stations were almost all operated as state-funded public services. However, the 1980s saw rapid changes in the way films were delivered to audiences, with many films becoming available on video cassettes for sale or for rental and with satellite and cable channels becoming widespread. Television was deregulated in Italy in the mid-1970s, in France and Spain in the 1980s, and in Russia after the fall of the Berlin Wall, so that commercial television channels became increasingly involved in both producing and screening cinema films. In Italy, for example, 80 per cent of feature films were financed by television by the end of the 1980s, while Canal Plus, one of the most dynamic of the new channels, which originated in France in 1984, had built up a production and distribution empire that covered much of Europe by the end of the 1990s. In anticipation of the completion of the Single Market in 1986, the European Commission addressed the question of cross-frontier broadcasting, or so-called 'television without frontiers', making it clear that the aim was to use television to create 'an increasingly integrated economic, social and political entity' in which questions of competition, particularly in relation to advertising and intellectual property, would require resolution. Thus a curiously contradictory situation arose. As competition between TV stations became more acute and revenues more and more dependent on the size of the audience, so television became another means by which American films, which were cheap to buy and popular, were distributed in Europe.

On the other hand, many European governments took a renewed interest in financing the cinema. In Britain, a government that was committed to privatisation and to shrinking the state, phased out tax breaks for investors in the film industry, abolished the Eady Levy and dismantled the National Film Finance Corporation in 1985, a year later establishing British Screen, a private company whose role was to lend money to finance film production. In France, the socialist government of the 1980s created three new television channels (two of them private), generating cut-throat competition for audiences and profit, which led to large increases in American imports, but at the same time increased the amount available for *avances sur recettes*, involved the Ministry of Culture directly in financing film production, and created a tax shelter system to encourage investment in films. In Russia in the early 1990s, immediately after the collapse of the Soviet Union, investment in film production became a preferred method of money-laundering while video-piracy made significant inroads into the distribution sector. More recently, the major television channels have operated a cartel for purchasing screening rights, which keeps the price of features artificially low and starves the film industry of funds for production. They devote one-third of their schedules to feature films but achieve high ratings by screening old Soviet films.

Cinema and the European Union

In Europe, state intervention in the film industries was invariably designed to prop up domestic industries or to encourage co-productions and it was often designed to support film-making in 'minority' languages. Until the completion of the Single Market in 1986 there was little thought of a European film policy, although, as we have seen, a unified television policy was adumbrated in 1984. However, in the 1980s and 1990s such a policy became both feasible and desirable. The fall of the Berlin Wall in 1989 and the re-unification of Germany in 1990 altered the perception of 'Europe' and gave western Europe economic and cultural responsibilities towards the former eastern bloc. The Treaty of Maastricht and the creation of the European Union made harmonisation and concerted action necessary both to manage competition, to ensure a strong European presence in the increasingly convergent telecommunications, computing and information markets, and in order to foster the cultural idea of Europe. The privatisation of television and telecommunications which began in the 1980s and gathered pace throughout the decade, the successive waves of mergers and takeovers in international media corporations, rapid technological change, and the birth of the information highway, all served to anchor cinema within the global media industries, which are, of course, dominated by the United States. Films made for cinema are used to attract customers to purchase other goods and services sold via the new media, and to underpin infrastructural investment, so that although film production forms a very small part of total media activity, it is an immensely significant element of the global media economy, as is the ownership of catalogues of films.

The global economic significance of the audio-visual sector was confirmed by the Uruguay round of negotiations which led to the 1993 GATT. The Americans sought a deregulation of the European market – an abolition of quotas and subsidies – in the cause of free trade, while the European Union, inspired by the French, argued that audio-visual products were cultural products and thus should be exempted from free trade provisions. The EU's refusal to shift its position almost caused a failure of the Agreement, which was finally concluded by omitting audio-visual products and by an 'agreement to disagree'.

The timing of this confrontation is interesting. In France it coincided with the release of Claude Berri's film of Emile Zola's novel *Germinal*, leading to an opposition between 'Cola' and 'Zola' which recalled an argument between the Europeans and the Americans that can be traced back, as we have seen, to 1945 if not to the 1930s. For Michael Chanan the argument is to be explained by the value of what was at issue (Chanan, 57). The 1980s saw transnational media corporations like Microsoft, News International and Time Warner massively increase their power. Thus the traditional argument between European and American film industries had been transformed in the 1990s into an argument about who would secure the multi-billion dollar profits from world media domination, in which cinema plays a small but significant part.

The GATT discussions gave further impetus to a series of Europe-wide initiatives tentatively begun in the 1980s when it was agreed that Europe's television channels would screen a fixed quota of EU-originated programmes. In 1989 the Council of Europe (whose members included eastern-bloc countries as well as those in the European Community) initiated the Eurimages programme, a fund for multi-lateral European co-productions between countries who are contributing members, which supports co-production through a loan mechanism and also supports documentaries, exhibition and marketing. Some of the most critically successful European films of the 1990s were supported by this fund. In addition, the European Community/Union has had two cinema initiatives, MEDIA I (1991–5) and MEDIA II (from 1995). While the former has been criticised for its 'scattergun' approach (Finney, 3), the second project, with a budget of 310 million ECU, concentrates on development, distribution and training as well as on the key industrial sectors of animation, new technology and heritage (Finney, 133). Its inspiration is clearly the Hollywood film industry, whose size is considered to offer significant economies of scale but, as important, a means to spread risk in what is an inherently uncertain business. Based on the knowledge that only 10 per cent of European films are screened in another European country, MEDIA II considered distribution to be a major weakness of the European film industries. A report by the consultants Coopers and Lybrand (cited in Finney, 141) identified the advantages of the American majors in respect of distribution, an illustration of which might be the extremely favourable deals imposed by George Lucas on theatres wishing to screen his prequel *Star Wars Episode 1: The Phantom Menace* (1999). Thus the European Union has made efforts to create industrial structures in the cinema to compare with and rival those of Hollywood, reinserting cinema into a commercial discourse from which it emerged in the aftermath of the Second World War, and reinforcing it by its policy of promoting fair competition.

Paradoxically, perhaps, new technologies have encouraged the production of new feature films and enhanced the value of back catalogues by increasing the outlets and demand for audiovisual products, so that the EU has been well placed to take advantage of the market expansion offered by globalisation. However, because the European Union also promotes cultural diversity, this creates uncertainty as to what should be the focus of public policy towards the cinema and whether, indeed, a common policy is feasible or desirable. What, if anything, defines 'European cinema' remains an open question, and it is this which forms the subject of the following chapter.

2

Ideology, Aesthetics and Style

The preceding pages have discussed the history of cinema in Europe from an economic and political point of view, stressing the importance national governments of all political persuasions came to attach to controlling and supporting what was, for much of the twentieth century, the most important audio-visual medium and the most significant form of mass entertainment. The Russian Revolution, the rise of fascism in Italy, Germany and Spain, the two world wars, the collapse of the Soviet Union, together with the creation and extension of the European Union, have all been seen to have had a profound impact on the cinema and to have affected the film industries in Europe.

The pages which follow will focus on questions of aesthetics and style and how these have been used to define the nationality of films. They will ask whether European cinema is merely the sum of different national cinemas or whether there are identifiable genres, styles, production norms and practices which differentiate European cinema from other regional cinemas and, especially, from Hollywood cinema. They will also consider whether the relationship between European cinema and Hollywood cinema can most productively be described as one of mutual creative tension, and what the cultural role of cinema in Europe will be in the context of twenty-first-century globalisation.

The Rise of National Cinema

In the 1920s the economic, political and ideological role of cinema was hotly debated and the idea of national cinema took root in Europe. In Italy, the Soviet Union, Germany and Spain, the context was the rise of nationalism and the increasingly totalitarian regimes in these countries. In other major European film-producing countries such as Britain and France, the nationalist emphasis was more obviously cultural than political. Elites were worried about the influence of the cinema in general and of the American cinema in particular. It has been argued that the standardisation and homogenisation of mass culture evident in American films purveyed a democratic egalitarianism which ran counter to the more hierarchical structures of European societies and posed a threat to bourgeois elites. Thus one commentator in Britain complained of

belonging to all classes whose experience of life is based largely on the
.... and frequently sordid plots of American films' (Thompson, 70);
another criticised the fact that in the America depicted in the movies, 'no sentiment is too sacred to be compared with the pleasures of the commodities displayed' (quoted in Ďurovičová, 140). A particular concern was that the emphasis
on material objects not only damaged European industries but was also particularly attractive to women, who were the 'ideal consumers' targeted by
Hollywood (Eckert, 16), and that this was subversive of their traditional place
in society. Hence another British writer's reference to 'women who, to all
intents and purposes, are temporary American citizens' as a result of watching
movies (Maltby and Vasey, 71). In response to the combination of moral and
ideological panic induced by the popularity of American films in Britain a
Commission on Educational and Cultural Films was set up in 1929 (Dickinson
and Street, 48), and in a report on *The Film in National Life*, called for the production of films which were 'an unequivocal expression of British life and
thought, deriving character and inspiration from our national inheritance'
(Maltby and Vasey, 72–3).

The 'America' of the movies was a utopia which 'presented itself less as a
geographical territory than as an imaginative one. It was a territory that deliberately made itself available for assimilation in a variety of cultural contexts,'
and it 'was not a foreign country to its aficionados whatever their nationality'
(Maltby and Vasey, 69, 79). American studio bosses made much of this utopianism and used the idea of a Hollywood 'melting pot' to promote Hollywood's universal appeal and to suggest that the American film industry was 'a
cultural microcosm gathering the best and the brightest from all continents'
(Ďurovičová, p. 141).

In seeking to offer economic protection to their domestic film industries,
European governments were led to attempt to define a national film since this
was both a form of distinctiveness and a useful counterweight to the supposed 'universalism' of Hollywood. The difficulties they experienced and the
solutions they devised offer an interesting approach to the question of
national cinema and its relation to European cinema.

The nationality of a film could be defined by where it is made and who
invests in its production and distribution (Higson, 36). But the various quota
systems introduced in Europe illustrate how ineffective this definition could
be. In Germany, for example, the American studios Paramount and Metro-
Goldwyn Corporation bought a large share of UFA in 1925, while in Britain
and Italy 'quota quickies' were filmed locally but using American money. The
fact that a film is shot in a particular country is no indication of who has
invested in it, who owns the finished product, or even who benefits from distributing it.

A second definition might concern the national origins of those who work on
a film. Thus the British 'Quota Act' of 1927 defined whether or not a film was
British by the 'proportion of labour costs paid to British nationals' (Maltby and

Vasey, 69). However, the film industry throughout Europe and the United States was extremely cosmopolitan. Hollywood employed individuals from all sorts of different national backgrounds – indeed, it was an industry in which immigrants were able to succeed with relative ease, whether as actors, directors, producers or technicians. Hollywood also proved a magnet to Europeans: some, like Chaplin, Hitchcock or Lubitsch, went to seek their fortunes; others emigrated for political reasons. The European film industries also employed waves of immigrants: Russians emigrated after the Bolshevik Revolution of 1917 to Berlin or to Paris where the Russian-owned and run Albatros Studios flourished in the 1920s; Alexander Korda, the most powerful film producer in England in the 1930s, was Hungarian by birth. When Hitler came to power in 1933 many Jews in the film business fled to France, England or America – Fritz Lang being perhaps the best known – and the German-trained cameramen who found work in France had an influence on the visual style of French films right up to the 1950s. When the Germans invaded France many French actors and directors, among them Renoir, Clair, Duvivier, Gabin and Jouvet, left for North or South America and did not return until after the war. Luis Buñuel went into political exile from Spain as a result of the Civil War and did not make a film there again until *Viridiana* in 1961; many Eastern European film-makers, like Roman Polanski or Milos Forman, emigrated to America during the Communist period; and since the fall of the Berlin Wall, many film-makers from Eastern Europe and Russia, such as Krzysztof Kieslowski, have worked in the west, especially in France, while large numbers of European film-makers, like Luc Besson, Ridley Scott and Wim Wenders, continue to work in Hollywood.

A more promising definition of national cinema might concern what it represents. Hollywood cinema is deliberately escapist and film studios became adept at creating sets to look like anywhere in the world, from Ancient Rome and Biblical Babylon, as in D. W. Griffith's *Intolerance* (1916), to modern Paris, London or Moscow. During the 1920s and 1930s, especially, set decorators worked from photographic records, embellished by their own invention, to re-create landscapes or cities thought to be typical of well-known locations like the cities of London, Paris, Berlin or New York. Indeed, the Paris photographic agency Seeberger Frères specialised in supplying Hollywood studios with images of 'typical' Paris street scenes and were thus influential in determining for decades how Paris would be represented by Hollywood. The need for a location to be recognisable often led to the flouting of verisimilitude. For example, Pabst's *Die Dreigroschenoper* (*The Threepenny Opera*) (1931), based on the eighteenth-century English play *The Beggars' Opera* by John Gay, was made in Berlin but set in a London in which, contrary to reality, the docks and Soho are contiguous. But these features are used as indices of London in much the same way as a meteorological commonplace such as the London fog in Hitchcock's *The Lodger*, or a monument such as the Eiffel Tower, which signifies Paris in *La haine*. Such features are incorporated into a shot to let the viewer know where the film is supposed to be set, which may be many thousands of miles away from where it is shot.

During the 1930s, European cinema often self-consciously shared Hollywood's utopianism, as can be seen in the extravagant sets of Italian spectaculars or the fantastic design of German expressionist films such as *Metropolis* or *The Cabinet of Dr Caligari*, as well as in the studio-produced historicism of internationally successful films such as Korda's *The Private Life of Henry VIII* (1933) or Feyder's *La kermesse héroïque* (*Carnival in Flanders*, 1935). Gradually, however, we can see the beginning of a movement towards realism, exemplified in Renoir's *La règle du jeu*, released just before the Second World War in 1939. This was taken up after the war in the Italian neo-realist cinema and gradually became a commonplace in European cinema in the 1960s. But even films shot 'on location' are not necessarily shot in the real location. Hollywood spectaculars such as Anthony Mann's *El Cid* (1961) or *The Fall of the Roman Empire* (1964) were shot in Spain, as were the so-called 'spaghetti westerns'. Today, modern technology makes it possible to create an authentic-looking location entirely within a film studio or on a computer screen, as was amusingly illustrated in Barry Levinson's *Wag the Dog* (1997). The result is that although the nationality of a film may be legally defined by where it is made, this definition may well be at odds with what the film represents and, therefore, what the audience believes, or is intended to believe, about its national origins. Hollywood 'represented' Europe and Europe fantasised about America.

Sound and Style

The arrival of the talkies at the end of the 1920s, however, seemed to offer an obvious way of defining a film's nationality. In the silent period language was certainly no guide to the nationality of a film. Many of the early film theorists considered that the silent cinema constituted an 'international language', either because it dealt with simple melodramatic or comic themes, which easily crossed national boundaries, or because its iconography and performance styles were based on a set of simplified, exaggerated and easily 'legible' codes. It was also suggested that cinema not only mobilised universal themes and genres but could also be used to promote humanist ideals. But films were primarily 'an international language' because they were exported as 'semi-finished products' (Maltby and Vasey, 77). For technical reasons European release prints were often made from negatives different from the ones used for American release prints and when they were exhibited it was in conditions which varied widely from place to place. There could be different musical accompaniments, and intertitles in the local language whose content was often radically modified to take account of local sensibilities; they could be projected at different speeds, with different colour tints; and they were often re-edited so that the versions screened could be of widely varying lengths. In the Soviet Union, when there was a dearth of imported films during the post-revolutionary blockade, a deliberate policy of re-editing imported films was developed both for aesthetic and for political reasons. The shortage of new imported films stimulated the 're-use' of those already in the country, which were often recut to make something new, while at the same time aesthetic experimentation in all the arts was predicated on the deliberate destruction of the old. The theories of montage, by which new aesthetic experiences are generated through the juxtaposition of different images, is said to have derived from this practice. But as well as existing in a range of sometimes quite different versions, adapted to local circumstances, silent films were 'naturalised' because audiences read into them whatever local interpretations they chose. Anthropologists have noted that groups unfamiliar with western narrative genres will appropriate western audio-visual material according to their individual world views (Michaels, 81–95), and a similar process probably took place with silent films. Sound cinema, on the other hand, made comprehension difficult, emphasised cultural specificity, and also offered greater opportunities for defining the nationality of a film.

Sound cinema had been technically feasible for some considerable time but it became commercially viable with the success of Crosland's *The Jazz Singer* (1927), starring the popular vaudeville singer Al Jolson. Designed to revive the flagging fortunes of the Warner Brothers Studio, which it did beyond all expectation, sound cinema also precipitated cut-throat technological and artistic competition. On the technological side, sound completed the industrialisation of cinema by introducing greater uniformity and standardisation. According to Williams, 'everywhere the coming of sound appears to have reduced diversity and acted against those who would oppose the classical Hollywood cinema with an alternative of their own' (Williams, 136). It also integrated the various elements of popular entertainment, such as song, music and dance, into the 'culture industries', and marked the beginning of the link, which is of immense significance today, between the film industry, the electrical and electronic industries, and big business. In Europe, sound reinforced national rivalries, stifled the cooperation that had been adumbrated in 'Film Europe', but also offered temporary protection from Hollywood. However, in Europe it was only in Germany that the link was made between big business and the cinema, through the investment of companies such as AEG and Siemens in the conversion to sound.

Artistically, many in Europe feared the standardisation that sound would bring not just to American films but to European cinema too, and believed that the constraints of filming on sound stages and the novelty of hearing people talk would put an end to visual experimentation. This was perhaps most acutely felt in the Soviet Union. Soviet films had often been conceived with musical accompaniments in mind – Eisenstein, for example, worked with the German composer Edmund Meisel on a specially composed score to accompany *The Battleship Potemkin* (Eisenstein, 177–8), and he maintained the habit of working closely with composers, as can be seen from his collaboration with

Prokofiev on *Alexander Nevsky*. But the organic development of musical accompaniments was a very different matter from the integration of dialogue. In 1928, Eisenstein, Pudovkin and Alexandrov published a 'Statement' on sound cinema in which they expressed concern that 'this new technical discovery may not only hinder the development and perfection of the cinema as an art, but also threaten to destroy all its present formal achievement' (Eisenstein, 257–9). They particularly feared that sound would destroy the aesthetic principles of montage, which was the national specificity of Soviet cinema and the foundation of 'the success of Soviet films on the world's screens', and they predicted, rightly, that sound would usher in 'an epoch of its automatic utilisation for "highly coloured dramas" and other photographical performances of a theatrical sort' and called for 'experimental work with sound...along the line of its distinct non-synchronisation with the visual images', for the 'contrapuntal use' of sound.

This 'Statement' is significant for a number of reasons. The first is that it embraces sound but not dialogue, whereas elsewhere the question of national cinema crystallised around dialogue in particular rather than sound in general. Secondly, it confirms a divorce, at this point, between the development of cinema in the west and in the Soviet Union. As Eisenstein and his co-authors acknowledged, it was to be several years before the Soviet Union was equipped for sound, and silent films continued to be made and distributed in that country until the Second World War (Nowell-Smith, 1996, 390), whereas in western Europe sound was initially viewed as an opportunity for national differentiation. But thirdly, as envisaged, when sound did eventually become general in Soviet films its advent took on political force as Socialist Realism was adopted as the party line and as Stalin's censorship bit hard: 'According to official doctrine, it was the scriptwriter rather than the director who was the crucial figure.... Publicists of the time insisted on the "iron scenario" strictly limiting the independence of the director and denounced the idea of directorial freedom as a remnant of formalism' (Nowell-Smith, 1996, 390). Indeed, it has been suggested that like Goebbels in Germany, Stalin 'micro-managed' the cinema and instituted himself as the supreme censor.

But in western Europe too, even where political totalitarianism was absent, artistic experimentation was killed off by sound. This is interestingly dramatised in one of René Clair's early sound films, *A nous la liberté* (1932), in which a gramophone-record factory is visually likened to a prison because both use the principles of mass production, in which tasks are measured, timed and infinitely repeated in order to achieve maximum efficiency. The film, which is said to have influenced Chaplin's *Modern Times* (1936), satirises the totalitarian slogan 'work is freedom' (later to be found over the entrance to concentration camps) and ends with its two heroes abandoning a life of industry-generated wealth for a life as tramps on the open road.

In the very early years of film with dialogue it appeared that the film industry might fragment into a series of national markets and audiences. Early sound films such as *The Jazz Singer*, in which music is much more important than spoken dialogue, solved the problem of language differences by projecting intertitles onto an adjacent screen, much as is frequently done for opera today (Thompson, 158). But subtitling or handing out a translation of the scenario somewhat undermined the novelty of films in which people spoke and could be understood. On the other hand, dubbing techniques remained unsatisfactory until the invention of the Moviola in 1930, when the mixing and accurate synchronisation of sound tracks became feasible. The result was that, for a brief period, films were often made in several different language versions. This was done either by setting up production facilities abroad or by hiring foreign actors to work in the domestic industry. The American studios were most active because they had most to lose. Paramount established a branch studio at Joinville just outside Paris, which came to be known as 'Babel on Seine'; MGM and Universal hired European actors to make foreign-language versions in Hollywood (Vincendeau, 1988, 29); but the Germans also operated abroad, with the Tobis studios at Epinay in the Paris suburbs, while many British and French actors travelled to Berlin to make films in their native languages.

The experiments with foreign-language versions are useful in considering whether language is axiomatic to defining national cinemas. The failure to respect language sensibilities led to riots in Prague in 1930, possibly discreetly fostered by American firms, when German-speaking films were screened, leading distributors to prefer French versions with Czech subtitles (Ďurovičová, 23, n. 25). Similarly, films made in Spanish in Hollywood, using Latin American actors, were ill-received in Spain because of its variety of linguistic communities. Sometimes there could simply be a failure of comprehension, as in Portugal where Brazilian speakers were not understood. Beyond this, dialogue increased social and cultural specificity both within films and between films and foregrounded the social and national origins of actors and characters. Films which Hollywood had passed off as 'universal', or in which nationality had not been an issue, now became identifiably American and therefore less amenable to local assimilation. In Britain where audiences ostensibly understood Hollywood's language, American idioms initially proved incomprehensible (they would not be today, thanks to the mass media), but on the other hand, audiences in the north of England and in Scotland preferred the apparently 'classless' accents of American actors to the relentlessly upper middle-class southern English accents of most British screen actors. Nationality differences were sometimes incorporated diegetically in order to allow different languages to be spoken. Thus Duvivier's *Allô Berlin? Ici Paris* (1932) is a comedy about male German telephonists falling in love with female French telephonists, based around language differences and stereotypical national behaviour. It is often said that the advent of sound destroyed many acting careers, but it was the making of others. Greta Garbo or Emil Jannings, who were bi- or multi-lingual, found their careers boosted by their transnational appeal, while Maurice Chevalier was apparently instructed not to lose his French accent, so that he could continue to incarnate a 'typical' French man in Hollywood.

Scholars have suggested that foreign-language versions were unpopular because audiences perceived them as somehow 'inauthentic', based as they were on a minimalist definition of the national as 'simply the difference between the least possible and the least necessary inflection of the basic text' (Ďurovičová, 144). In a film industry built around stars it was pointless to replace a well-known figure simply in order that the film's dialogue could be understood. More significantly, foreign-language versions underscored the fact that cultural discourse was just as important as dialogue in the reception of a film. Nataša Ďurovičová cites the fascinating example of the Swedish version of a Hollywood film in which 'the sense of comfort with which the Swedish actors speak their lines is essentially incompatible with the non-Swedish social mannerisms, surroundings and psychological types of the characters' (146). With the coming of sound, the corporeal expressiveness of silent cinema gave way to a certain 'casualness' which became the mark of authenticity and realism, but this was a way of 'being in the world' which was culturally specific. In this way sound cinema required films to adopt a recognisable cultural idiom so as to appear authentic.

Sound was also instrumental in shifting the origin of language from a geographical to a technological space (Ďurovičová, 142). The two methods quickly perfected for distributing foreign-language films were dubbing and subtitling (preferences for one or the other varied from country to country) and both could be used to promote national requirements. Italy, France and Germany all required dubbing to be carried out in those countries and not, for example, in America or Britain. The requirement that all foreign films screened in Italy should be dubbed into Italian was both a protectionist measure and a nationalist one since it imposed on Italian cinema a linguistic uniformity which the Italian state, with its many and varied regional dialects and languages, did not have (Nowell-Smith, 1968, 146). It also began the tradition of post-synchronisation which persists in Italian cinema today. The Italian used in dubbing was, in the main, a 'standard Italian' designed to eradicate dialect and foreign words, but more recently, for the dubbing of a film such as *Trainspotting*, a kind of colloquial Italian is used which is largely self-referential (that is, rather than mirroring how people actually speak, it signifies 'the colloquial register in cinema'). From 1941 onwards, Spain likewise imposed dubbing into Spanish (Bosch and del Rincón, 119), and on occasion this proved an extremely useful tool of censorship. In Franquist Spain, for example, all references to Rick's (Humphrey Bogart's) participation in the Spanish Civil War in Curtiz's *Casablanca* (1942), were simply excised (Bosch and del Rincón, 122–3). But even where political censorship was non-existent, references which were considered obsure were frequently 'naturalised' and the film's meaning was often altered in the process (Nowell-Smith, 1968, 147). In such cases it would be difficult to argue that audiences in different countries were seeing the 'same' version of a film.

To sum up, therefore, sound cinema required the 'proper bodies' to make the 'proper noises'. Usually the proper noises were the national language, which could be a dialect invented for the purpose, as in Italy, or, as in Britain, a foreign dialect such as 'American English', which had the advantage of not being regionally specific. The 'proper bodies' were often more problematical because the norms to which they were required to conform were, and are, less well codified: the 'grammar' of physical comportment is less highly developed than the grammar of spoken dialogue.

Film-makers sometimes used national stereotypes to comic effect. Knowing that the west was both suspicious and curious about the post-revolutionary Soviet Union, the Russian film-maker Lev Kuleshov made a spoof entitled *The Extraordinary Adventures of Mr West in the Land of the Bolsheviks* (1924), in which Bolsheviks dress up like the tribal bandits the Americans imagine them to be in order to fleece the American visitors. Similarly, the Spanish film-maker Luis Buñuel, making *Cet obscur objet du désir* (*That Obscure Object of Desire*, 1977) in France, investigated the themes of Frenchness and Spanishness through body language and speech in 'a film by a Spaniard who has lived in France adapting a French novel (Pierre Louÿs's *La femme et le pantin*) whose Spanish protagonist is transformed by Buñuel into a Frenchman played by a Spaniard and dubbed by a Frenchman' (Shohat and Stam, 50). Conversely, in Claude Chabrol's film of Simone de Beauvoir's novel *Le sang des autres* (*The Blood of Others*, 1984), made in English for the American cable network HBO and starring American and Australian actors, the question of nationality is not foregrounded, so that both the body-language of the actors and the confrontational dialogue, as well as the fast-paced editing, combine to produce a representation which more closely resembles *Dallas* than Paris in the 1950s.

The European Film Studios

Most film historians attribute the world-wide success of American cinema to the studio system. 'By concentrating production within vast, factory-like studios and by vertically integrating all aspects of the business, from production to publicity to distribution to exhibition, they created a model system – the "studio system" – which other countries had to imitate in order to compete' (Gomery, in Nowell-Smith, 1996, 43). Indeed, the use of the word 'studio', which simultaneously connotes an artist's workshop and the place where the pupils and followers of a great artist produce imitations of his work, neatly encapsulated the cinema's role as industry masquerading as art.

As we have seen, the studio system was a key factor in helping the Americans to consolidate their European domination at the time of the First World War, when American products proved technically and artistically superior to those in Europe. It was also crucial after the advent of sound cinema when technological superiority was achieved through the involvement of big corporations, especially those from the electrical industries, in the modernisation and expansion of the studios. Is it the case, however, that the Europeans had to 'imitate the Americans' in order to compete?

It is certainly true that they thought they did. In France during the 1930s, when film-production companies came and went bankrupt with alarming rapidity and when it appeared impossible to achieve continuity in film production, Jean Renoir, Marcel L'Herbier, and several other film-makers tried to persuade the government to create a 'Hollywood on the Côte d'azur'. Ironically, this was only achieved during the Occupation when the mass exodus from Paris of people involved in the film business led to the creation of a prototype film school and production centre near Nice (Bertin-Maghit, 42–8). In Italy, Luigi Freddi, the Fascist Party's head of propaganda, went to Hollywood to study the organisation of the film industry and, after he became head of cinema, promoted vertical integration in the Italian industry and secured state funding to build the new Cinecittà studios, opened in 1937.

In the Soviet Union the Hollywood model proved equally seductive although it operated within the overall context of state control. Boris Shumyatsky, appointed head of Soyuzkino by Stalin in 1930, visited Hollywood. He applied its lessons by successfully managing the transition to sound, by re-organising Soviet film production on Hollywood lines. Similarly in Germany, after the Nazis came to power, Goebbels worked closely with the film industry to concentrate film production into a small number of highly capitalised, efficiently organised studios which successfully produced high-quality entertainment, often inspired by Hollywood genres, for Germany's expanding market. These examples, and that of Tobis-Klangfilm or Paramount, who built studios in Paris in order to exploit their respective sound systems, suggest that some European studios were, indeed, vehicles for factory-style mass production.

However, this was not always the case, nor is it necessarily what they are best remembered for. Babelsberg, owned by UFA, became celebrated for a distinctive style of film-making based initially on complex and intriguing sets and lighting, and later, on a style of 'cold' cinematography which was exported to France and to America through the emigration of cinematographers after the Nazis came to power. The Albatros film studio at Montreuil near Paris was taken over in 1920 by the Russian émigré Ermolieff. It became the vector through which much contemporary Russian art and design and a certain orientalism reached a wide public in western Europe, while its leading actor, Ivan Mosjoukine, became one of the first film stars to emerge in Europe (Albera, 19–31). The Tobis-owned Epinay film studio in the Paris region became known, under the designer Lazare Meerson, for its elaborate sets, seen in many of René Clair's films, as did the Victorine studios in Nice where *Les enfants du paradis* was shot. The UFA and Albatros models are arguably more typical of European film studios, which were primarily artistic or stylistic communities rather than factories of films. With the exception of the Soviet studios, which were devoted to catering for the masses, their major function was not to serve as the centre of vertically integrated businesses but to provide an artistic home and a means of artistic expression for communities of like-minded individuals.

The 1920s and 1930s were probably the period when studio styles had the greatest influence on cinema in Europe. After the Second World War, under the influence of the Italian neo-realists who shot their films on location rather than on elaborate sets, their influence declined, but it did not disappear. In Britain, Michael Balcon used the Ealing Studios, which he took over in 1938 but whose period of greatest celebrity was the late 1940s and early 1950s, to promote an ideology more than an aesthetic through the genre of comedy, consciously putting 'film to work in the national interest' (Barr, 7) and aiming to make films 'projecting Britain and the British character'. But perhaps the most celebrated of all post-war European studios was Rome's Cinecittà, the 'Hollywood on the Tiber' that Pasolini called 'the belching stomach of Italy'. It created its own star system of 'sex-pot divas' such as Gina Lollobrigida and Sophia Loren, who subsequently became world famous thanks to Hollywood, and it specialised in mass producing a rapidly changing range of 'B' features and genre films – popular melodramas, comedies, horror films, sword and sandal epics and, most famous of all, 'spaghetti westerns'. The increasingly parodic self-reflexiveness of the spaghetti westerns underlined the ambiguous function of a film studio attempting to copy pre-war Hollywood in the post-Second World War era. The conflicts between a 'European' artistic community and 'American' big business inherent in Cinecittà's approach to film-making is also dramatised in Jean-Luc Godard's film *Le mépris* (*Contempt*, 1962), itself a Franco-Italian co-production shot at Cinecittà and on location in Italy. However, François Truffaut's *La nuit américaine* (*Day for Night*, 1983), whose ambiguous title 'the American night' does not come across in English, is a nostalgic evocation of studio-based film-making which suggests both the positive and negative aspects of the studios, as does Federico Fellini's equally nostalgic *Ginger e Fred* (*Ginger and Fred*, 1985). Such exercises in nostalgia underline the important but frequently neglected contribution of studios to European film-making.

Hollywood, For and Against: Art Cinema and Popular Cinema

As we have seen, for much of the twentieth century European countries were concerned about the threat of 'Americanisation', or to be more specific, 'Hollywoodisation'. 'Americanisation' was synonymous with 'Hollywoodisation' because of the US motion picture industry's success at exporting its films all over the world and the assumption that films carried cultural meanings: Uncle Sam invades Europe. The dilemma hinged on the extent to which separation from Hollywood was possible or, indeed, desirable. For many in Europe, particularly cultural and political elites who feared the impact of mass exposure to Hollywood's messages of democracy, this was something to be taken seriously (Maltby, in Nowell-Smith and Ricci, 104–15). Throughout the twentieth century the existence of Hollywood as a major international competitor has exerted a profound influence over the direction of European film industries as European states have sought to protect their national cinemas against Hollywood competition. In the totalitarian states the film industries were carefully developed and nurtured for nationalist economic and cultural reasons, either by massive state investment, as in the USSR, or, as in Germany, through the close involvement of the banks in financing the film industry. Indeed, with Goebbels's encouragement, the cinema developed into the fourth largest industry of the Third Reich (Petley, 86). In France and Britain, pre-war state involvement was patchy and in the main confined to forms of import regulation.

At the end of the Second World War, European governments became more actively involved in the promotion of cinema through various forms of state subsidy, and later, through the regulation of television and the mechanisms of the European Community/Union. France took the lead in the 1950s, followed by Germany and, after Franco's death, Spain, in promoting the art film or *auteur* film, which some scholars would consider a characteristic form of European cinema. The art film existed alongside the popular film genres which continued to be produced in Europe, but for a period of about twenty years from the late 1950s art cinema came to be seen as distinctively European because it was the form of cinema in which states invested the greatest financial support and which they promoted abroad.

In an interesting article published in 1979, Bordwell suggested that art cinema was a post-war 'mode of film production' which grew up 'as the dominance of Hollywood cinema was beginning to wane' (Bordwell, 57). He attempted to define art cinema by stating what it is not – in other words by positing Hollywood as the classic or the 'norm' and describing how art cinema deviates from it. According to Bordwell, in Hollywood cinema the *mise en scène*, editing, sound, and cinematography all function to advance the narrative and to create compositional unity so that the narrative represents a 'cause-effect chain'. Classic Hollywood cinema is thus transparent, easy to read, goal-oriented, and structured around narrative closure. Art cinema, on the other hand, rejects cause and effect and favours narratives motivated by realism and authorial expressivity. Its protagonists are psychologically complicated, reality is ambiguous and subjective, while the author is foregrounded as a structure in the film's system.

The aesthetic origins of art cinema are undoubtedly to be found in European modernism. The narrative structures and the focus on subjectivity, as well as the self-reflexiveness, which are typical of art cinema, all have their counterpart in the experimental European novel of the 1920s to the 1960s, while the playfulness, intertextuality and fragmentary nature of much art film is equally central to modernist writing whether prose or poetry. Thus a typical art film might be Antonioni's *L'Avventura* (1960), with its apparently inconsequential narrative, unexplained shifts of focus, and characters who are engaged in a compelling but unresolved quest. Similarly, Truffaut's first two feature films, *Les quatre cents coups* (*The 400 Blows*, 1959) and *Tirez sur le pianiste* (*Shoot the*

Pianist, 1960), the former the subjective narrative of the adolescent Antoine Doinel, the latter with its playful references to Hollywood gangster films, its narrative flashbacks, its abrupt shifts of tone and strange mixture of genres, fall centrally within the modernist narrative and aesthetic tradition. The art film addressed its audience in a different way from the Hollywood film and the audience it addressed was different. Hollywood sought to federate its spectators and, in Steve Neale's words, 'succeeded in...producing a unified and unifying mode of textual address, a genuinely popular form of entertainment with a mass rather than a class-based audience' (Neale, 29). Art films, on the other hand, reflecting the fact that the cinema audience in the post-war world was no longer a mass audience, deliberately sought out the fraction that was more middle-class, better educated and more receptive to narrative experimentation.

The existential quest, the interrogation of subjectivity, and experiment with narrative form which appear to lie at the heart of art cinema mirror a structure of production in which the director is the linchpin of the film. The film is a personal statement by the director, who has himself invented the project, probably written the script, raised the finance, used his house as a location and cast his friends and family in the leading roles. Making a film thus becomes more like writing a private diary than manufacturing a car, and the camera becomes the instrument for writing rather than a machine for producing. The film is sold on the director's name rather than that of the star and it remains the intellectual property of the director rather than that of the studio, as in the Hollywood tradition.

Is Bordwell right to suggest that 'realism' is also characteristic of art cinema? In the 1950s, the British and Italian film studios continued to construct fantasy worlds and utopian environments while the French cinema frequently invested in costume dramas and adaptations of nineteenth-century novels. But at the same time the neo-realist movement in Italy adumbrated a new approach to subject-matter, to performance and to setting. This is exemplified in Visconti's *Ossessione*, which takes a theme that is treated in a heightened, melodramatic manner in the American cinema and adapts it to the circumstances of Italian village life. By the 1960s, territories such as Spain, which remained politically and culturally isolated, continued, as Buñuel's *Viridiana* (1961) suggests, to give a national inflection to artistic traditions. But elsewhere the realist approach had become general in European cinema and it can be found in films as diverse as the French New Wave and the 'kitchen sink' dramas of British 1960s cinema. The realism in question often consisted in choosing subjects from everyday life, enacted by ordinary people in settings which were not obviously glamorised, so that one of its extremely significant features was a naturalistic approach to performance that often relied on young, relatively unknown actors, anti-heroes and anti-stars whose consciousness rather than their public role was the mainspring of the film's action and who lent the films a degree of authenticity.

An important aspect of this new authenticity was a willingness to depict sexual relations more openly and realistically, and this was to prove a major selling point for European cinema at a time when Hollywood films were still too frightened of public reaction to do so. The typical plot of a New Wave film concerns the relationship of a young man and a young woman, while much of the foreign reputation of the French cinema in the late 1950s was based on the corporeal freedom symbolised by Brigitte Bardot who, of course, quickly became a star in the Hollywood sense of the word, able to sell films on the basis of her appearance in them. In Godard's film *Le mépris*, Bardot becomes the pretext for a confrontation between the European art film and the American popular cinema, since *Le mépris* depicts the American producer of an Italian film who wishes to seduce the wife (Bardot) of the French scriptwriter and to people the film adaptation of a world literary classic, *The Odyssey*, with naked mermaids as in a sex film.

Neale suggests that the representation of the body was a site of crucial difference between art cinema and Hollywood cinema. Whereas 'the body in Hollywood became simultaneously the incarnation of fictional characterisation and the nodal site of a fetishistic regime of eroticisation and sexual representation... [t]ogether with a reticence of gesture and (later) vocal delivery', European cinema exploited a freedom which was the result of a tradition stretching back to the 1920s, and which can be seen in Eisenstein's use of 'types', Renoir's stress on the artifice of acting in *La règle du jeu*, Visconti's use of non-professional actors in *La terra trema* (1948), and so on (Neale, 31). From the mid-1950s onwards, this freedom enabled European films 'to trade more stably and commercially both upon their status as "adult" art and upon their reputation for "explicit" representations of sexuality' (33), so constituting a recognisable export genre within world cinema trade.

Bordwell's thesis that art cinema is a 'mode of production' must therefore be placed alongside Neale's view of art cinema as a 'mode of consumption'. Neale points out that the exhibition basis for art cinema was provided by the film clubs developed in the 1920s to view censored Soviet films. Film education was an important element of fascist film policy in Italy in the 1930s and was instrumental in the careers of the neo-realist directors. Similarly, in France in the 1950s, film clubs sprang up whose initial purpose was to educate the public in the critical interpretation of films through the organisation of screenings and discussions, and through film magazines, such as *Cahiers du cinéma* and *Positif*. Eventually, as in Italy, it was from these groupings that the new generation of film-makers emerged as the New Wave. In Germany, a little later, the conscious attempt to create a 'film culture', that is a domestic audience capable of appreciating and understanding the films that were produced as art, was, as Elsaesser has pointed out, an absolutely central element in the success of the New German Cinema both domestically and internationally: 'Almost as important as the films, the film schools and cinémathèques and the contacts with an avant-garde cinema were the new writing about the cinema, the publishing ventures and other local and regional media initiatives – all of which revalued the experience of going to the cinema' (Elsaesser, 1989, 27).

Whilst Nowell-Smith may be right to dismiss attempts to treat art cinema as a 'distinct genre analogous to those that flourished in Hollywood and other mainstream commercial cinemas' as a 'mockery', on the grounds that art cinema is too heterogeneous, it certainly is the case that 'art cinema' became a useful marketing device capacious enough and flexible enough to accommodate the differential promotion of films according to the audience targeted (Nowell-Smith, 1996, 569). Thus it is perfectly possible, indeed quite common, for a film which is sold as 'popular' in its home territory to be designated 'art' when exported. This is particularly true of the so-called 'heritage' or 'nostalgia' film which became fashionable in the 1980s and 1990s in Britain, France, Italy and, slightly later, in Russia. Such films play on the anxieties of modernisation, particularly acutely felt at a time of rapid industrial change, and set out to re-create a lost era which, they imply, was better, more agreeable and more exemplary of the national experience than the present. A film such as Claude Berri's *Jean de Florette* (1986) was an immense popular success in France and overseas, but in France this was based on the re-creation of a regionalism which had disappeared with the post-war rural exodus, whereas abroad the film addressed an audience who liked to consume French products, including holidays in the French countryside. Not surprisingly, an imitation of the film, using the same music, was used in a commercial for Stella Artois beer.

Cinema and the National Question

The heritage film points to another distinguishing feature of European art cinema, namely its engagement with the national question, which in cinema terms takes the form of a dialectical relationship with Hollywood cinema. In French film writing of the 1950s, Hollywood cinema is seen as embodying a classicism which is the guarantor of its cultural centrality, rather as French eighteenth-century literature had embodied a classicism which claimed to represent universal truths and values – hence its use as an intertext by Renoir in *La règle du jeu*. If Hollywood represents the classical, then the French or any other European cinema necessarily has a marginal existence which is defined only in relation to the centre. Another version of this belief is found in the 'colonial paradigm' identified by Elsaesser as typical of the relationship of German cinema to Hollywood, and embodied in the famous statement in Wim Wenders's film *Im Lauf der Zeit* (*Kings of the Road*, 1976) that 'the Yanks have colonised our subconscious'. Like 'minority' literatures, or writers who come from 'minorities', European cinema inevitably places the national question at its centre since this is what defines both its structure and its content.

The national question is, of course, more acutely felt by some film-makers than by others, but it is nevertheless a constant of European cinema and it finds a range of expressions. One is the reworking or re-appropriation of genres felt to be typically American, as seen in the Italian spaghetti western, the French crime film or *polar,* or the German road movie. Another is the attempt to repossess the national history, a particularly acute problem in relation to Germany and Russia. Thus Edgar Reitz wrote: 'the most serious act of expropriation occurs when people are deprived of their history', and explicitly conceived *Heimat (Home,* 1984) 'as a riposte to [the American TV series] *Holocaust'* (Elsaesser, in Nowell-Smith, 1996, 143), while Mikhalkov turns to the history of Tsarist Russia as a source of values for the contemporary spectator. Indeed, revisionist history, the desire to use film to tell a different version of past events, is an important strand of film-making not just in Germany and Russia but in Italy and France too. The national question may be a pretext for experimental uses of colour and iconography, as in Godard's recourse to a tricolour palette (blue, white, red) or his oblique references to Joan of Arc and Marianne as symbols of France and the Republic, while the dialectical relationship with Hollywood may account for the split or fragmented narratives which are a common feature of many art films, the double narrative of Godard's *A bout de souffle (Breathless,* 1959) being a case in point.

Perhaps the most interesting representation of the national question is through the sensibilities, and above all, over the bodies, of women. We have already noted how, in *Le mépris,* the body of Brigitte Bardot became the site of a cultural contest between Europe and America, the locus of both pleasure and conflict. In the New German Cinema, and especially perhaps in films such as Rainer Werner Fassbinder's *Die Ehe der Maria Braun (The Marriage of Maria Braun,* 1978) or Helma Sanders-Brahms's *Deutschland bleiche Mutter (Germany, Pale Mother,* 1980), the suffering, sometimes prostituted, woman becomes the symbol of the state of Germany, while in Spanish cinema of the 1980s and 1990s, in the work of the director Almodóvar, sexually mobile bodies establish 'a new cultural stereotype for a hyperliberated Spain' (Kinder, 3) in films like *Matador* (1986) and *La ley del deseo (The Law of Desire,* 1987).

The inscription of the relationship with Hollywood underlines the double address of national cinemas, simultaneously speaking to a domestic audience and embodying the national stereotype for foreigners. This frequently gives rise to complex texts. For example, in *Kings of the Road* mentioned above, the reference to colonisation is, as Elsaesser reminds us, both approving and critical. In Luis García Berlanga's *Bienvenido Mister Marshall (Welcome Mr Marshall,* 1952), an *españolada,* or folkloric comedy, is rendered satirical by having the inhabitants of a village dress up as Andalusian peasants in order to look like the Spaniards the American visitors expect to see, while the Hollywood intertext is used for subversive purposes to circumvent censorship and criticise the Franco regime.

While it would be tempting to view Europe as simply being imposed upon by Hollywood, it is important however to appreciate that American films were popular, and, as Martin Scorsese acknowledges, that directors of the 'new'

Hollywood were inspired by European cinema (Scorsese, in Thompson and Christie, 14). Scorsese was a film student from 1960 to 1965, during the height of the French New Wave, and his films, as well as others produced by his generation of film-makers, pay homage to European cinema as well as to the traditions of Hollywood genre cinema. Those who used political rhetoric in their arguments against 'cultural imperialism' and 'the Hollywood invasion' often neglected to appreciate the complexities of Hollywood's relations with Europe or to recognise that most of Hollywood's personnel were descendants of European immigrants. European cinema is often explained in terms of its resistance to Hollywood styles, its determination to offer an artistic alternative to crass commercialism, but it is also productive to consider European cinema in terms of the overlaps, distinctive qualities, genres and stars which resulted from operating in a position of market inferiority that nevertheless was also characterised by cultural symbiosis. Foregrounding this dynamic broadens analysis to encompass questions about the relationship between art and popular cinema and the existence of popular European genres and stars. In part, these are a facet of Europe's response to Hollywood, but they also relate to national cultural traditions.

Popular European Cinema: Genres and Stars

Hollywood developed film studios and genres into a highly sophisticated and resilient system which was designed to ensure continuity of production on a 'factory' basis, streamlined into an operation which worked to reduce the high element of financial risk involved in film production. Film genres were integral to the functioning of this system since they provided a key dynamic to the challenge of judging which films would be popular. European cinemas also thrived on film genres that were popular with domestic audiences, many of which share affinities with American genres in their ability to change and develop over several decades, yet at the same time display a set of consistent themes and preoccupations, for example musicals, comedies, melodramas and crime thrillers. Thrillers are an interesting case in point in terms of their overlap with American styles and themes and, in exchange, the incorporation of European sensibilities into Hollywood cinema. The crime/thriller genre was popular throughout Europe: in Britain crime was a staple genre, particularly the 'spiv' films of the 1940s featuring characters who were swindlers and blackmarketeers; in Spain the *Cine Negro* genre, which dramatised social discontent in the 1950s and 1960s, was akin to both American *films noirs* and French *polars*, while the post-war German *Trümmerfilme* (ruin films) also demonstrated close affinities with *film noir*. Similarly, contemporary Russian *chernukha* ('made black') films depict a bleak reality with the killer as hero. From this perspective, variations of *noir* thrillers can be examined as a pan European genre which shares similarities but is also integral to each particular country's national output.

The French *polar* or crime film, bearing close resemblance to the American *film noir*, is interesting because it often contained explicit reference and even homage to its Hollywood counterparts. This was particularly evident in the 1950s films of Jacques Becker, or of Jean-Pierre Melville who in turn is much admired by Quentin Tarantino. Similarly, many of the early films of Godard and Truffaut, like *A bout de souffle* and *Tirez sur le pianiste*, contain references to, or pastiches of, *film noir*. In more recent years the so-called *cinéma du look* exemplified in films such as Beineix's *Diva* (1980) or Besson's *Nikita* (1990) has been highly influenced by Hollywood images, evincing a fascination with youth, fashion, 'trash' culture and the aesthetic of music videos and commercials. These films contain slick images, bright colours, and crisp editing which are influenced by television commercials. Similarly, much of Kassovitz's *La haine* is filmed in the so-called MTV style.

By contrast, pre-1945 German cinema was on the whole more resilient to the absorption of external styles and influences, in part owing to the strength of its system of economic protectionism and the exclusion of American films during the Nazi period, and in the 1920s German films were successfully exported, particularly the spectacular costume films directed by Ernst Lubitsch. Although box-office earnings and the number of films produced by the German expressionist movement were not especially high, their international reputation ensured that they were thereafter considered to be the most significant development in German cinema of the 1920s. German expressionist cinema had a profound impact on Hollywood, particularly the *film noir* genre, and directors including Fritz Lang, who fled from fascism in the 1930s, carried this style with them and provide a key example of how the influence of European cinema is present in many of Hollywood's films. German expressionism's distinctive, 'unrealistic' *mise en scène* functioned as a focus for a film's overall artificial, constructed look and gestural acting styles. In Germany, Lang directed the expressionist classic *Dr Mabuse, der Spieler* (*Dr Mabuse, the Gambler*, 1922), a film which is very similar, in its obsession with guilt, innocence and fear of mental illness, to *Ministry of Fear*, which he made in 1943 in Hollywood.

American stylistic influence can also be traced in the work of European *auteurs*; for example, the films of Pedro Almodóvar deploy comedic and melodramatic traditions that combine an acute sense of national specificity with cultural fascinations which cross national boundaries. Martin Scorsese, whose films are a point of reference for the French characters in *La haine*, has acknowledged his debt to European art cinema of the 1960s as has Tarantino, whose obtrusive displays of cinematic allusion in his films frequently reference classics of European cinema. Similarly, Wim Wenders's *Alice in den Städten* (*Alice in the Cities*, 1974) is an exploration of European identity *vis à vis* America. The relationship, therefore, between Hollywood and Europe is clearly at best a productive example of cultural cross-fertilisation and at worst an attempt to simply ape an economically successful formula at the expense of indigenous experiment.

As argued above, European cinema is frequently taken to be synonymous with art cinema. The concept of art cinema has provided Europe with a set of distinctive directors and genres and is broadly associated with experimentation with the film medium. The impact of German expressionism, Soviet montage, French impressionism, Italian neo-realism, Spanish surrealism, and the avant-gardes of Europe has been profound and sustained, so much so that in international terms art cinema *is* popular cinema. As a result, however, for many years the dominant critical position held by *auteur* theories privileged art cinema above 'entertainment' genre cinema, resulting in an often distorted notion of a nation's cinematic output. Indeed, the films which influenced Scorsese were made by celebrated *auteurs* including Godard, Truffaut, Antonioni, and Powell and Pressburger. No mention is made of American film schools showing their students films by other, less-renowned directors.

Films that were more popular at the box office but not much admired by critics tended to be forgotten in histories which attempted to emphasise European cinema as a superior alternative to Hollywood. It is possible, however, to view art cinema as part of a nation's generic heritage ('expressionism', for example, can be referred to as a German cinematic genre, as can Italian neo-realist films), so that it can be examined alongside popular films which were not so easily exportable and are therefore less well known. Arguably, it is these films which made fullest use of national traditions and, by dint of their box-office success, say much about a particular country's collective psyche. In France, while most film histories quite properly chronicle the work of Jean Renoir and Marcel Carné, the box office in the 1930s was dominated by musicals (filmed operettas) and screen adaptations of boulevard theatre. As this book demonstrates, while *La règle du jeu* is undoubtedly a key film of 1939, we nevertheless need to be aware of the commercial and political context of its release – it was a box-office failure and was banned for most of the Second World War – and its relation to the overall corpus of French national film production. In Britain most critics praised David Lean's *Brief Encounter* (1945), but it is only in recent years that film historians have recognised the social importance of a more risqué film, Leslie Arliss's *The Wicked Lady* (1945), a Gainsborough melodrama which outstripped *Brief Encounter* at the box office. That edge of popularity prompts the conclusion that contemporary audiences preferred the image of unrepentant female transgression which pervades most of *The Wicked Lady*, as opposed to the guilt-ridden depiction of marital infidelity presented in *Brief Encounter*. Considering art cinema alongside popular cinema and appreciating the links between the two is not to detract from a country's accepted cinematic heritage; it is rather to dismantle the artificial division between 'high' and 'low' art.

In the 1920s, while the classics of German expressionist cinema, *The Cabinet of Dr Caligari* and *Nosferatu* (1922), were receiving international acclaim, the *Strassenfilme* ('street' films) was another significant genre. The *Strassenfilme* were associated with particular directors, including G. W. Pabst (particularly *Die freudlose Gasse* (*The Joyless Street*, 1925)) and Bruno Rahn (*Dirnentragödie*

(*Tragedy of the Street*, 1928)), and the films depicted life in the urban milieu, providing a location for narratives which associated the city with vice and temptation. As the chapter on Hitchcock's *The Lodger* demonstrates, this representation of the city was highly influential in Britain in the mid-late 1920s. While Germany's most popular genres were light entertainment comedies or *Lustspielfilme*, and musicals, *Heimat* films came to prominence in the 1950s and were distinctive for their engagement with issues of national identity. Also operating as a critique of city life, the *Heimatfilm* genre drew on Germanic folklore, celebrating traditional values and a conservative rural utopia with the effect of 'sustaining cultural boundaries and boundedness' (Morley and Robbins, 2–3). Again, we see an interesting example of how genres relate to each other, and can conclude that a dominant theme in the European cinematic imagination has been the often fraught tension between the city and the countryside.

In Spain an indigenous genre of musicals known as the *folklóricas*, rooted in traditional values, again depicted the city as vice-ridden, and promoted flamenco performances. Saura's *Carmen* exploits this strongly national tradition. In Italy, the figure of the athletic slave, Maciste, first seen in *Cabiria*, proved so popular that it gave rise to an entire series (Nowell-Smith, 1996, 129), while elevation of the past to a mythic level was also a staple of one of Italy's most popular film genres, the 'peplum' adventure spectacles of the late 1950s and early 1960s. These films glorified the ancient world and the films featured heroes including Spartacus and Hercules. Italian westerns, known as 'spaghetti westerns', were also extremely popular and received international acclaim in the 1960s. They retained some qualities of the 'peplum' films but also resembled American westerns before developing into the most dominant strain of cinema in Italy, with its greatest *auteur* being Sergio Leone, director of *Per un pugno di dollari* (*For a Fistful of Dollars*, 1964), *Per qualche dollari in più* (*For a Few Dollars More*, 1965) and *Il buono, il brutto e il cattivo* (*The Good, the Bad and the Ugly*, 1966). In these films the negotiation of geographical 'spaces' (they were filmed in Spain) came to be invested with national overtones as the films became less 'Hollywoodised' and more rooted in Italian or European culture and concerns.

In the 1920s and 1930s the Soviet Union also had its fair share of *auteurs* and popular genres. Eisenstein's contribution to world cinema is well known, and *The Battleship Potemkin* (1926) was a popular (particularly in international markets) and artistic success. Although it has a clear narrative structure the film indirectly critiques Hollywood's methods by employing symbolism as ironic counterpoint and utilising the technique of ideological montage. While the Soviet state was anti-capitalist and critical of America, there was, as we have seen, considerable admiration for the efficiency of Hollywood's studio system, and Alexandrov's popular musicals such as *The Circus* (1936) and *Volga-Volga* (1938) were intended to combine propaganda with entertainment and were part of an attempt to 'Hollywoodise' Soviet cinema in the 1930s. Again, it is important to view this connection with Hollywood as a key dynamic in art and genre cinema, something which could be drawn upon, adapted and critiqued.

Another way to examine the specificity of European cinema is to look at its film stars. In the early twentieth century several stars were associated with a particular national genre; for example, in Italy female stars Lyda Borelli and Francesca Bertini were known as 'divas', while in France the Russian émigré Ivan Mosjoukine embodied a certain orientalism. These stars were the focus of their films, which encouraged fans to worship them and admire their lavish costumes and lifestyles, both on and off screen. Frequently associated with genre and popular cinema, stars acquire iconic status and come to represent the essence of a national cinema for the export market. Thus in the 1930s, for instance, Arletty and Jean Gabin conjure up French cinema; in the 1940s Margaret Lockwood and James Mason suggest a conception of British cinema; and after the Second World War Marcello Mastroianni *is* Italian cinema, at least for foreign audiences. While considerable academic enterprise has been expended on examining Hollywood's stars, their personas and their social function, less attention has been paid to stardom in a European context.

European cinema had, and continues to have, many important film stars. Like Hollywood's stars, they were followed by loyal fans and were part of an industrial infrastructure which produced fan magazines, photographs and merchandise. Stars give particular films a sense of 'national essence' and it is clear that more than one star can occupy the role of communicating this 'essence' even though they might be completely different performers and represent very different aspects of that 'national essence'. In Britain, Gracie Fields and Anna Neagle could not be more opposed in their acting styles, personas and class appeal, yet in their distinct ways they embody particular aspects of 'Britishness': Gracie Fields as the down-to-earth working-class singer with a good heart and Anna Neagle as the upper middle-class 'lady' who was plucky, refined and moral. Both national and international popularity has been attained by Gérard Depardieu, who represents what Ginette Vincendeau describes as 'an idealised masculinity, merging working-class virility with romanticism' (Vincendeau, 1995, 111). On the other hand, actresses like Catherine Deneuve and Isabelle Adjani can be said to represent different facets of French femininity, respectively elegance and glamour, underlined by their employment as models to advertise the perfume and cosmetics manufactured by the French couture houses.

Interesting divergences emerge when international reputation is compared with internal box-office success. While, at an international level, French cinema of the 1960s is associated with stars such as Jean-Paul Belmondo and Simone Signoret, in terms of box-office success the biggest star of the period was Louis de Funès, who appeared in popular comedies rather than the showcase New Wave films. There was a similar tendency in Italian cinema. It is ironic, considering the anti-American aims of the neo-realist project, that Anna Magnani and the 'stars' of neo-realism were well known world-wide and came to represent

Italian cinema, even though at the domestic box office they were eclipsed by other less critically applauded stars, including the popular comic actors Erminio Macario and Walter Chiari. Similarly, the British actors Alec Guinness and Laurence Olivier are far better known internationally than stars such as Will Hay and George Formby, who consistently topped the domestic box office in the 1930s and 1940s. The star, of course, conveys his or her identity through a particular acting style which can be associated with their country. In Spain, the *folklóricas* films were characterised by musical performance interludes which would have been most familiar to, and easily understood by, domestic audiences. A key star in relation to this type of performance is Lola Flores, who was an extremely well known Spanish dancer, singer and actress in the 1950s. It is important, therefore, to appreciate the extent to which stardom can operate in different ways and on several levels according to national and international circulation.

In spite of the Soviet cinema's apparent rejection of Hollywood's norms and the capitalist associations of star systems, there were popular stars in the 1920s, like Igor V. Ilyinsky, who managed to develop an individual comic persona and at the same time to fulfil the propagandist function of playing a classic 'type', the bureaucrat. Britain shared this ambivalence towards copying Hollywood's formulas. This arose partly because of the assumption that Hollywood's stars were manufactured and that 'good acting' could never result from such a system, for it was believed that 'good acting' had its origins on the stage. Many of Britain's most famous screen actors had established stage careers, including Ivor Novello, Laurence Olivier and John Gielgud. In France, as in Britain, there were strong links between stage and film careers, for example Jean-Louis Barrault (perhaps his most famous role was as Baptiste in *Les enfants du paradis*), Jules Berry, Harry Baur and Pierre Brasseur are just a few of the many stars who were known as theatre and film actors. Reservations apart, these actors were involved in the pursuit of screen stardom, but at the same time film producers were keen to differentiate them from popular Hollywood stars. One way to achieve this was to incorporate aspects of Hollywood's publicity methods but colour them with specific national associations. The Rank Organisation did this in Britain in the 1940s and 1950s when it developed 'The Charm School', which involved figures such as Diana Dors, Phyllis Calvert, Stewart Granger, Margaret Lockwood, James Mason and Patricia Roc. Actors and actresses under contract were required to attend film premières and publicity events. The aim was to inject glamour into British cinema but at the same time identify this as unmistakably British. British stars were to be associated with class and decorum whereas American stars were represented in fan magazines as much more ambitious and mercenary. In this way we can see another instance of Europe's ambivalent attitude towards Hollywood, simultaneously trying to incorporate and to reject many of its norms.

The diversity which characterised European cinema increased as the century progressed towards the Millennium and as globalisation erased national boundaries in economic and ideological terms. Cinema is now part of a huge, multinational system which consists of television networks, the pursuit of new technologies in media production, and co-productions between countries. Inevitably, the existence of this system militates against the perpetuation of rigid national boundaries and the ossification of nationalist conceptions of identity. This state of flux is reflected in much contemporary cinema. As Everett has put it: 'European cinema is not a monolith, but a series of expressions of different ways of questioning and portraying itself and the world' (Everett, 5). While many elements of identity are historical and draw upon references of collective cultural memory, globalisation has the dual and frequently contradictory effect of erasing national barriers but at the same time prompting a defence against, or negotiation with, its perceived reality as yet another development in American economic and cultural hegemony: 'Coca-Cola' culture has an economic, cultural and ideological face.

The pursuit of overseas markets encourages European films to present narratives that will 'travel' well, such as the films of Luc Besson, or Wim Wenders's internationally acclaimed works, particularly *Paris, Texas* (1984). Yet it is paradoxical that despite the push towards globalisation and hybridity, films that do best in overseas markets are often quite specific in their engagement with issues of national identity. Both *La haine* (1995) and *Trainspotting* (1996) are examples of films which contain particular conceptions of 'Frenchness', 'Britishness' and 'Scottishness' but these may well be essential components of their international appeal. This is not to say that globalisation has intensified the defence of traditional nationalism; rather it is to observe that contemporary cinema articulates the crisis experienced by European identities when challenged by the economic and cultural forces of globalisation. This crisis has been aptly described by Antoine Compagnon (in Petrie, 113): 'Europe is everywhere and yet invisible; the circumference is everywhere and the centre nowhere.' Indeed, negotiating a cultural space for the fluid, unstable and ever-changing facets of European identity is the challenge which faces cinema in the twenty-first century.

References and Suggestions for Further Reading

Albera, François 1995: *Albatros: des Russes à Paris, 1919–1929*. Milan: Edizioni Gabriele Mazzotta.

Bance, Alan (ed.) 1997: *The Cultural Hegemony of the British Occupation in Germany*. Stuttgart: Verlag Hans-Dieter Heinz.

Barr, Charles 1993: *Ealing Studios*. London: Studio Vista.

Bertin-Maghit, Jean-Pierre 1989: *Le Cinéma sous l'Occupation*. Paris: Olivier Orban.

Bordwell, David 1979: 'The Art Film as Mode of Film Practice'. In *Film Criticism*, 4, 1, 56–64.

Bosch, Aurora and del Rincón, Maria Fernanda 1998: 'Franco and Hollywood'. In *New Left Review*, 232, 112–127.

Chanan, Michael 1994: 'What was GATT About?' In *Vertigo*, Spring, 57–58.

Danilowicz, C. de 1924: 'Les projets de Monsieur Wengeroff'. In *Cinémagazine*, 10, October, 54–56.

De Grazia, Victoria 1989: 'Mass Culture and Sovereignty: The American Challenge to European Cinemas, 1920–1960'. In *Journal of Modern History*, 61, 1, 53–87.

Dickinson, Margaret and Street, Sarah 1985: *Cinema and State: The Film Industry and the British Government, 1927–84*. London: British Film Institute.

Ďurovičová, Nataša 1992: 'Translating America: The Hollywood Multilinguals'. In Rick Altman (ed.), *Sound Theory, Sound Practice*. London: Routledge, 138–153.

Eckert, Charles 1978: 'The Carole Lombard in Macy's Window'. In *Quarterly Review of Film Studies*, 3, Winter, 1–21.

Eisenstein, Sergei 1957: *Film Form, Film Sense*. Edited and Translated by Jay Leyda. New York: Meridian Books.

Elsaesser, Thomas 1989: *New German Cinema: A History*. London: Macmillan.

Elsaesser, Thomas 1996: 'Germany: The Weimar Years'. In Geoffrey Nowell-Smith (ed.), *The Oxford History of World Cinema*. Oxford: Oxford University Press, 136–51.

Everett, Wendy (ed.) 1996: *European Identity and Cinema*. Exeter: Intellect Books.

Finney, Angus 1996: *The State of European Cinema*. London: Cassell.

Forbes, Jill 1992: *The Cinema in France: After the New Wave*. London: Macmillan.

Gomery, Douglas 1996: 'The Hollywood Studio System'. In Geoffrey Nowell-Smith (ed.), *The Oxford History of World Cinema*. Oxford: Oxford University Press, 1996, 43–52.

Guback, Thomas 1969: *The International Film Industry*. Bloomington: Indiana University Press.

Guback, Thomas 1974: 'Cultural Identity and Film in the European Economic Community'. In *Cinema Journal*, 14, 1, 2–17.

Hartnoll, Gillian and Porter, Vincent 1982: *Alternative Film-Making in Television: ZDF A Helping Hand*. London: British Film Institute.

Higson, Andrew 1989: 'The Concept of National Cinema'. In *Screen*, 30, 4, 36–46.

Jeancolas, Jean-Pierre 1993: 'Blum-Byrnes: L'Arrangement, 1945–48'. In *1895*, 13, 7–21.

Jordan, Barry and Morgan-Tamosunas, Rikki 1998: *Contemporary Spanish Cinema*. Manchester: Manchester University Press.

Kepley, Vance 1991: 'The Origins of Soviet Cinema: A Study of Industry Development'. In Richard Taylor and Ian Christie (eds), *Inside the Film Factory*. London: Routledge, 60–79.

Kepley, Vance and Kepley, Betty 1979: 'Foreign Films on Soviet Screens 1922–31'. In *Quarterly Review of Film Studies*, Fall, 428–442.

Kinder, Marsha (ed.) 1997: *Refiguring Spain: Cinema, Media, Representation*. Durham, NC, and London: Duke University Press.

Lindeperg, Sylvie 1997: *Les Écrans de l'ombre*. Paris: CNRS Editions.

Maltby, Richard 1998: '"D" for Disgusting: American Culture and English Criticism'. In Geoffrey Nowell-Smith and Ricci, Steven (eds), *Hollywood & Europe: Economics, Culture, National Identity, 1945–95*. London: British Film Institute, 104–115.

Maltby, Richard and Vasey, Ruth 1994: 'The International Language Problem: European Reactions to Hollywood's Conversion to Sound'. In David Ellwood and Rob Kroes (eds), *Hollywood in Europe: Experiences of a Cultural Hegemony*. Amsterdam: VU University Press.

Michaels, Eric 1994: 'Hollywood Iconography: A Warlpiri Reading '. In *Bad Aboriginal Art: Traditions, Media and Technological Horizons*. Minneapolis: University of Minnesota Press.

Morley, David and Robbins Kevin 1990: 'No Place like Heimat: Images of Home(land) in European Culture'. In _New Formations_, 12, Winter, 1–23.

Neale, Steve 1981: 'Art Cinema as Institution'. In _Screen_, 22, 1, 11–39.

Nowell-Smith, Geoffrey 1968: 'Italy Sotto Voce'. In _Sight and Sound_, 37, 3, 145–147.

Nowell-Smith, Geoffrey (ed.) 1996: _The Oxford History of World Cinema_. Oxford: Oxford University Press.

Nowell-Smith, Geoffrey and Ricci, Steven (eds) 1998: _Hollywood & Europe: Economics, Culture, National Identity, 1945–1995_. London: British Film Institute.

Petley, Julian 1979: _Capital and Culture: German Cinema, 1933–45_. London: British Film Institute.

Petrie, Duncan (ed.) 1992: _Screening Europe: Image and Identity in Contemporary European Cinema_. London: British Film Institute.

Puttnam, David 1997: _The Undeclared War: The Struggle for Control of the World Film Industry_. London: HarperCollins.

Richards, Jeffrey 1984: _The Age of the Dream Palace: British Cinema and Society, 1930–1939_. London: Routledge.

Sadoul, Georges 1947: _Histoire générale du cinéma_, vol. 2: _Les Pionniers du cinéma, 1897–1909_. Paris: Editions Denoël.

Shohat, Ella and Stam, Robert 1985: 'The Cinema after Babel: Language, Difference, Power'. In _Screen_, 26, 3–4, 35–59.

Taylor, Richard and Christie, Ian 1988: _The Film Factory: Russian and Soviet Cinema in Documents, 1896–1939_. London: Routledge & Kegan Paul.

Thompson, David and Christie, Ian (eds) 1989: _Scorsese on Scorsese_. London: Faber.

Thompson, Kristin 1985: _Exporting Entertainment: America in the World Film Market, 1907–1934_. London: British Film Institute.

Thompson, Kristin and Bordwell, David 1994: _Film History: An Introduction_. New York: McGraw-Hill.

Vasey, Ruth 1997: _The World According to Hollywood, 1918–1939_. Exeter: Exeter University Press.

Vincendeau, Ginette 1988: 'Hollywood Babel'. In _Screen_, 29, 2, 24–39.

Vincendeau, Ginette (ed.) 1995: _Encyclopedia of European Cinema_. London: British Film Institute: Cassell.

Wagstaff, Christopher 1984: 'The Italian Cinema Industry during the Fascist Regime'. In _The Italianist_, 4, 160–74.

Williams, Alan 1992: 'Historical and Theoretical Issues in the Coming of Recorded Sound to the Cinema'. In Rick Altman (ed.), _Sound Theory, Sound Practice_. London: Routledge, 126–37.

Part II

Case Studies

52

1 *The Battleship Potemkin*
The massacre on the Odessa steps.

Bronenosets Potemkin/ Potyomkin (The Battleship Potemkin)

Birgit Beumers

Voted the best film of all time by an international critics' poll conducted in 1958, Sergei Eisenstein's *The Battleship Potemkin* (*Bronenosets Potemkin/Potyomkin*, 1926) was produced in the Soviet Union at a time when that country was pioneering a new form of social and economic order: socialism. In the nationalised Soviet film industry the state controlled film production, a situation which highlights the relationship between art and politics during the early years of the Soviet regime. Indeed, many Russian artists, especially those of the left-wing avant-garde movements of the 1910s, hailed the 1917 Revolution and actively supported its cause, some by taking up posts in the political structures, others by putting their art at the service of the new ideals. At this time the state also realised cinema's potential for agitation of the masses and for political propaganda. It is within this context that an analysis of *The Battleship Potemkin* must be located.

Cinema of the Soviets

The state took control of the film industry in 1919 and in 1922 Lenin declared: 'of all arts, the cinema is for us the most important'. However, as a consequence of the civil war, film stock was in very short supply at the time and future film directors like Lev Kuleshov (1899–1970) were reduced to experimenting in acting studios without actually filming. Sergei Eisenstein (1898–1948) had trained as a set designer before he studied with the theatre director Vsevolod Meyerhold (1874–1940) to become a director. Meyerhold's theatre was based on the idea that theatre would enlarge and enhance certain fragments or episodes from reality; for this purpose, he restructured plays into fragments and episodes and set his productions in Constructivist designs. He perceived theatre as having a social and political function and went out to factories to perform plays whilst closely monitoring audience response in order to heighten the comic and agitational elements. His actors were trained in 'bio-mechanics' (the science of rational movement), so that movements on stage would be choreographed and paced (rather than motivated by the psychological identification of the actor with his role) and bring man closer to a perfect, machine-like state. He thus created *types* rather than characters with psychological depth. Both the concept of fragmentation and that of 'typage' through body language and choreographed movement are important for Eisenstein's work in the cinema. For his staging of Ostrovsky's *The Wise Man* (1922) Eisenstein made his first film, a short called *Glumov's Diary*, which he used in the production.

Goskino (the State Committee for Cinematography) was established in 1922 to organise cinema matters centrally after the Treaty of Rapallo between Germany and the Soviet Union had, among other things, guaranteed imported supplies of film stock. With these incentives in place, many young artists were anxious to apply their experiences in theatre and the visual arts to the newer medium of film, and to devote their work to the socialist cause.

The Battleship Potemkin is Eisenstein's second full-length film, commissioned by the state in 1925 to commemorate the twentieth anniversary of the abortive 1905 Revolution. It was intended to create a positive image of the country's revolutionary past in order to justify the rule of the Bolsheviks at a time which followed prolonged suffering of the population during the civil war.

Eisenstein worked on the scenario and soon embarked on the filming of 'The Year 1905' in St Petersburg. When weather conditions made it impossible to continue, he and his film crew moved down to Odessa to shoot what was intended as a minor episode in the film, the mutiny on the battleship *Prince Potemkin*. The 'minor' sequence turned into an entire film, which was shot (to a modified screenplay) over three months in Odessa, partly on the *Potemkin's* sister-ship *Twelve Apostles* since the *Potemkin* itself had been dismantled. *The Battleship Potemkin* was officially premiered at a gala screening in the Bolshoi Theatre on 21 December 1925 and released in January 1926. During the twelve days of screening in Moscow in January and February 1926 it attracted almost 30,000 spectators, a number that had, at the time, only been achieved by American films. The film made a profit through export to Germany, France and the USA, enabling the state-run industry to purchase new equipment and film stock from the west, and it was to be promoted as the pride of Soviet cinema. Indeed, its immense success in Berlin in April and May 1926 played a particular role in its promotion both at home and abroad.

It was also in Berlin that the music for *The Battleship Potemkin* was composed by Edmund Meisel, the first violinist of the Berlin Philharmonic Orchestra. Meisel composed the music not as a mere accompaniment to the film, but – at Eisenstein's request – to stress moods, such as tension and triumph, and to echo the rhythm and noise of the engines in the last part of the film. This version is normally used in international distribution. A second version, restored in 1976, uses the score written by the Russian composer Dmitry Shostakovich, whilst the film itself has been re-edited by Sergei Yutkevitch to match this score.

In the years following the October Revolution artists thus put their art to the service of politics, while the state used (and later abused) its control over the funds needed for film production to finance films that would advance the ideas of socialism. Shortly after the Revolution, theatre directors had begun to mount mass spectacles in the streets in celebration of the event: *The Storming of the Winter Palace* (1918) marked the anniversary of the Revolution, involving 100,000 actors. Eisenstein's film *October* (1927), which commemorated the tenth anniversary, required a cast of 120,000 people although there had been far fewer people around the Winter Palace on 25 October 1917. In this instance, and in other films of the 1920s, historical facts were manipulated, certain events being 'magnified' and appropriated in order to glorify the Soviet regime. The cinema of Eisenstein played a key role in this approach to the past and constituted a crucial element of Lenin's propaganda policies for the arts.

Propaganda and Myth-Making

In 1928 Eisenstein and Alexandrov wrote: 'The first basic function of our films is to interpret the theses and decrees, to reveal them and make them infectious through a visual demonstration of their significance in the general cause of socialist construction' (in Taylor and Christie, 218). Eisenstein perceived theatre and film as means to convey a political message and to 'cinefy' the theses of the Party and the state. He used the devices of fragmentation and montage (discussed below) to construct worlds which would allow for parallels to be drawn between the past and the present. In his films of the 1920s, *Stachka* (*The Strike*, 1925), *The Battleship Potemkin*, and *Oktiabr'* (*October*, 1927), Eisenstein related history with the help of images which he cut, fragmented, edited, and reassembled, thereby creating a new text. By merging the past and the present, he created the perfect world of a socialist utopia.

The Battleship Potemkin clearly reveals the impact that the 1917 Revolution had on the subsequent assessment of Russian history. Since the reality of a country stricken by a civil war and struggling with new forms of economic management was far too grim, but since film-makers still wanted to support socialism, they represented history in an idealised way. In *The Battleship Potemkin* Eisenstein created the myth of a successful 1905 Revolution in order to re-affirm and consolidate the new Soviet regime, whereas what had actually happened in 1905 had been far from successful. This Revolution had failed but it was to prove a key event in the years leading up to the fall of the Romanov dynasty and was therefore to serve as a precursor to the Bolshevik Revolution of 1917.

The Battleship Potemkin portrays the 1905 Revolution in the light of the successful 1917 Revolution: the final success of the revolutionary ideals is more important than contemporary historical accuracy. The demonstrations of people petitioning for civil rights and equitable wages in St Petersburg on 9 January 1905 ended in a massacre: the Tsarist troops panicked, and over 200 people were shot on 'Bloody Sunday'. However, despite the failure of the 1905 uprising, the spirit of the Revolution spread. The event caused a wave of strikes and demonstrations all over Russia, among them the mutiny on the battleship *Potemkin*. The Revolution propelled Tsar Nicholas II to grant the right to establish a parliament, the Duma, but he was to remain in charge of the armed forces and to instruct them to crush the revolutionary movement. In June 1905, the Odessa uprising coincided with the mutiny on the battleship *Potemkin* just outside the port. The crew turned to the citizens of Odessa for supplies and deposited in the port the body of the martyr-sailor Vakulinchuk who had been shot during the mutiny. It was less the news of the mutiny (the citizens of Odessa were also hard up and suffered injustice from the regime) than the presence of the vessel which boosted the citizens' confidence. Growing civil unrest, combined with looting in the town, eventually led to a massacre when the Tsarist troops shot indiscriminately into the crowd. During the massacre on the night of 15/16 June the *Potemkin* failed to fire a single shot; it was only on the next day that the vessel fired some volleys into the air, missing the Odessa Theatre. The *Potemkin* was isolated among the fleet and later left for Romania for coal and supplies. This uprising, then, was anything but successful, and some historians have noted that a more active and forceful part by the *Potemkin* in these events might have led to the triumph described in the film and even triggered a revolution.

Eisenstein stops his version of the historical events at a convenient and advantageous point: 'We stop the event at this point where it had become an "asset" of the Revolution,' he commented (Eisenstein, in Taylor, 60). In the film the vessel's guns aim, fire and hit a target: the military headquarters located in the classical building of the Odessa Theatre. Eisenstein conflates two moments in time: the massacre on the night of 15 June takes place during the day (much more convenient for filming), and through montage he brings the gunfire forward in time to make it coincide with the events on the Odessa Steps. Other details also differ from factual accounts of the events. For example, Eisenstein neglects the fact that some crew members were agitators who belonged to the radical movement, preferring to locate their dissatisfaction in injustice rather than ideology. Instead of the battleship being left in isolation at the end, it is supported by the squadron, and there is no sign of unrest or looting in Odessa before the arrival of the vessel in the bay. In Eisenstein's rigorous construction of the film there is no room for any interaction among the opposing forces (the soldiers versus the people or the sailors), since he operates within a strict dialectical principle of opposition. All the action develops from the individual to the crowd, from the part to the whole (*pars pro toto*). The individual is never concerned with himself, but fights for the sake of others, excluding himself, and thereby annihilating himself as an entity. Eisenstein treats film form in the same way: he films not the individual but the people, and he edits the sequence of frames, not the individual frame. Eisenstein thus distorts historical fact through fragmenting and reassembling the fragments to create a new entity.

Stars or Types, Individual or Mass?

Eisenstein's emphasis is placed on the masses, not on individuals. 'The shot itself as star,' he wrote, '[w]e must look for the essence of cinema not in the shots but in the relationship between the shots, just as in history we look not at individuals but at the relationships between individuals, classes, etc.' (Eisenstein, in Taylor and Christie, 147). The revolutionary spirit of the people is seen as victorious in the light of the October Revolution and, as a sign of triumph, the soldiers on the battleship even raise a red flag, which was hand-coloured in each print of the black and white film. The masses are elevated to heroic status and only the agitators on both sides – Vakulinchuk, Matiushenko, the senior officer Giliarovsky, the captain, and the doctor – are individualised. The masses are portrayed heroically in their suffering and their sacrifices for the revolutionary cause in order to legitimise the October Revolution, an event which was started in the name of the people but was steered by one man alone: Lenin. The depiction of the masses as supportive of their leaders and agitators is an important feature in Soviet films of the 1920s, since it serves to justify the socialist principle of the rule of a leader over the masses.

Eisenstein used 'types', people with expressive faces and an interesting physiognomy, rather than professional actors. As in Meyerhold's theatre he utilised physical expression and choreographed movement for action rather than psychological motivation. While for some directors, such as Trauberg and Kozintsev, the movement and facial expression within the frame was important, for Eisenstein the emphasis at that time lay on the juxtaposition of different movements within one frame or within sequences, on choreography and (arranged) chaos, on the lines and circles of movement. In his famous sequence of the Odessa Steps the linear movement of the soldiers is juxtaposed to the unorganised, chaotic and elemental movement of the people, who were described by one critic as 'bouncing down the steps like cherry stones'.

In *The Battleship Potemkin* Eisenstein made his assistant Grigori Alexandrov play Giliarovsky, the priest was played by a gardener, while the doctor, played by a stoker who was working on the set, bears a striking resemblance to the great dramatist Anton Chekhov, who was a medical doctor by training. Villains are mostly portrayed with a touch of the grotesque, for example the priest pretends to be dead when he falls down the stairs yet he winks in the following shot, while the workers and sailors are shown in a realistic manner.

Eisenstein uses stereotypes in the characterisation of groups of society, so that the bourgeoisie are characterised by their fashion accessories, whereas the sailors are muscular and strong. Women usually endure and suffer (a mother is shot, a child is trampled on), while only men fight with weapons. There are also sexual implications in the imagery of the battleship's guns, filmed from above to stress their phallic shape. They fire only under the command of the sailors, implying that while the Tsarist regime is impotent and infertile, the energy and force of the sailors makes the guns potent.

Composition and Structure, Fragmentation and Montage

Eisenstein's contemporary Lev Kuleshov outlined, in 1917, how the director should approach film composition: 'The essence of cinema art lies in the creativity of the director and the artist: everything is based on composition. To make a picture the director must compose the separate filmed fragments, disordered and disjointed, into a single whole and juxtapose these separate moments into a more advantageous, integral and rhythmical sequence' (Kuleshov, in Taylor and Christie, 41). The film narrates the events in chronological order: the sailors on board the battleship *Potemkin* are discontented and protest when they are given rotten meat. When they are threatened with execution, the brave cry of the sailor Vakulinchuk makes the firing squad realise that they are about to shoot at their 'brothers'. This heroic deed costs Vakulinchuk his life: while the sailors seize control over the ship he is shot by the senior officer Giliarovsky after a decktop chase. His body is taken to the port of Odessa, where the citizens soon flock to the pier in mourning and begin to send supplies to the battleship. The Tsarist troops try to control the crowds gathering around the tent with the dead sailor, and, advancing from the top of the Odessa Steps, shoot at the citizens. The battleship's guns fire at the staff headquarters (the theatre) to defend the people of Odessa. The next day, the rebellious battleship is met by the fleet, which, after a period of anxiety about the fleet's attitude to the mutiny, supports the *Potemkin* by letting the vessel pass.

Eisenstein uses the classical structure of Aristotelian tragedy by dividing the film into five parts: Part 1: Men and Maggots; Part 2: Drama at Tendra;[1] Part 3: Appeal from the Dead; Part 4: The Odessa Steps; Part 5: Meeting the Squadron, with exposition, peripetia, and dénouement. Broadly speaking, he observes the unity of time, since the action takes place over twenty-four hours, and place, since it takes place in one location, and there are no sub-plots which would distract from the main story. He designs a rigid compositional principle of opposing images and moods within each sequence and within each part. The action within each of the five parts is very neatly organised in that each part contains a change of mood: (1) from quiet suffering (passivity) to declared dissatisfaction (active resistance); (2) from the fear of execution (submissiveness) to mutiny (aggression); (3) from mourning over the dead sailor (passive) to anger at the injustice (active); (4) from sending boats to demonstrate solidarity with the sailors on the ship (building bridges) to the slaughter on the Odessa Steps (destruction) that triggers the gunfire from the battleship (action); and (5) from anxiety over the fleet's response (passive, subdued, insecure) to triumph (safety, active response, red flag). Each part moves from passive to active, from subdued to triumphant, from submissive to aggressive, thus ensuring both the juxtaposition of opposing principles (thesis/antithesis) and the dialectical conclusion: progress (synthesis). This principle also determines the structure of the filmic sequences so that 'any two frames juxtaposed inevitably combine into a new concept' (Eisenstein, in Taylor and Christie, 145).

The appeal for solidarity ('brothers') resounds twice: as an appeal when the firing squad is about to fire and as a cry for solidarity when the fleet joins the battleship in its revolt. At these two points the film moves from the part to the whole, from the sailors to the other 'workers' on the battleship (the firing squad) and then from the battleship to the entire fleet. The spirit of the Revolution spreads first on the ship, then across the fleet. Yet it also spreads to Odessa when the body is taken there on a boat and the Odessans symbolically send their boats to the ship with supplies. There is a reciprocal movement from sea to shore and shore to sea, implying that the Revolutionary spirit of the citizens spurs on the sailors, and that the sailors will rush to the citizens' defence. The episode of the boats sailing from the port to the battleship and the sequence of the gunfire from the battleship at the theatre are therefore filmed from camera positions both on the shore and on the boat. The parallel between land and sea, city-dwellers and sailors, is enhanced by the split-level structure which can be found both on the battleship (upper deck and lower deck) and in the city (top of steps and pier, bridges and arches).

The neat symmetry in the composition is reflected in the creation of parallels and contrasts in the scene before the uprising, when the sailors, sleeping in their hammocks, resemble lumps of meat (which is the source of their complaint), whereas after the rebellion, they sleep on sofas and in chairs. Similarly, and continuing with the theme of parallels and contrasts, while the meat is infested by maggots, the officers later thrown overboard go 'down to feed the maggots'. During the rebellion the sailors are threatened with being hanged from the yard-arm, a threat which is visualised; later they are shown triumphant on the very same yard-arm. The priest strikes the cross with the same gesture as that used by the officer with his dagger and when the priest falls, the cross is thrust into the floor like a dagger. Both the priest's response to the rebellious sailors and the officers' response to the meat ignore the facts and aim only at maintaining the status quo, thus creating a parallel between military and religious oppression.

Such formal unity lends meaning to the film as a whole, while it destroys the fragments which are parts of the whole. Eisenstein's principle of a movement from the small cell to the whole is also expressed in the intertitle 'all for one, one for all', which appears twice in the film – when Vakulinchuk has died for the sailors, and when the battleship has scored a victory for the entire fleet. Since it is a silent film the narrative of *The Battleship Potemkin* is communicated not through spoken dialogue but through the five-part structure, through the intertitles which supply the most important parts of narrative and dialogue, and through the relationship between the contents of each frame. The way in which frames with different content are assembled is known as the principle of 'montage'.

Montage is the juxtaposition of images, usually of a contrasting nature, and it can imply conflict between two opposing principles. In Part 4, the chaotic movement of people on the steps is juxtaposed to the disciplined movement of the soldiers; the organised movement of many soldiers downward is countered by the upward movement of a single figure, the mother; the white uniforms of the soldiers are contrasted with the dark garments of the citizens, and the numerous bayonets of the soldiers are opposed by the single shot fired from the battleship's gun. Montage can also create the illusion of setting things in motion: the people on the steps, representatives of all classes – bourgeois, workers, beggars – are portrayed in a jump cut sequence (frame to frame without coherence) as though a static picture was being animated and set in motion through a gradual increase in the number of frames devoted to each single action. Society is fragmented, while the Tsarist forces move in unison, and their movement requires a greater number of frames. Montage can produce movement artificially, as in the three shots of the lions – sleeping, waking, rising – which not only give the illusion that a single lion rises, but also appear to make the lion roar, thus transgressing the boundaries of the visual.

Eisenstein later defined five types of montage: *Metric montage* determines the absolute length of a piece, and refers to the rhythm or pace of a sequence. In the last part, the number of shots per minute increases along with the battleship's speed. Similarly, in the 'Odessa Steps' sequence, the shots change more frequently as the chaos increases. Both sequences create the illusion of accelerated pace and enhance the sense of panic and chaos. *Rhythmic montage* refers to the movement within the frame, to its actual length. The 'Odessa Steps' sequence begins with a shot of the motionless citizens and the soldiers. The camera subsequently focuses on the feet of the soldiers advancing downward and of the crowd trampling over bodies, and finally we see a baby carriage rolling down the steps – a movement which in itself is faster than the steps of the soldiers or the running of the crowd. This gradation serves to create a crescendo, so again Eisenstein manages to cross the boundary of the visual, giving the impression of an outcry (sound) through images alone. This is achieved by the way in which visual images are punctuated by different movements and speeds so that when we see the woman scream as she falls, the lack of conventional soundtrack is not a problem.

Tonal montage refers to the choice of tone or colour, light or gloom, within a frame. On the steps the soldiers in their white uniforms and with their bayonets cast a dark shadow which pierces the figure of the mother before she is actually shot. The fog outside the tent reflects the doomed, gloomy mood of mourning and, as a final reference to Vakulinchuk's passing away, the light that penetrates the tent from outside is eclipsed by a passing vessel at the end of the sequence.

Intellectual montage implies the juxtaposition, or comparison, of one situation to another. When the battleship fires, the lion rises. The statues of the lions are not part of the architecture of the Odessa Theatre (they are pictures taken of the Tsar's palace at Alupka on the Crimea), nor do they belong in the narrative of the film; they are non-diegetic images (not part of the space or time of the narrative) which symbolise the beginning of the revolt. Similar examples can be found in other Eisenstein films, such as the sequence in *The Strike* when the features of human faces are compared to those of animals using shots of a monkey, an owl, and a fox which intersect the narrative to portray a character. Finally, *overtonal montage* is a synthesis of different forms of montage: in the Odessa Steps sequence the pace of the action increases both in terms of the length of the frame and in terms of the movement within the frame (metric and rhythmic montage), light opposes darkness and shadows (tonal montage), the movement of the soldiers is opposed to the movement of the crowd in its direction and in its quality (linearity/chaos) to render a sense of the conflict escalating. Eisenstein frequently uses the device of overlapping editing: he would shoot a sequence from different angles and overlap the frames in editing, thus prolonging the duration of the action. This is very clearly visible in the sequence of the sailor smashing a plate, where part of his movement is repeated to underline the thrust behind this gesture.

Eisenstein's principle of montage is complemented by that of 'attractions'. He had already elaborated on the concept of attractions during his time in the theatre:

> An attraction is any aggressive moment in the theatre, ... calculated to produce specific emotional shocks. ... These shocks provide the only opportunity of perceiving the ideological aspect of what is being shown, the final ideological conclusion. ... Our present approach radically alters our opportunities in the principles of creating an 'effective structure' instead of a static 'reflection' of a particular event dictated by the theme ... and this gives rise to a new concept: a free montage with arbitrarily chosen independent effects (attractions) but with the precise aim of a specific final thematic effect – montage of attractions.   (Taylor and Christie, 87–9)

'Attractions' are scenes which shock the spectator, which are provocative, and may even be repulsive, such as the near-execution of the sailors covered by a tarpaulin, the maggots in the meat (enlarged through the doctor's pince-nez), and the slaughter of the innocent people on the steps. 'Attractions' thus challenge the spectator to take action and defend the unjustly treated. At the end of the film he offers another striking 'attraction' when the spectators appear to be bombarded by the battleship, whose keel splits the frame in half.

By creating 'attractions' (as in the circus) Eisenstein challenges the spectator intellectually rather than leading him/her into the illusion of a make-believe world as created in the traditional Hollywood plot. This device, known as 'estrangement' (*ostranenie*), was derived from Russian formalism and was to translate into German theatre theory as Brecht's *Verfremdungseffekt* (alienation effect). The estrangement or alienation from the usual is achieved by displaying the devices, reflected to a certain degree in Eisenstein's concern with montage, which can serve to make the spectator aware of the manipulation of images for the purpose of telling a story through images alone. The techniques of fragmentation and montage, of challenging the audience intellectually by juxtaposing images and concepts which propel them to act, of alienation and estrangement to ensure rational judgement, were common features for many avant-garde artists working all over Europe in different spheres during this period.

Avant-garde and Tradition

In the 1910s, artists across Europe had begun to fragment the world that surrounded them and reassemble it in a different way, in order to estrange the spectator from traditional, habitual ways of perception and to offer a fresh view. The stage of construction endowed artists with the power to create a world more perfect than reality; to make history more glorious in the light of subsequent developments and to build through their work the world that the socialist Revolution had promised. This allowed the artist to appropriate the past and conquer the future. However, the power to appropriate the past could also make artists servants of a particular ideology, and this was to degenerate into a totalitarian system under Stalin in the 1930s.

In *The Battleship Potemkin* Eisenstein stands between tradition and the avant-garde. The film offers continuity with tradition in its narrative, but a rejection of tradition in its formal fragmentation. Bearing in mind the techniques of montage discussed above, it is important to note that Eisenstein uses a classical five-part structure; he takes traditional shots with a largely stationary camera; he constructs a narrative through a series of intertitles; and finally, he relies on traditional vocabulary to formulate a revolutionary message. In his traditional story-telling Eisenstein is closest to the realism that would dominate Soviet arts in the 1930s, when he would succumb to the call for realism after the method of montage had came under fire in the late 1920s for being too formalistic, too intellectual, and too sophisticated for the masses. At this point, in order to be able to make films, Eisenstein had to bow to Stalin's orders for historical films which would legitimise the use of absolute power in certain moments of history.

The Battleship Potemkin was designed to serve the state and promulgate the Revolution first and foremost to Soviet audiences, yet its complex form meant that it did not appeal to the mass audiences in the Soviet Union. Abroad, however, the opposite occurred. The film enjoyed considerable success in intellectual circles, especially in Germany, and through its use of a new medium it created a lasting image of the new Soviet state for western audiences. Indeed, for years to come, Eisenstein's version of the 1905 Revolution and his use of cinema for an intellectual reflection on history were to dictate the manner in which Soviet history would be perceived.

References

Taylor, Richard (ed.) 1998: *The Eisenstein Reader*. London: British Film Institute.
Taylor, Richard and Christie, Ian (eds) 1994: *The Film Factory*. London: Routledge.

Suggestions for Further Reading

Aumont, Jacques 1987: *Montage Eisenstein*. Bloomington, IN: Indiana University Press.
Barna, Yon 1973: *Eisenstein*. London: Secker & Warburg.
Bordwell, David 1993: *The Cinema of Eisenstein*. Cambridge, MA, and London: Harvard University Press.
Eisenstein, Sergei 1949: *Film Form*. Edited and translated by Jay Leyda. New York: Harcourt Brace.
Kenez, Peter 1992: *Cinema and Soviet Society, 1917–1953*. Cambridge: Cambridge University Press.
Taylor, Richard (ed.) 1998: *The Eisenstein Reader*. London: British Film Institute.
Taylor, Richard 1979: *The Politics of the Soviet Cinema, 1917–1929*. Cambridge: Cambridge University Press.
Taylor, Richard 1999: *The Battleship Potemkin*. London: I. B. Tauris.
Taylor, Richard and Ian Christie (eds) 1994: *The Film Factory*. London: Routledge.

Note

1. This title is sometimes mistranslated as 'Drama on Quarterdeck'. Tendra is the place-name of a sandbank in the Black Sea to the south-east of Odessa.

Credits

Director	Sergei Eisenstein
Production	Goskino
Scenario	Sergei Eisenstein
Director of Photography	Eduard Tissé
Editor	Sergei Eisenstein

Art Director	Vasili Rakhals
Music	Edmund Meisel

'Mosfilm version' restored by Naum Kleiman and Sergei Yutkevich (1976), to the music by Dmitry Shostakovich

Cast

Alexander Antonov	Vakulinchuk
Grigori Alexandrov	Officer Giliarovsky

Sailors of the Navy, citizens of Odessa, actors of the Proletkult Theatre (Moscow)

Filmography

Stachka (The Strike, 1925)
Bronenosets Potemkin (The Battleship Potemkin, 1926)
Oktiabr' (October, 1928)
Staroie i novoe (The General Line / The Old and the New, 1929)
Que Viva Mexico! (1932)
Bezhin lug (Bezhin Meadow, 1935)
Aleksandr Nevskii (Alexander Nevsky, 1938)
Ivan grozni (Ivan the Terrible, 1943–6)

2 *The Lodger*
Expressionist imagery in *The Lodger* shows Hitchcock's debt to German cinema.

The Lodger
Sarah Street

The Lodger, a British silent film directed by Alfred Hitchcock, was produced in 1926 and released in 1927. It starred Ivor Novello as a mysterious young man who lodges in a London home at a time when a number of blonde-haired young women have been murdered in the city. It was one of the most significant British films of the decade, praised by critics who in particular appreciated Hitchcock's importation of German techniques which were used to create suspense and atmosphere. *The Lodger* was released when the British film industry was struggling to survive, and it represented a sophisticated response to the problem of producing distinctive film drama at a time when the market was more or less dominated by Hollywood's films. Hitchcock's adaptation of a popular story, based on the Jack the Ripper murders, can be linked to contemporary fears of, and ambivalence about, modernity and city life, and is distinctively British in its settings. As this chapter will also argue, it raises questions of gender identity which featured in many German films of this period (Petro, 1989).

For many years *The Lodger* was studied primarily in terms of its relation to Hitchcock's later, more celebrated films in Britain and America (such as *The Thirty-Nine Steps*, 1935; *The Lady Vanishes*, 1938; *Strangers on a Train*, 1951; or *Vertigo*, 1958), as evidence of his young talent, the beginning of a brilliant trajectory which was slowly ripening to maturity. British film director Lindsay Anderson expressed this view very clearly:

> Considered in relation to Hitchcock's subsequent career, *The Lodger* is particularly interesting. Its realistic settings, its lower middle class locale (presented without any false glamour) are those which were to form the background to Hitchcock's famous series of melodramas in the thirties. Most, indeed, of the later films' ingredients are here; the ingenious visual touches, the acute and sometimes caustic observation, the imaginative economical style, the long build up of suspense, the climactic violence. In all these *The Lodger* pointed forward to its director's great future. (Anderson, in Manvell, 378).

Other critics argued that as an 'early work', *The Lodger* was blighted by the prevailing modes of silent cinema which foregrounded melodrama over realism:

> I do not think that the silent film, although it was photographic, was expected by its popular audiences to reconstruct the scenes and situations of real life.

The silent film offered you a fancy world, impressive but remote, the genuinely realistic films (*Birth of a Nation*, *Potemkin*, *Drifters* etc.) were outstanding
because they were so exceptional. The silent images normally belonged to
the fantasy of sentiment or of melodrama, and occasionally they produced
their own genuine poetry. Their measure was not that of the street outside
or of the crime columns of real newspapers; they derived mostly from the
vagaries of lady novelists, or from the ingenious imaginings of the creators
of haunted houses.   (Manvell, 378)

The quotations from Anderson and Manvell illustrate the prevailing critical
orthodoxy of the 1950s when film critics privileged two dominant value-systems,
the appreciation of the *auteur* and the praise of realism above melodrama.
While Anderson's view reveals how an auteurist approach automatically
demarks areas for analysis – the identification of 'visual touches', 'acute and
sometimes caustic observation', 'economical style', 'suspense' and 'climactic
violence' – the more dismissive view of Manvell reproaches silent films such
as *The Lodger* for their lack of realism and their origins in 'the fantasy of sentiment or of melodrama ... derived mostly from the vagaries of lady novelists'.
This chapter aims to challenge both these critical approaches, arguing that *The
Lodger* should be analysed in relation to other European and American films
(as opposed to its evaluation solely in terms of Hitchcock's films) and in the
immediate context of its release. The place of melodrama in British cinema will
also be a focus of the analysis, interpreted not in Manvell's terms as an inferior
mode to realism, but as an integral aspect of the address of silent cinema and
the photographic emphasis of Ivor Novello's star persona.

    The Lodger is related to a tradition of British cinema in the 1920s which drew
inspiration from films from France, Germany, the Soviet Union and also from
Hollywood. This eclectic mix of styles was an integral aspect of the economic
and cultural aspirations of 'Film Europe' which was an attempt in the 1920s to
promote co-operation among European film-producing countries to counter
the domination of American films. Germany took the initiative, encouraging
films to be made in a 'European' rather than a national style, and Hitchcock's
first feature film, *The Pleasure Garden* (1925), was a British–German co-production
shot in Germany. *The Lodger* was shot in Britain but stylistic homage to German
expressionism, French impressionism and Soviet montage has been noted (Ryall,
24–30). Whereas many of the films made under the 'Film Europe' banner lost
their sense of national identity in the spirit of co-production and internationalism
(Bordwell and Thompson, 185), *The Lodger* managed to utilise a range of European
and American techniques and at the same time preserve a sense of 'Britishness'
which is located in its London story and setting, in its characters, and by featuring the top British box-office star of the period, Ivor Novello. A convincing
case can therefore be made that *The Lodger* is both a European *and* a British film.

    As far as the evidence for Hitchcock's familiarity with German expressionism
is concerned, he had been to Germany in 1924 as a member of the production

team of *The Passionate Adventure*, a co-production between Michael Balcon's Gainsborough Pictures and Germany's major film conglomerate, UFA. While in Germany, Hitchcock familiarised himself with the techniques of F. W. Murnau, director of *Nosferatu* (1922), and Fritz Lang, director of *Dr Mabuse, the Gambler* (1922), who were both associated with expressionism. Their films took inspiration from the reaction against nineteenth-century realism which was evident in painting and theatre from about 1908. Expressionist art aimed to convey inner emotional experience through distorted images and unrealistic colour. The films used studio-built sets to create an extreme sense of stylisation, for example the sets used in Robert Weine's *The Cabinet of Dr Caligari* (1920) created a *mise en scène* which expressed its characters' confused state of mind. Large, distorted structures appeared to blend in with the characters' costumes and gestural acting style. The purpose of lighting in expressionist films was not to create the illusion of realism but instead to convey dark moods, fear and foreboding. Hitchcock's first two films involved European settings (*The Pleasure Garden* and *The Mountain Eagle*, 1926). *The Mountain Eagle* starred Bernard Goetzke, a distinguished German actor who had been directed by Fritz Lang in *Der müde Tod (Destiny)* in 1921, and in this film Hitchcock experimented with lighting effects. But it was *The Lodger*, made in 1926 when Balcon and Hitchcock returned to London, which paid the most sustained homage to the themes and techniques of German expressionism with the construction of a three-sided house with narrow walls and ceilings to facilitate the varied lighting effects in the film.

Hitchcock's familiarity with European cinema also stemmed from his membership of the Film Society, formed in 1925 by left-wing intellectual Ivor Montagu and actor Hugh Miller to show imported art films and films which were not screened in London's commercial cinemas because of censorship. Private clubs could ignore the rulings of the British Board of Film Censors and bans effected by local authorities. In this way Hitchcock and other members of the Film Society saw banned films including *Nosferatu* and *The Battleship Potemkin*. Ivor Montagu, an admirer of the Soviet regime and of Eisenstein's films, re-edited some scenes in *The Lodger* after the film's distributors were concerned about its commercial viability. Montagu and the Film Society represented the trend of cultural modernism which also manifested itself in *Close-Up*, an art film periodical which reviewed many European films (Street, 150–4). So when Hitchcock returned to London in 1926 the film-makers he had studied in Germany were also being discussed and written about by those who wanted to promote European cinema as an artistic vanguard against the perceived commercialism of Hollywood.

As *The Lodger* reveals, however, Hitchcock was not as critical of Hollywood's methods and techniques as his modernist colleagues who wrote articles for *Close-Up*. He had always admired American films and his first film-related job was working as a title designer for Famous-Players-Lasky (an American film company which later became Paramount) at their Islington studios in London.

In the mid- to late 1920s Hollywood was interested in developments in European art cinema and several film-makers including Ernst Lubitsch (director of popular German comedies in the 1920s), Mauritz Stiller (a Scandinavian who had discovered Greta Garbo), Paul Leni (director of the expressionist classic *Waxworks*, 1924) and F. W. Murnau went to Hollywood to make films. There is much evidence, therefore, of stylistic cross-fertilisation between Hollywood and Europe in the 1920s and *The Lodger* demonstrates an appreciation of 'art' cinema and at the same time admiration for Hollywood's narrative techniques and acknowledgement of the need to entertain the film audience. In keeping with 'classical' Hollywood cinema, the narrative displays a clear trajectory organised around the principle of 'problem-resolution'.

The narrative of *The Lodger* is 'classical' in the sense that the film poses, and answers, a basic question: who is 'the Avenger'? The most obvious candidate is the Lodger (Ivor Novello), but there are also grounds for suspecting Joe (Malcolm Keen), who is associated with sexual banter with Daisy (June) and comments early on in the film 'I'm keen on golden hair myself, same as the Avenger is'. Like many films based on patterns of classical narrative the film introduces its 'inciting incident' when the Lodger arrives at the Buntings' house looking for a room to let. On top of the mystery already established about the murders, another crucial layer is added which presents us with the possible culprit, who has a strange reaction to the paintings of fair-haired women which are on the walls of his room. Further suspense is created when we know that fair-haired Daisy lives in the house and is therefore a potential victim for the Avenger.

The composition and structure of *The Lodger* would appear to be fairly straightforward. It consists of ten sequences which deal with murder number seven; the reporting of the murder; introduction to Daisy as she hears the news at work with other chorus girls; introduction to the Buntings and Joe; the arrival of the Lodger; the development of the 'love triangle' between Daisy, Joe and the Lodger; murder number eight; the Lodger is suspected; Joe closing in on the Lodger; the Lodger's arrest; followed by the final sequence of the Lodger and Daisy in their home after the discovery of his innocence. Despite this clear pattern there are, however, several layers of ambiguity which raise the story from a simple 'whodunnit'. The main site of ambiguity, especially for audiences watching the film in the 1920s, concerns the Lodger, who was played by Ivor Novello, a well known and loved star. Apart from our knowledge of his star persona and contemporary popularity he is coded completely differently from the other male characters. What might be construed as sinister about him can also be interpreted as sensitive, well-bred and attractive. Several incidents are puzzling – for example, what does the Lodger have in his bag and where does he go at night? These enigmas serve as devices to propel the narrative from one plot event to the next. Novello's star persona is discussed at more length below, but it is important to note here his ambiguous function in a narrative context.

The narrative uses various mechanisms to link particular incidents and themes, the most noticeable being associative and parallel action. In the first sequence we see not just the discovery of a murder but the introduction of the crowds who later play an important part in hounding the Lodger when he is mistaken for the Avenger. In the fifth sequence, when the Lodger is introduced, his arrival is intercut with a comedic episode with Mr Bunting standing on a chair to put money in the meter above the door because the light has gone out. The Lodger is startled when he hears a crash (as Bunting falls off the chair) and the light suddenly goes on again. The parallel action here serves two purposes: a comedic one which is consistent with the characterisation of the Bunting family as previously presented, and as a mechanism of suspense which becomes associated with the Lodger. The light is also significant in that it goes out just before the Lodger first arrives, cueing us to expect something sinister and setting up a key motif which recurs throughout the rest of the film. In the penultimate sequence, when the Lodger takes Daisy to a dark street, they sit on a bench under a lamp; he meets her again later at the same place when he has escaped from Joe. The light surrounded by darkness here serves to focus even more attention on the Lodger and Daisy in these two key scenes, when they appear to be vulnerable innocents who find the city threatening and dangerous.

Another narrative device is the way in which scenes progress into sequences (a sequence being made up of a series of linked scenes) by advancing from the general to the particular, establishing a state of affairs, developing the situation and ending with a particular event or suggestion. The second sequence, for example, which deals with the reporting of the murder on the wireless, in newspapers and by word-of-mouth, begins with a general shot of editors scanning a wire in the newsroom. It then progresses to the publication of the news in papers, in neon and via radio, and ends with the particular reception of the news by the crowds. Similarly, the following sequence, which shows how the dancers and Daisy learn the news, begins with their general discussion of the crimes and builds up to their particular reception of the news of murder number seven. Similarly, in the sequence which introduces the 'love triangle' theme between Daisy, Joe and the Lodger, a complex dynamic between the three characters is established by progressing from a general observation about Daisy and the Lodger's increasing friendliness and intimacy, to Joe's jealousy and symbolic linking of the murders with his plans to marry Daisy. Here the handcuffs serve as a symbol of sexual violence: when Joe catches the Avenger he will marry Daisy (a 'rope around the Avenger's neck' is equated with 'a ring around Daisy's finger'). Into the conventional mystery another layer of ambiguity is therefore inserted. As a character we are not encouraged to like Joe, who is less handsome and refined than the Lodger. The incident with the handcuffs associates his desire for Daisy with the violence of murder, which is given an extra sexual edge with the persistent use of the pulsating neon flashes of 'Tonight. Golden Curls' which recur throughout the film.

Narrative structure and *mise en scène* are used to explore the film's major themes of guilt and innocence, communication, the dangers of the city, and gender/sexuality. The identity of the Avenger is the major question posed by the narrative. It is important, however, to appreciate how the revelation that he has been caught (we never see him) reminds us that although we have been anxious to learn his identity we have been encouraged to suspect both the Lodger and Joe. In so doing we learn other things about them, which raises the question that either of them *might*, in different circumstances, have been capable of murder. On several occasions the Lodger is built up as suspicious: his dramatic, wincing reaction to the paintings of fair-haired women when he enters his room; the intertitle: 'Be careful, I'll get you yet' when he is flirting with Daisy in his room; his restless pacing in his room, which we see from the point of view of the Buntings from below (using the celebrated technique of the thick plate-glass ceiling); the coincidence of timing that the Lodger is out at the time that the eighth murder is committed; the discovery of the map, press cuttings and photograph in his bag and, finally, aspects of Novello's acting style and Hitchcock's visual composition of the actor in the frame.

These last two points suggest comparison with Murnau's *Nosferatu*. On several occasions Novello's slow, gestural acting style is reminiscent of expressionist acting techniques. His movements are deliberate and studied and his hand gestures reveal long fingers that are similar to those of the vampire in *Nosferatu*. When the Lodger has arrived at the Buntings' house and is installed in his room there is a shot of him from outside the window. As he looks out, the window pane forms a frame-within-a-frame around his face and the lighting effects create a streak of vertical light down his face. This image is very foreboding, particularly of the scene at the end of the film when the Lodger's handcuffs have got caught on the railings. In *Nosferatu* the vampire is also filmed so that his face is framed by window panes, his fingers are unnaturally long and the visual construction of his image shows consistent patterns of a trapped individual, contributing to the film's suggestion of sympathy for the vampire. Novello's white make-up also gives him a vampiric quality, while Daisy's instantaneous attraction to him is reminiscent of the classic representation of the vampire whom women are compelled to desire.

As previously noted, Joe is also a suspect although he is a policeman. His relationship with Daisy is coded with overtones of violence and fetishism (the handcuff incident) and his desire to capture the Avenger becomes acute when he realises that he can obliterate his rival at the same time by identifying him as the Avenger. The motif of the triangle is a plot device which links the murderer with the serial killings of the fair-haired women and provides clues for the location of the most likely spot for the next murder. Its other crucial function is to symbolise the three-way love contest between Daisy, Joe and the Lodger. When it becomes clear that Daisy is attracted to the Lodger, Joe becomes all the more intent on linking him with the killings, as we see from a montage of subjective shots which convince him that the Lodger is the Avenger. The inference is that patterns can be detected when you want them to be, and were it not for the news that the real Avenger has been caught, the film could have ended with the crowd lynching the Lodger, even though we (and Daisy) know about his sister via the two flashback scenes of the story of his sister's murder at a ball and of his mother on her deathbed. The fact that the film's ending is ostensibly 'happy' does not, perhaps, remove every doubt about the characters' potential to be violent.

The film contains many montage sequences of communication, communication systems and communication between people. The opening sequences deal with the murder and how the news spreads via modern technology (the wire and mass production of newspapers) and word-of-mouth. This provides an opportunity for some documentarist sequences that bear a close resemblance to images of modern technology in Soviet films. This representation of modernity as progressive and efficient was consistent with European modernism's fascination with machinery as a progressive force. Consequently, in the second sequence, we learn *how* the news is spread from the newsroom to the crowd. This montage is not strictly necessary for the advancement of the plot, but it provides an opportunity for yet another style to be incorporated into the film. The impression is of pace, but the machines which print the newspapers are lingered on for their aesthetic qualities, encouraging the spectator to admire not only their efficiency but also their beauty. Once the news reaches the crowds, however, its details are distorted, exaggerated and engulfed by the by-standers, who are both shocked by and fascinated with the Avenger's deeds. The inference is that although modern technology can make news travel fast it has no control over how it is received, what interpretations people will construct from its 'neutral' factual bulletins. The by-standers' discussion of the murders also permits an opportunity for humour, as in the scene when someone pretends to be the Avenger by pulling a scarf over the lower half of their face. When the chorus girls and Daisy's colleagues at the fashion house hear the news they devise schemes to thwart the Avenger by wearing dark wigs to disguise their fair hair. Their banter is fearful but excited, which contributes to the sexual theme that pervades the entire film.

The Lodger can be linked generically to films which portray the city as threatening and vice-ridden. While avant-garde cinema embraced technology it could often be critical of the structures which sustained modernity, including the city. Many films in the 1920s, such as the German *Strassenfilme* ('street' films), depicted the city as a dangerous place, and G. W. Pabst was one of the key directors who worked with this genre. Perhaps his best known film is *Pandora's Box* (1929), which succeeded *The Lodger* by three years but contains many of the same preoccupations, including the Jack the Ripper theme at the end of the film. As already noted, the scenes in *The Lodger* when Ivor Novello and Daisy (June) are under the streetlamp are reminiscent of many European images of the city as dense, threatening, in this case fog-ridden (which also has a metaphorical function), and mysterious. The city is represented as a dangerous place for women and the film's insistence on the Avenger's victims being fair-haired relates to the tradition of the *femme fatale* which was incorporated into American *films noirs* of the 1940s. This complicates the impression that the victims are innocent: the women we see discussing the murders are mostly young, attractive, and work in city-related occupations on the stage and in glamorous fashion houses. As in Murnau's *Sunrise* (1927), women who live in the city are portrayed as vulnerable, tempting and a source of male anxiety, anger and even violence; the neon-flashing 'Tonight. Golden Curls' encapsulates the impression of the city as full of promise but with a dangerous edge.

Related to the theme of women and the city is the broader issue of gender and sexuality. Ivor Novello's portrayal of the Lodger is tinged with sexual ambiguity. His appearance is somewhat androgynous: his hair is sleek, he has a pale face and dark eye make-up. He is the direct opposite of the rougher, more conventionally masculine Joe. Two intertitles intimate that the Lodger may be homosexual: 'I'm glad he's not keen on the girls' and 'Even if he is a bit queer, he's a gentleman'. Novello's portrayal of the Lodger also demonstrates a classic representation of gay male sexuality of the period: the sad young man who is a misunderstood outsider. Although Ivor Novello's own gay sexuality was not widely known at the time, the film's ambiguous narrative and the way the star is photographed in long, languorous close-ups which emphasise his good looks, large dark eyes, and hair, permit a reading which places sexual ambivalence at the centre rather than at the margins of the film. At the time, Novello was the most popular British male film star. As well as being an actor he was a songwriter and playwright and had acted in Hollywood in the early 1920s, returning to star in a successful film adaptation of his stage play *The Rat* (Graham Cutts, 1925). Audiences would have been familiar with Novello's stage and screen work and, according to Donald Spoto, Hitchcock could not end the film on an ambiguous note, leaving it unclear as to whether the Lodger was the Avenger or not because the distributors were convinced that Novello's fans would not tolerate him being depicted as a villain (Spoto, 85).

In terms of film style, *The Lodger* utilises many techniques of silent cinema at its most visual and graphic. The sparse, but adequate intertitles (in keeping with German films) were designed by McKnight Kauffer, a painter and poster designer. As the first frames of the film appear, the originality of the designs is striking and they continue to punctuate the narrative throughout. Other textual insertions are important: the repeated flashing in neon of 'Tonight. Golden Curls' creates a link between the murder of blonde women and the city which exploits them for sex. The news bulletin giving the details of the seventh murder provides the spectator with vital plot information. The film's *mise en scène* is employed to the full for the advancement of plot and suggestion of sub-plot. The triangle with 'The Avenger' written in its centre is a key plot device which also symbolises the three-way love contest.

Costume is used in intriguing ways to confuse our expectations about the characters. When we first see Daisy she appears to be a well-to-do woman dressed in a fur coat, emerging from a doorway. We then cut to a wide shot which reveals that she is in fact a model for expensive clothes in a fashion house. The Lodger's first appearance codes him as mysterious, dressed exactly as we would expect the Avenger to be, wearing a long, black cloak, dark hat and with a scarf covering the lower half of his face. The clothes we see him in later suggest to us that he is upper class, an observation which is later confirmed by the flashback of his sister's 'coming out' ball and the penultimate scene when the Buntings visit his palatial mansion. The Lodger's bag is important for the plot in that we see from very early on, when he first goes to his room at the Buntings, that it must hold something vital because he locks it in the sideboard. Later on, when Joe arrests the Lodger, the bag is opened to reveal maps, press cuttings about the murders, and the photograph of his sister. This condemns him in the eyes of Joe but vindicates him according to Daisy, who believes his story about his sister being the Avenger's first victim. Used here primarily as a plot device, the bag is nevertheless deployed in a way that is similar to how bags feature in Hitchcock's later films – as a character's private space where secrets can be hidden. While a bag is usually a woman's property, in this instance the nature of its use links it with the theme of sexual ambiguity. Novello is identified with 'the feminine' in the film – the way he is filmed, his association with sensitivity, his clash with the uncomplicated 'masculine' Joe, his inability to communicate his story – and this use of conventionally feminine *mise en scène* in connection with the Lodger is therefore not surprising.

Novello's acting style was typical of silent cinema. His melodramatic gestures and slow, deliberate movements are, however, rather different from those of the other characters. In *The Lodger* the Buntings' acting style is also melodramatic, but the camera singles them out less than Novello. As Christine Gledhill has argued, British cinema of the 1920s engaged with traditions inherited from popular late nineteenth-century stage melodrama in such a way as to adapt them to suit cinematic techniques. In stage melodrama, acting was non-naturalistic, typified by large, often slowish and languid movements to give presence to characters who were representing extremes of good and evil. While cinematic representation did not require the use of such grand gestures, acting traditions taken from the theatre were clearly present in early screen acting. The close-up, for example, could convey the dramatic equivalent of a fulsome melodramatic stage gesture and at the same time communicate a scene's emotional core. Thus melodrama had not disappeared in silent cinema but had simply been accommodated by the film medium, and Novello's style is therefore very appropriate for the camera in terms of both his physical movements and his suitability for close-ups.

It has been argued in this chapter that *The Lodger* engages with many styles and techniques which were prevalent in both European and Hollywood cinema of the 1920s. In what ways, therefore, is it a 'British' film? The traditions inherited from late nineteenth-century stage melodrama are important in that the film can be linked to a longer trajectory of British popular theatre. The film was an adaptation of a novel by Mrs Belloc Lowndes, written in 1913 about the Jack the Ripper murders, which had taken place in Whitechapel in the 1880s. A more direct source for the film was *Who Is He?*, a stage adaptation of the novel, which Hitchcock had seen. As well as its link with popular mythology surrounding Jack the Ripper, a sense of 'Britishness' comes mainly from the use of London settings in *The Lodger*. The lower middle-class milieu of the Buntings' house, the foggy street scenes and the scenes of communal activity (the street tea-dispenser, the pub) connote London life, as do the inter-titles of dialogue, particularly those conveying the colloquial speech of the crowds and the Buntings ('dearie'; 'the way that fiend did her in').

The film was a popular and critical success and was released at a time when the British film industry was being singled out as a candidate for state assistance to bolster production and counter American domination. The Cinematograph Films Act, 1927, stipulated that renters and exhibitors should handle and show a certain percentage of British films in relation to the total number they distributed and exhibited. *The Lodger* was highly praised as an example of a standard to which other British films should aspire. The trade paper *The Bioscope* even went so far as to suggest it was 'possibly' the finest British production ever made. *The Lodger* represents both the sophistication of silent cinema and the prevailing trends towards co-operation and internationalism which were cut short by the upheavals wrought by the coming of sound in the late 1920s. From this perspective it is a key film which illustrates the eclecticism of European film production and its accommodation with Hollywood.

References

Gledhill, Christine 1999: 'Taking it Forward: Theatricality and British Cinema Style in the 1920s'. In Linda Fitzsimmons and Sarah Street (eds), *Moving Performance: Theatre and Early Cinema in Britain*. Wiltshire: Flicks Books.
Manvell, Roger 1951: 'Revaluations'. In *Sight and Sound*, January, 378.
Petro, Patrice 1989: *Joyless Streets: Women and Melodramatic Representation in Weimar Germany*. Princeton, NJ: Princeton University Press.
Ryall, Tom 1986: *Alfred Hitchcock and the British Cinema*. London: Croom Helm.
Spoto, Donald 1986: *The Life of Alfred Hitchcock: The Dark Side of Genius*. London: Collins.
Street, Sarah 1997: *British National Cinema*. London: Routledge.
Thompson, Kristin and Bordwell, David 1994: *Film History: An Introduction*, NewYork: McGraw-Hill.

Suggestions for Further Reading

Barr, Charles 1997: 'Before *Blackmail*: Silent British Cinema'. In Robert Murphy (ed.), *The British Cinema Book*. London: British Film Institute.

Barr, Charles 1999: *English Hitchcock*. London: Cameron & Hollis.
Higson, Andrew 1993: *Waving the Flag: Constructing a National Cinema in Britain*. Oxford: Clarendon Press.
Low, Rachel 1971: *The History of the British Film, 1918–1929*. London: Allen and Unwin.

Credits

Director	Alfred Hitchcock
Assistant Director	Alma Reville
Producer	Michael Balcon
Production Company	Gainsborough Pictures
Screenplay	Eliot Stannard, from novel by Marie Belloc Lowndes
Editor/Titling	Ivor Montagu
Director of Photography	Baron [Giovanni] Ventimiglia
Art Director	C. Wilfrid Arnold, Bertram Evans
Title Designs	E. McKnight Kauffer

Cast

Marie Ault	Mrs Bunting
Arthur Chesney	Mr Bunting
June	Daisy Bunting
Malcolm Keen	Joe
Ivor Novello	The Lodger

Filmography (Hitchcock's British Films)

The Pleasure Garden (1925)
The Mountain Eagle (1925)
The Lodger (1926)
Downhill (1927)
Easy Virtue (1927)
The Ring (1927)
The Farmer's Wife (1927)
Champagne (1928)
The Manxman (1928)
Blackmail (1929)
Juno and the Paycock (1930)
Murder! (1930)
The Skin Game (1930–1)
Number Seventeen (1931)
Rich and Strange (1932)
Waltzes from Vienna (1933)
The Man Who Knew Too Much (1934)

The Thirty-Nine Steps (1935)
Secret Agent (1935)
Sabotage (1936)
Young and Innocent (1937)
The Lady Vanishes (1937)
Jamaica Inn (1938)

3 *La règle du jeu*
Christine (Nora Gregor) and Geneviève (Mila Parely) in fancy dress with Octave (Jean Renoir).

La règle du jeu
Jill Forbes

Filmed in the spring of 1939 and first released in July of that year, Jean Renoir's
La règle du jeu is a magnificent summary of an era that was about to come to an
end, both in the history of France and in the French cinema. When Renoir
began the film he was at the height of his fame and fortune. His adaptation of
Zola's novel *La bête humaine*, starring Jean Gabin and Simone Simon, had
opened at the end of 1938 to universal acclaim and, with his brother Claude,
his assistant director André Zwoboda, and several other associates, he had
formed a production and distribution company called La nouvelle édition
française, which he hoped would operate rather in the manner of the United
Artists Company in the United States, promoting the work of its owners rather
than the fortunes of the studios or big business. *La règle du jeu* was the company's first project, and an ambitious one, described by Renoir as 'a precise
description of bourgeois people of our period' (Curchod and Faulkner, 10).

The film tells the story of the daring aviator André Jurieux, who flies the
Atlantic, single-handed, for love of Christine, Marquise de La Chesnaye. But
when he lands at Le Bourget airport, to the rapturous acclaim of the assembled
crowds, he is not met by Christine, as he had hoped, but by her family friend
Octave. And instead of behaving as the national hero the waiting crowd
desires, he gives a radio interview, heard by Christine and her husband at
home in Paris, in which he petulantly expresses his disappointment at Christine's absence. His despair is such that shortly afterwards he attempts suicide
by trying to crash his car.

These episodes serve as a prologue which introduces us to Octave, Christine, her husband Robert de La Chesnaye, and Robert's mistress, Geneviève, a
world of wealthy 'bourgeois' with useless aristocratic titles, innumerable servants,
and assorted hangers-on. We accompany this group to a weekend house
party given at the La Chesnaye country seat, La Colinière, and momentarily
appear to be transported back in time to a world that was frequently represented in the comic theatre of the eighteenth and nineteenth centuries by
playwrights such as Beaumarchais, Marivaux and Musset. The central preoccupation of all the characters, whether masters or servants, is an elaborate
series of games, played, as the title of the film suggests, according to rules
which everyone understands and which must not, under any circumstances,
be broken. One of these games is hunting, which is depicted in an exquisitely
beautiful and poignant sequence of the film, shot on location in the Sologne

countryside; another is play-acting, in evidence in a series of gruesome music-hall turns performed by the hosts and guests at La Colinière for the benefit of the assembled household. Most of all, the game in question is that of love – conjugal or adulterous – in all its vagaries and permutations. But whatever the game, it seems that the form is more significant than the content and that the observation of the rules is an end in itself, an end which is more important than winning or losing.

This eminently theatrical and highly artificial setting, as well as the invention of characters whose concerns are apparently entirely frivolous and solipsistic, seemed an extraordinary subject for a film in 1939 and especially for Renoir, who was known both for the 'realism' of his films and for his support for left-wing causes. The political context was, indeed, sombre. In France, the Popular Front government, elected in 1936, had ended in failure, brought down by violent opposition from the extreme Right but also by a series of strikes by the Left, and in 1938 the Frontist Prime Minister Léon Blum had been replaced by Édouard Daladier. Outside France, events were moving with frightening speed. In March 1938 came the Anschluss, when Germany invaded Austria and annexed it to the Third Reich, clearly signalling that war was imminent. On 29 September 1938, Hitler, Chamberlain and Daladier met in Munich and signed the agreement which, Chamberlain declared, secured 'peace in our time' – or, at least, a breathing space – but in March 1939, as Renoir was shooting the first sequences of the film, Germany invaded Czechoslovakia. On 1 September Germany invaded Poland and on 3 September war was declared.

The principal characters in *La règle du jeu* seem blithely unaware of the impending conflagration and resolutely turn their faces against the realities of politics. The Marquis collects mechanical musical instruments, one of which he proudly demonstrates to his assembled guests; the General cares only about preserving appearances; the aviator cares only whether Christine loves him; Geneviève is preoccupied by the belief that Robert will leave her; Jackie cares only for André, who does not love her; and her mother seeks only to marry off her daughter. The servants, too, share their employers' preoccupations, mirroring their solipsism and introversion. There is, apparently, no character in the film who speaks for 'the people' or 'the common man' or who is capable of offering an outside perspective on this group determined to sink with their ship.

Understandably, Renoir was criticised from all sides. From the Right came the accusation that the film caricatured and ridiculed the very people on whom France depended for its defence. The Army is represented here by the General, who is an aimiable buffoon, while the Air Force is – at least potentially – represented by André Jurieux, who is totally unwilling to place his country above his personal preoccupations. Thus such military heroes as the film contains are decidedly unsatisfactory and, with hindsight, we may say that Renoir's view of the military capabilities of France in 1939 was more prescient than his critics on the Right admitted publicly. Perhaps this knowledge explains why the film came in for virulent attacks from the right-wing press and provoked violent incidents when it was screened. But from the Left, too, came criticism that was certainly more muted but which nevertheless expressed unease at Renoir's essentially sympathetic portrayal of the foibles of a group of people who were rich, idle and exploitative. During the 1930s, there was much criticism on the Left of the so-called 'two hundred families' who were said to be ruining France. *La règle du jeu* apparently depicts one of these in all its magnificent irresponsibility.

The strength of Renoir's films in the 1930s, and indeed the feature on which much of his reputation rested, was his humanism, his creation of sympathetic communities, the notion that runs from film to film of the nation as a collectivity in which each person has a part to play, and of the way that individualities contribute to a richly variegated totality. We see this in films such as *Le crime de Monsieur Lange* (1935), which rests on working-class solidarity, or *La Marseillaise* (1938) where the community is extended to the nation as a whole. *La règle du jeu* apparently conforms to this approach both ideologically and cinematically since it is a film without stars and without a principal character or characters. But the difficulty, at least for critics on the Left, was that the community in question, with its 'upstairs downstairs' relationships and its impermeability to outside forces, more closely resembled that of an eighteenth-century château than that of France in 1939.

Clearly, *La règle du jeu* was not what audiences in 1939 expected from France's most celebrated director. After its initial screening Renoir shortened the film in an attempt to make it more accessible, but even so its first run only lasted a few weeks. Thereafter, the turn of events removed it from commercial release for over two decades, leaving it to acquire an underground reputation which, if anything, reinforced its political impact. The film was banned under wartime censorship in 1942 and may have been banned as early as 1940 in the category of films considered 'depressing, morbid, immoral and likely to corrupt young people' (Curchod and Faulkner, 21–2). In November 1940, its director left France for the United States where he remained until 1952, while its negative was destroyed by Allied bombing in 1942. It was not until 1958 that the version we see today was pieced together by two devoted film scholars, and it was not until 1965 that it was commercially re-released. Though the present version is longer than the one released commercially in 1939 it is shorter than Renoir had originally intended, with the result that several episodes seem incoherent or unexplained (notably André Jurieux's suicide attempt and the intimacy of the relationship between Christine and Octave). But perhaps the most important effect is to alter the balance of the film, to make it appear less of a psychological drama which turns on the emotions of characters such as Jurieux and Octave, and to make the house party at La Colinière the structural centre and focus of the film.

The house party is a metaphor commonly used to signify a society in microcosm, enabling a cross-section of social types and interests to be brought

together in one place. It was a particularly common device in boulevard
theatre but its ultimate origins lie in the Aristotelian unities of time, place and
action. The fact that La Colinière has become the centre of the film emphasises
both its literary origins and its satirical import. While *La règle du jeu* depicts
a weekend rather than twenty-four hours, it appears to achieve a dramatic
unity: for a short period of time an assorted group of people, representing
a microcosm of French society, are brought together under one roof. A carnivalesque atmosphere prevails in which it is difficult to distinguish servants
and masters, and cases of mistaken identity occur – one thinks of similar revelries
in Shakespeare's *Twelfth Night* or *A Midsummer Night's Dream* – until finally
a dramatic action brings the crazy atmosphere to an end, order is restored and
everything returns to 'normal'.

However, it was not just the theatre in general to which Renoir referred but
specific literary sources. In order to see how this is explored we must return
to the beginning of the film and its epigraph from *Le mariage de Figaro* (*The
Marriage of Figaro*), a play by Beaumarchais (1732–99) first performed in 1784:
'Cœurs sensibles, cœurs fidèles/Qui blamez l'amour léger/Cessez vos plaintes
cruelles/Est-ce un crime de changer?' (Sensitive hearts, faithful hearts/Who
condemn fickle love/Cease your harsh complaints/Is it a crime to change?).
The epigraph seems to anchor the film securely in French eighteenth-century
culture, in the world of the *ancien régime*, ruled by an aristocracy which invented
the concept of politeness and good manners and where sexual and social relationships were conducted according to strict codes of behaviour. We might
also note similarities of title and plot to another eighteenth-century play, *Le jeu
de l'amour et du hasard* (1730) by Marivaux (1688–1763), in which a noblewoman
changes places with her maid in order to observe her suitor who, unbeknown
to her, has changed places with his manservant for the same reason. This was
not the first time that Renoir had evoked the eighteenth century on film. In *La
Marseillaise*, in which he played the role of an artist, casting himself as the
painter of the Revolution Jacques-Louis David, he explored the origins of the
French national anthem by following a group of Marseillais as they travel to
Paris to support the Revolution.

It seems fair to assume that Renoir's fascination with the eighteenth century
was in part because it was a period of revolutionary change, the time when
a corrupt aristocracy was overthrown by popular action rather as many had
hoped would occur in 1936. But the eighteenth century had other attractions
too: the formalism of its literature, its fondness for structural games and *mises
en abyme*, and its reflexivity, all of which are also mirrored in *La règle du jeu*.
However, the film was initially conceived as an adaptation of Alfred de Musset's
play *Les caprices de Marianne* (1840), in which Marianne, who is married to
Claudio, is having an affair with Octave, and in which Célio, who also loves
Marianne, goes to a rendezvous in place of Octave and is killed on the orders
of Claudio. This provided Renoir with part of his plot and the name of his own
character as well as a further theme, embodied in the name Marianne, which

links the exploration of the state of the nation – Marianne was the female figure of the Republic – with that of the role and status of women. What can we learn from this complex of intertexts which were and are extremely familiar to French audiences? And how do they reinforce the political impact of the film?

Perhaps the strongest theme to emerge from them is that of social satire. It is a commonplace of literary history to view *Le mariage de Figaro* as a prefiguration of the Revolution, which took place five years after it was first performed and which overturned the social structure it depicted. Beaumarchais subversively satirised the customs and habits of a declining aristocracy by showing the essential similarity between its behaviour and that of its servants. With hindsight, Beaumarchais appeared premonitory in exactly the same way as, with hindsight, Renoir appeared premonitory. The analogy works, provided one accepts that the France of 1939 was ruled by a kind of *ancien régime* which was swept away by the revolutionary forces of post-war modernisation, and it is an analogy that critics in the 1950s and 1960s were understandably eager to embrace in order to distinguish post-war France from the period of shameful appeasement and occupation in the 1930s and 1940s.

In French cinema we frequently find film-makers using the body of a woman to symbolise the body politic, and in wishing to adapt Musset's play about 'Marianne' it may well be that Renoir had something of the kind in mind. Women's inconstancy is often said to be the subject-matter of *Les caprices de Marianne* and, to some extent, *Le jeu de l'amour et du hasard* but a modern reading would probably emphasise that the subject is women's freedom of choice. Certainly, plays and film juxtapose inclination and duty, doing as you please and doing as you should, frivolity and seriousness, comedy and tragedy. However, it is interesting that Renoir's 'Marianne' is not French but Austrian, since one of the vital questions posed in the film is the nature of identity. What makes people what they are? Can they change? And can one judge essence from external appearances? Renoir's literary sources make great play with carnivalesque disguise and inversions of identity: in Beaumarchais the implication is that a servant can become a master; in Musset the *quiproquo*, or mistaken identity, leads to a tragic outcome. And in *La règle du jeu* such questions have a strongly political dimension.

A great deal of dressing up goes on in the film. This is of course most obvious during the evening's theatricals when Geneviève wears gypsy costume, Christine wears Tyrolean costume, and Octave puts on a bearskin. Perhaps these costumes are intended to reveal 'true' identity rather than to disguise. Octave, for example, seems stuck inside his bearskin, which turns him into a permanent pantomime character against his will and makes a mockery of his later confession of musical ambitions and his love for Christine. If so, what are we to make of the performances of the other guests at La Colinière and the songs they sing? One of these, *En r'v'nant d'la revue*, was a late nineteenth-century musical-hall song which became the anthem of supporters of General Boulanger who, in the late 1880s, attempted a military coup d'état against the

Republic. Is Renoir implying that the performers at La Colinière would support such an anti-Republican act and that they thought one was needed? Arguably, when Marshal Pétain became head of state the following year, that is exactly what happened, and such people did support him. The second song performed, *Nous avons l'vé le pied*, was a so-called music-hall 'patter song' and it is sung by Berthelin, La Bruyère, L'Inverti (the Homosexual) and the South American, disguised as office workers with enormous and clearly false beards. Its ironies are harder to interpret but Keith Reader has suggested that these are burlesque representatives of a class which is absent from the film, that of the petty bourgeoisie, whose social instability had proved the downfall of the Popular Front. By the time the ghosts and the skeleton come on stage to cavort to the music of Saint-Saëns, spookily provided by a piano that no-one plays, it is clear that the theatricals are not, or no longer, harmless play-acting, for during this performance the whole tone of the film shifts from the comic to the tragic. The intimate relationships in the household are reconfigured during the *danse macabre*, so that its placing gives it a premonitory function as it points forward to the tragedy that will occur. Renoir referred to French society, in the context of *La règle du jeu*, as 'dancing on a volcano' and perhaps that is indicated by this dance of death.

If the significance of dress and identity are overdetermined in the theatricals, they are also crucial elsewhere in the film. For example, Marceau the poacher is issued with a servant's livery and is transformed, at least in theory, commenting with what for the audience is heavy irony, 'I've always dreamed of being a servant'. The double case of mistaken identity is caused by nothing more complicated than coats: Lisette lends Christine her cape so that Christine is mistaken for Lisette by Schumacher and Marceau as she is embracing Octave; Octave lends Jurieux his coat in order for him to run away with Christine, so that Schumacher mistakes him for Octave whom he mistakenly thought had been embracing his wife. André's death is sacrificial, restoring calm and order and allowing everyone to return to their 'rightful' place and their 'true' identity.

However, true identity is not always as clear-cut as some of the characters might wish. Christine is Austrian – indeed, she speaks French with a marked accent – and is played by the actress Nora Gregor who was a real refugee from Hitler's Anschluss. Christine comes from a musical family (we learn from Octave that her father was a conductor), and we are reminded of the Austrian tradition he represented by the musical quotations of Mozart's *Marriage of Figaro*. It is a tradition quite different from the bellicose and predatory one symbolised by the Anschluss and embodied in Hitler, another Austrian. It is not clear whether Christine has put her Austrian origins behind her. Her assimilation into French society is initially imperfect and she does not understand the rules of the game Robert is playing. Above all, she does not know, initially, that he has a mistress. She is perhaps nostalgic, too, for her country of birth, because she likes to dress up in Tyrolean costume. In her person she therefore embodies the conflictual Austrian destiny: Hitler or Mozart, *Realpolitik* or music.

Her husband is not what he seems either. He has an aristocratic title but, as the General points out, 'his grandfather's name was Rosenthal'. The Marquis is a man of exquisite taste who knows how things should be done; he has immense style but he is, in the cook's words, a 'métèque' (that is, of mixed race). France was, and had been for over a century, a country that welcomed immigrants of all kinds and granted them civil rights, and this was one reason why the pre-war Jewish population in France was both numerous and assimilated. In addition to obliquely referring to Renoir's earlier, pacifist film *La grande illusion* (1937), in which Dalio, the actor who plays Robert, had played a character named Rosenthal, the remarks by the General and the cook reflect the anti-Semitism that was widespread in France across many social classes in the 1930s and that was to be allowed to flourish under the Vichy regime and the German Occupation. Indeed, during the Occupation a portrait of the actor Dalio, by now a refugee in the United States, was used to 'help' people identify Jews. But despite Renoir's evident critique of anti-Semitism, the character Robert also embodies some caricatural aspects of Jewishness, both in his wealth and in his exaggerated adoption of the outward signs of Frenchness. For Robert is an actor – his white make-up, it has been suggested, is clown-like – he performs the part of a host, a lover, a theatrical impresario, and an aristocrat, and Dalio's performance as the Marquis brilliantly and convincingly conveys the impression of inauthenticity, which the audience is free to interpret positively or negatively.

The final component of this international jigsaw is Schumacher. As an Alsatian he embodies the dual or split identity and divided loyalty which is common to many in the house. Alsace is the province in eastern France which had been a political football since 1870 when it had been captured by Germany. Its loss had been a humiliation for the French army and its recovery by France, enacted under the Treaty of Versailles (1919), had become a nineteenth-century patriotic *cause célèbre*. Alsace's 'dual nationality' is wittily referred to when Christine pronounces Schumacher's name with a German inflection in contrast to Robert's French stress. It is a double allegiance which is mirrored in Schumacher's status: he is both of the household and outside it; he is not quite a servant but not quite a master. He is said to like order, and indeed organises the hunt in a military fashion, suggesting a caricaturally Germanic trait; but he is a man of deep emotions, and everywhere he goes he creates chaos. Above all, perhaps, he is the agent of tragedy, as was the province he comes from.

Throughout the film Renoir calls attention to the artificial and theatrical nature of its contents and to his role as a film-maker in their production and *mise en scène*. This is signalled in the role of Octave, a wry but sympathetic portrait of the artist as a sometimes clumsy manipulator of events, someone who stands outside the main action, differentiated from the real players by his poverty and his class. Not for the first time, as we have seen, the role of the artist is played by Renoir himself and this serves to emphasise the degree to which the film is intended as an interrogation of his art.

In addition to the obviously theatrical numbers, Renoir establishes an important contrast between interiors and exteriors. During the hunting scene, nature is almost tangibly sensuous. We observe the shimmering play of light on the landscape, we hear the leaves rustling, we see the animals playing, the guests admire the antics of a squirrel through their binoculars in a shot which is held much longer than is narratively necessary in order to appreciate the beauty and grace of the animal. We also see the bloody destruction of this beauty as the beaters progress in grimly deliberate formation and the scene builds up to a crescendo of carnage while the camera lingers on the quivering bodies of dying rabbits and birds. The hunt sequence has rightly been called an anthology piece; a tour de force of sound, image, and movement; a palette of blacks, whites, and greys which confirmed Renoir's pre-war mastery of his art. But in the post-war, post-Holocaust Europe, its connotations have become sinister and have served to underline, once again, the political impact of the film.

There are other exteriors too, truncated in the final version of the film, which are far from being a poem to nature but are, rather, a hymn to the communications revolution of the 1930s: aeroplanes, automobiles and radio are evident in the crowd scenes at Le Bourget and the scene where André tries to crash his car. Cinema belonged to this revolution and Renoir had, in *La vie est à nous* (1936), assisted his communist friends in using the cinema for propaganda purposes. Thus in *La règle du jeu* we find juxtaposed the various uses to which the medium can be put: to convey the news, to influence the masses, to represent nature, and to offer entertainment in the form of theatrical spectacles. The latter are to be found in the film's interiors; unlike the hunt scenes, which were shot on location, these were filmed for the most part on an elaborate set at the Joinville studios in Paris (although the arrival at La Colinière was filmed at a stately home near Orléans). Here Renoir is participating in a debate which had raged in film circles since the advent of the talkies: had sound destroyed the naturalism of cinema and the essence of its art by requiring the use of studios?

Like many film-makers in the 1930s, Renoir inscribes the artificial and constructed nature of the set into the diegesis by filming the successive arrivals at La Colinière as a prologue, using a rainstorm to emphasise the contrast between the world outside and the space of the diegesis, and by reminding the audience, at intervals, that the events depicted are taking place inside an artificial space. This is clearly apparent in the scene where Octave, standing on a flight of exterior steps leading to the house, turns his back to the camera/audience and conducts an imaginary orchestra which would be situated inside the château. It is also to be seen in the closing moments of the film. André has been shot in the conservatory, a space which is half inside and half outside, half 'real' and half 'theatrical'. By interpreting this tragic dénouement as an 'accident' and inviting his guests to accompany him back into the house, Robert reassimilates the tragedy into the domain of the theatrical, defusing its impact and diminishing its significance. In this way Renoir asks what is the ultimate significance of spectacle, entertainment and performance when even death can be accommodated within it.

Above all, perhaps, Renoir seems eager to suggest that appearances, especially those offered by cinema, can be deceptive. *La règle du jeu* is a cinematic tour de force. In both the interiors and exteriors Renoir uses the deep focus which was later to be praised as such an innovative feature of Orson Welles's *Citizen Kane* (1941), to create an illusion of three-dimensional space – emphasised by aspects of the set design such as the chequered floor in the corridor of La Colinière, which is used to create an apparently distant vanishing point – and to heighten the naturalism of the hunt scene. Yet certain moments in the film indicate that we should not necessarily trust what we see, especially when it is shown to us by the cinema or other technologies of viewing. Thus during the *danse macabre*, in an extraordinarily long and fluid movement, the camera seems to be mirroring the quest of the guests as they seek out their preferred sexual partners, but just when they (and we) think they have lighted on the right person the camera shows us, instead, a reflection in a mirror. Even more tellingly, during the hunt sequence Christine changes the direction and focus of the binoculars she has been using to observe the squirrel, and brings into view a different kind of game – the figures of her husband and Geneviève embracing in the distance. Christine does not know that this is their farewell embrace and that the spy-glass has served to create another *quiproquo*. On the other hand, although the interpretation it allows her to place on their current relationship is false, it simultaneously allows her to make sense of the past in a way that would not otherwise have been possible. This extraordinary moment sums up the ambiguities of the truth of the spectacle we see, precisely by emphasising the beauty of the image and the satisfying character of the narratives it conveys. By posing questions about the nature of cinematic reality, by asking whether we can trust the products of the new technologies, by assimilating the traditions of eighteenth-century French culture into the cinema and using them to make a contemporary political statement, *La règle du jeu* has come to stand as the masterpiece of French cinema of the pre-war period.

However, Renoir owed much of his post-war reputation and celebrity to the critics of *Cahiers du cinéma* who were to become the film-makers of the New Wave. These critics and film-makers, and Truffaut in particular, adopted Renoir as a model and precursor of their own film practices. In fact Truffaut's film *Tirez sur le pianiste* (*Shoot the Pianist*, 1960) opens with shots of piano keys in tribute to *La règle du jeu*. Renoir's craft-based approach to film-making, his rejection of grandiose subjects and use of actors who were not stars, and his authorial control of his material, all differentiated him from the immediate predecessors of the New Wave and turned him into a suitable patron of its cinematic revolution. In *La règle du jeu*, Renoir uses many of the actors who had regularly appeared in his films and who had become part of his 'team' or his family, rather like British character actors in films of the 1950s. Here we see

Carette perform his 'turn' as Marceau the poacher with an accent that is improbably Parisian; Gaston Modot does his number as the impossibly rigid Schumacher; Paulette Dubost flounces her way through the film as Lisette the maid. Recurrent actors and roles were part of the appeal of cinema in the 1930s and such 'family' preferences were also to become commonplace in New Wave film-making as the same actors and actresses reappear from film to film.

Nevertheless, it is in some ways odd that *La règle du jeu*, which for the most part is highly theatrical and non-naturalistic, and whose sources are evidently literary, should have appealed so strongly to post-war audiences. The reason lies, perhaps, in the fact that it functions as a summum not just of French film-making but of a certain idea of French culture. It is a film which faces both ways. At the same time as it points to the future, it looks back over the 1930s with a degree of nostalgia, criticising both French society of the period and French film-making with considerable affection and assuming a cultural heritage which embraces the *ancien régime* as well as the new order.

References and Suggestions for Further Reading

Andrew, Dudley 1995: *Mists of Regret: Culture and Sensibility in Classic French Film*. Princeton, NJ: Princeton University Press.

Bazin, André 1971: *Jean Renoir*. Paris: Éditions Champ Libre.

Crisp, Colin 1993: *Classic French Cinema*. Bloomington, IN: Indiana University Press.

Curchod, Olivier and Faulkner, Christopher 1999: *La règle du jeu. Scénario original de Jean Renoir*. Paris: Nathan.

Faulkner, Christopher 1979: *Jean Renoir: A Guide to References and Resources*. Boston, MA: G. K. Hall.

Faulkner, Christopher 1986: *The Social Cinema of Jean Renoir*. Princeton, NJ: Princeton University Press.

Reader, Keith 1999: 'Chaos, Contradiction and Order in Jean Renoir's *La règle du jeu*'. In *Australian Journal of French Studies*, 36, 1, 26–38.

Sesonke, Alexander 1980: *Jean Renoir: The French Films*. Cambridge, MA: Harvard University Press.

Vanoye, Francis 1995: *La règle du jeu*. Paris: Nathan.

Credits

Director	Jean Renoir
Producer	Jean Renoir
Production Company	La Nouvelle Édition Française (NEF)
Screenplay	Jean Renoir, Carl Koch
Director of Photography	Jean Bachelet
Editor	Marguerite Houllé-Renoir
Art Directors	Eugène Lourié, Max Douy

Cast

Marcel Dalio	Robert de La Chesnaye
Nora Gregor	Christine de La Chesnaye
Jean Renoir	Octave
Roland Toutain	André Jurieux
Mila Parely	Geneviève de Maras
Paulette Dubost	Lisette Schumacher
Gaston Modot	Schumacher
Julien Carette	Marceau
Anne Mayen	Jackie
Pierre Nay	Saint-Aubin
Odette Talazac	Charlotte de La Plante
Pierre Magnier	The General
Georges Forster	Dick
Richard Francoeur	La Bruyère
Claire Gérard	Mme La Bruyère
Nicolas Amato	Cava
Eddy Debray	Corneille
Léon Larive	Cook

Filmography

La fille de l'eau (*Whirlpool of Life*, 1924)
Charleston (1927)
Marquitta (1928)
La petite marchande d'allumettes (*The Little Match Girl*, 1928)
Tire-au-flanc (1929)
Le bled (1929)
On purge bébé (1931)
La chienne (1931)
La nuit du carrefour (1932)
Boudu sauvé des eaux (*Boudu Saved from Drowning*, 1932)
Chotard et cie (1933)
Madame Bovary (1934)
Toni (1934)
Le crime de Monsieur Lange (1935)
La vie est à nous (*People of France*, 1936)
Une partie de campagne (*A Day in the Country* / *Country Excursion*, 1936/46)
Les bas-fonds (*The Lower Depths* / *Underworld*, 1936)
La grande illusion (1937)
La Marseillaise (1938)
La bête humaine (*Judas was a Woman*, 1938)
La règle du jeu (*The Rules of the Game*, 1939)
Swamp Water (1940)
This Land is Mine (1943)

Salute to France (1944)
The Southerner (1945)
Diary of a Chambermaid (1946)
The Woman on the Beach (1947)
The River (1950)
La Carrozza d'oro (*Le carrosse d'or / The Golden Coach*, 1952)
French Cancan (1954)
Eléna et les hommes (*Paris does Strange Things*, 1956)
Le déjeuner sur l'herbe (*Picnic on the Grass / Lunch on the Grass*, 1959)
Le testament du Docteur Cordelier (*Experiment in Evil*, 1959)
Le caporal épinglé (*The Elusive Corporal*, 1961)
Le petit théâtre de Jean Renoir (*The Little Theatre of Jean Renoir*, 1971)

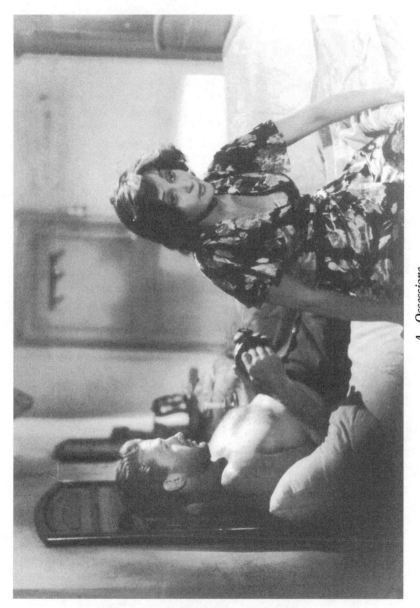

4 *Ossessione*
A dishevelled Giovanna (Clara Calamai) reflects on her life while her lover Gino (Massimo Girotti) looks indifferently on. Note the lighting of Gino's torso and face.

Ossessione

Derek Duncan

When Luchino Visconti's first film, *Ossessione*, was released in the spring of 1943, Mussolini had been Italy's head of state for twenty years and the country had been at war for three. In the summer of that year Mussolini's fascist government would be overthrown and the country torn apart by civil war. In retrospect, it is perhaps surprising that at this point Italy still had a thriving film industry. It is estimated that in 1942 no less than 117 feature films were produced and many had been made with government support. Mussolini's government had in fact promoted the Italian film industry throughout the 1930s in a variety of ways (Wagstaff, 160–74). Legislation was introduced that offered subsidies to the most successful film-makers, the network of film distribution was re-organised to favour Italian products, and restrictions were placed on the importing of films from the United States. Other initiatives such as the setting up of the Venice Film Festival in 1934, the creation of a film school, and the building of Cinecittà, the studio facility near Rome intended to emulate Hollywood, demonstrate the commitment of the fascist regime to the industry. Overall, these measures must be judged successful in significantly increasing the number of films produced in the course of the following decade. Although fascism operated a censorship policy the regime seems to have been more concerned with developing a profitable industry than with regulating the content of specific films. In general terms, this fitted in with the fascist economic policy of 'autarchia', or self-sufficiency, which proved disastrous in some areas of the economy but seems to have given the film industry a substantial and necessary boost.

While the regime sought to limit its influence, American cinema's financial success and technical proficiency along with its audience appeal remained a model. Italian films often imitated those of the United States; light comedies and historical costume dramas were popular, and Italian film stars copied the style of their American counterparts. Until the 1970s film critics derided the films made under fascism as either escapist nonsense or propaganda. Many films of that period have been destroyed but enough remain for more recent critics to have revised this purely negative assessment. While some films such as Giovacchino Forzano's *Camicia nera* (*Black Shirt*, 1933) clearly aim to show the regime in a positive light and others such as Carmine Gallone's *Scipione l'africano* (*Scipio Africanus*, 1937) offer a thinly veiled celebration of Mussolini's imperialistic forays into Africa in the mid-1930s, the political message of most was a low-key one of social conformity (Hay, 1987; Landy, 1986). Critics have also acknowledged certain technical innovations made by these film-makers such as the use of non-professional actors and outside locations, features often thought to characterise, and to have been invented by, the more celebrated neo-realist movement of Italian cinema in the post-war period.

Some of the most vociferous advocates of an autonomous national cinema in Italy were involved with the journal *Cinema*, which attracted a number of left-wing critics despite the fact that its editor was Mussolini's son Vittorio. These critics argued for a greater level of realism in Italian cinema, an argument that on the one hand drew on contemporary Soviet and French ideas about film, but also referred back to the realist tradition in Italian literature that sought, amongst other things, to portray accurately ordinary life. They believed style and politics to be closely linked. Visconti himself became involved with this group after returning from France where he had worked as a costume designer with Jean Renoir on *Une partie de campagne* (*A Day in the Country*, 1936). He had never worked in cinema before and the collaboration with Renoir proved decisive. He visited Hollywood in 1938 and was working again with Renoir on a film version of Puccini's opera *La tosca* in Rome in 1940 when Italy entered the war on the side of Germany and the left-wing French director was forced to leave the country. Renoir's influence was crucial in another respect for he had given Visconti a copy of the novel on which his first film would be based, the thriller *The Postman Always Rings Twice* (1934) by the American writer James Cain.

Visconti's choice of an American text as the source for his film is particularly interesting because of the complex and contradictory cultural position the United States occupied in Italy in the 1930s. The United States had attracted an enormous number of Italian emigrants earlier in the century and although tight immigration controls ended that era of mass emigration many Italians still believed it to be a land of opportunity and escape from the terrible poverty that affected much of the country. Left-wing writers such as Elio Vittorini and Cesare Pavese, perhaps surprisingly, viewed the United States positively as a new nation, full of possibilities. A very different version of the American experience is offered by the fascist writer Emilio Cecchi in the screenplay of *Harlem* (1943), a film that featured Massimo Girotti, the star of *Ossessione*, as an immigrant boxer whose dream turns into a nightmare in the streets of New York. In the 1930s, however, the United States was most commonly known through its own glamorised self-portrayal in films. Claretta Petacci, Mussolini's mistress, is reported to have had an American-style kitchen, indicating the appeal of the United States at every level of society, and the extent of its integration into everyday life. Even fascist concern about the representation of Italians as mafia criminals in American cinema of the period did not seriously damage its allure.

This story of adulterous and murderous passion was not Visconti's first choice of subject however. Originally, he had wanted to make a film based on a short story by the nineteenth-century realist writer Giovanni Verga. The short story itself was based on a newspaper item about a Sicilian bandit but the script was blocked by the fascist censor. Fascist censorship of the press was not solely directed at stifling political opposition but also suppressed the reporting of aspects of contemporary Italy that might reflect badly on the regime; censorship was as much about disguising the nation as about suppression. By drawing on a source that had few obvious links with what was going on in Italy, Visconti was able to elude the censors and develop his own critique of fascism, in turn masking the reality of what is represented on screen.

Cain's novel is set in California and is a contemporary tale of fatal passion, murder, and betrayal. The story is told by Frank, a rootless drifter who happens to turn up one day at a small restaurant run by Nick, a Greek-American, and his unhappy, frustrated wife Cora. Frank and Cora begin a passionate affair and they decide to run off together. Cora, however, changes her mind, unable to abandon the financial security that Nick gives her. A chance meeting brings Frank back into her life and the murder of Nick seems the only way out of their situation. Their relationship is finally destroyed through fear and suspicion, and Frank is charged with Cora's murder after she dies in a car accident, pregnant with their child. The first person narrative/voice-over turns out to be Frank's confession from his prison cell as he awaits execution. The Italian censor probably saw little to concern him in the way Visconti re-worked this melodramatic plot. The basic elements of Cain's novel remain; Gino, a young and handsome drifter, arrives one day at the trattoria run by Bragana and his wife Giovanna. Gino and Giovanna are immediately drawn together by a passion that will lead to the murder of Bragana and ultimately to her own accidental death. Yet within this familiar structure Visconti makes some subtle but significant changes.

In retrospect, Visconti said that he had wanted to make a film that was 'absolutely Italian' and that gave the audience a 'picture of Italy'. On the most superficial level, the story's setting is changed from California to the Po Valley, in the north of Italy. The flat river landscape features prominently in the film as do the cities of Ancona and Ferrara where some of the action is shot. In this sense, the film is recognisably Italian. Nevertheless, there is perhaps little in the film to locate the events in a country marked by twenty years of fascism. No direct reference is made to the political situation nor does the viewer see any evidence of it. There are, however, less obvious intimations of fascism's presence that contribute in no small measure to the film's unsettling effect. From the beginning, Gino and Giovanna use the familiar 'tu' form of address when they talk to each other, suggesting the commanding nature of their nascent passion. Later, when they meet in Ancona, the presence of Bragana demands that they appear less intimate. Rather than resorting to the traditional 'lei' form of address employed between strangers, Gino adopts the normally plural 'voi' form promoted by the fascist regime. Such details escape a foreign audience reliant on subtitles, but are resonant of the period. Similarly, apart from a brief glimpse of uniformed children towards the film's conclusion, there is no visual evidence of a regime that cultural historians argue was heavily dependent on spectacle and public ritual for its success (Gentile, 1996).

The image of Mussolini himself, which seems to have been omnipresent in fascist Italy, is absent. He figured prominently in the newsreels that accompanied every film-showing during the 1930s. These newsreels were used as propaganda to show how fascism had improved and modernised the country, and in addition, they attempted to instil a sense of patriotism in the Italian people. Like print journalism and film, what the newsreels did not show were images of Italy that in some way undermined the regime's wholesome and heroic image of itself. These images also provide one way of understanding the effect of Visconti's film when it was shown in Italy at that time; audiences left the cinema in uproar, and local party officials, often acting with representatives of the Church, succeeded in having the film banned, even though Mussolini himself was famously unperturbed by it. Compared with the Italy usually seen on the cinema screen *Ossessione* represented another country, and even without overtly criticising the regime, the fact that unsavoury aspects of the nation such as murder and adultery were shown at all constituted a challenge to how people were allowed to see Italy. Rather than holding a mirror up to a known reality, Visconti makes the spectator look again and question what passes for reality at the cinema, and also in the fascist nation.

While the novel's basic plot is retained, certain alterations to the way it unfolds provide an implicit critique of the fascist state. A large section of Cain's book deals with the role of the police and the legal system in the administration of justice. Visconti omits the courtroom drama that is central to the novel and also gives the police a less prominent and effective role. Although they are not convinced of the accidental nature of Bragana's death in the car crash, suspecting Gino and Giovanna from the outset, they are only able to act against them when two lorry drivers, who witnessed the incident, unexpectedly turn up at the police station. Gino is arrested after the second car crash, in which the pregnant Giovanna is accidentally killed as the lovers try to flee. They are punished by ironies of fate rather than by the order of law. The absence of an effective system of order and justice is a notable element of the film. Similarly, the Church lacks any moral authority; the priest, Padre Remigio, is primarily concerned with hunting and fishing, and when he is called upon to intervene in the irregular domestic arrangements of Giovanna and Gino after Bragana's death, suggests only a feeble, albeit pragmatic, compromise to their situation. Bragana, the patriarchal figurehead, is blustering and ineffectual, impervious to the needs of his wife and the threat posed by Gino, a slave to base carnal desire and infantile pleasure. This absence of any effective form of authority is an especially challenging element of Visconti's claims to be painting an authentic picture of Italy. Fascism prided itself on having restored law and order to the country and having established a strong regime with the figure of Mussolini as its symbolic and literal embodiment of authority. Not only is the iconography of fascism missing from Visconti's film but so too are many of the values through which fascism expressed itself and its sense of the nation.

Patriotism was one of fascism's key values. For Mussolini, fascism and Italy were synonymous, and the state tried to promote a positive sense of national identity in a number of ways. Often this was done through the organisation of mass public events and spectacles, or through impressive projects of public building. The education system had a crucial role in encouraging young Italians to identify with the nation, and was the hub of the youth organisations that combined the diffusion of nationalist propaganda with the pleasures of sport and subsidised entertainment. Such projects and activities appear wholly absent from the Italy of *Ossessione*. Yet, they do receive covert acknowledgement through the treatment of Bragana. Before he appears on screen, he is heard singing (rather well) a song from Giuseppe Verdi's romantic melodrama *La traviata*. His physical appearance belies the part of romantic hero, an irony that is taken even further with the motley range of competitors at the singing competition in Ancona. Implicitly too, the work of Verdi, considered Italy's national composer because of the symbolic importance of his work during the nineteenth century before Italy unified and became independent, is cast in an ironic light. Through its association with Bragana, and the indifference to it of the other main characters, it is turned into something comic and grotesque. Only Bragana demonstrates any attachment to the Italian state as his pride in having completed his national service in the 'bersaglieri' indicates. Yet his patriotism is merely an aspect of his buffoonery and discredits rather than enhances him. In Cain's novel, Nick, the husband, is mocked because of his Greek origins; Cora from the beginning is anxious to assert her pure American identity. Visconti manages to reverse the racism of the novel by making Bragana's patriotism the butt of humour whereas Gino, Giovanna, and the minor characters, lo Spagnolo and Anita, more marginal to the Italian state, are viewed with greater sympathy.

If, on a number of levels, the absence of fascist values characterises Visconti's film, the presence of unfamiliar elements equally threatens the image of Italy framed by fascism. As a political system, fascism had enormous ambitions to intervene in and transform the lives of the Italian people. This was nowhere more apparent than in its attempts to regulate aspects of sexuality and reproduction. The imperative to reproduce was most clearly directed at women; fascism saw women as mothers, reinforcing the traditional view of the Church (De Grazia, 1992). The family as an institution was in fact the key to the nation's development. Men were uneasily positioned within fascist ideas about gender; on the one hand they too were essential to the family, yet on the other, the fascist rhetoric of virility that developed round the figure of Mussolini himself suggested a more aggressive and adventurous model of male behaviour. This type of masculinity was also a common feature in Italian films of the period; Massimo Girotti, the star of *Ossessione*, in fact found fame embodying this sort of role where the emphasis was on action and on the actor's physical, rather than acting, prowess.

One of the primary mechanisms for the diffusion of ideas about gender at this time was the cinema, but there are limits to what this tells us about men and women of the period. Rather than showing cinema audiences what men and women were really like, films contributed in very powerful ways to creating an idea of what they perhaps should be like. Recent film critics have argued that while few Italian films of the time were overtly political, they were at their most reactionary in their portrayal of women. Women who obeyed society's rules were rewarded with a successful marriage and a happy family life whereas more independently minded women were invariably punished in some way. In this the Italian cinema of the period was noticeably more conservative than that of Hollywood, which did allow its female protagonists some measure of freedom (Landy, 72–117).

Visconti's film proposes representations of gender which were very different from those that commonly circulated under fascism; the manner in which the film is shot, the unfolding of the film's plot, and the casting of the actors, all contribute to an erosion of one of fascism's fundamental set of beliefs. The married couple so central to fascist ideology is parodied by the sham of Giovanna's relationship with Bragana. She married him to escape a life of poverty and semi-prostitution only to find herself trapped by the tyranny of domesticity and an old man whom she finds physically repellent. She abhors the idea of bearing his children but is trapped by her own need for the security he offers. If Giovanna is self-serving, Bragana is an oafish bully as far removed from the role of staunch patriarch as she is from that of loyal wife. Giovanna is immediately drawn to the handsome stranger, whose difference from her husband is quickly established; she comments at once on Gino's muscular body, underlining his desirability compared with her husband and drawing attention to the fact that it is Gino's body that will be on display throughout the film.

The casting of Clara Calamai and Massimo Girotti as Giovanna and Gino is very significant of the ways in which Visconti plays with accepted representations of gender. Both were established stars; Calamai was best known for playing the femme fatale in historical costume dramas and bourgeois comedies; as already noted, Girotti, a former swimming star, had starred in action and adventure movies. Calamai was also famous for being the first woman in Italian cinema to appear topless in a film, *La cena delle beffe (Joker's Banquet)* (1941). Her star persona was glamorous and sophisticated and she was not Visconti's first choice for the part. In *Ossessione*, however, she plays a character who goes against audience expectations of the familiar image of the female star. Here she is a working woman, worn down by a life of hardship and deprivation. Until she inherits Bragana's money, she appears down-at-heel and dishevelled. Her clothes are old and slightly grubby. After working hard all day in the trattoria she collapses exhausted, too tired to eat the plate of pasta she prepares for herself. Italian audiences were not used to seeing a star like Calamai stripped of her glamour. Visconti's exploitation of the ten-year age gap between the two stars also accentuated the dowdy desperation of her performance. Her acting style too contributes in no small measure to the effect of the film. Although the film contains many realistic elements it draws equally generously on the popular Italian tradition of melodrama. Calamai plays Giovanna in the style of a diva of the silent screen, a grand theatrical rather than smaller-scale cinematic style of performance – her exaggerated eye movements towards the camera point to a world beyond her tawdry provincial existence. Calamai herself was very distressed when she first saw herself in the role and it took her some time before realising how her unglamorous appearance added to her performance, and to the film's power.

The physicality of Girotti is as important however. In the opening scene, the bodily difference between the young, handsome Gino and the older, fatter Bragana, is immediately established. Gino is also more quick-witted and less self-satisfied. However, in some respects Bragana, initially at least, remains more attractive to Giovanna. On account of his relative wealth, he stands for security whereas, for his wife, Gino represents the precarious life she knew before. This is why she abandons their initial attempt to flee, preferring the material comfort her husband can provide to the erotic sustenance offered by Gino. Later, she sees the fulfilment of her passion for Gino in running the trattoria, but he resists such domestic confinement; the tension between freedom and the imprisonment by conventional ideals structures the film.

Gender and politics are thoroughly enmeshed in *Ossessione*. After Giovanna returns to her husband, Gino meets, again by chance, a character known only as lo Spagnolo (the Spaniard). He is the only character who has no parallel in the novel and originally, as is suggested by a name that alludes to the Spanish Civil War, was meant to embody the voice of socialism and personal freedom. Like Gino, he appears to be a drifter and they meet when he offers to pay the penniless Gino's train fare. They become friends, largely at lo Spagnolo's behest, and go on the road together until Gino's chance encounter with Bragana and Giovanna at a fair in Ancona. Most critics see lo Spagnolo as homosexual and even misogynist, for he tries to convince Gino that there is more to life than chasing after women. Yet perhaps it might be more tellingly argued that his attack is less on women as such than on a specific style of heterosexuality popularised under fascism, promoting the interests of the lower middle classes by means of the regulation of sexuality and reproduction. He contrasts with Giovanna, who accepts these values not because she is a woman, but because she identifies with certain class interests. This becomes clearest when she collects Bragana's life assurance policy; although she claims ignorance of its existence, Gino suspects that she used him as an accomplice. Her claims lack credibility because early in the film Bragana had referred to a document which would provide for her after he was gone, a fairly clear reference to the policy. This suggestion of betrayal has also been attributed to lo Spagnolo who is seen, at one point, in the police station. The episode is obscure yet it does not lead directly to the arrest of the couple, which occurs only after the chance arrival of the truck drivers and the second fatal accident. That Giovanna also contrasts with Anita, the dancer/prostitute whom Gino meets in Ancona, further indicates that Visconti does not simply associate femininity and heterosexuality with confinement, and male homosexuality with freedom. Unlike Giovanna, Anita gives herself freely and asks nothing in return, in sharp contrast to Giovanna who represents not femininity but the material values of a fascist lower middle class.

This tension between freedom and confinement also emerges through Visconti's treatment of space. He uses exterior shots (notably in Ancona where Gino and lo Spagnolo sit smoking on the sea wall, and later when Giovanna and Gino fall asleep on the beach) to indicate an absence of constraint and the positive enjoyment of the natural world. The ill-lit, dingy trattoria resonates with the claustrophobia of Giovanna's desires and Bragana's ignorant mean-spiritedness, a comment on the Italy that the two represent.

Such contrasts form a structure within which the narrative develops; the meaning of events emerges from the play of oppositions as much as through any narrative logic or motivation. Everything centres round the figure of Gino who does little to initiate events. His past is never fully explained and he remains enigmatic throughout the film, a screen onto which other people can project their fantasies. For most of the film it is Giovanna's desire that drives the plot. She sees Gino as someone who can rescue her from her predicament. After they make love for the first time, she describes the horror of her marriage to Gino, yet only the spectators are listening to her for he has ears solely for the sound of distant waves in a seashell he picks up in her bedroom, as she goes on to orchestrate the plan first to leave her husband and then to kill him. Similarly, she wants to stay and run the trattoria whereas all Gino wants to do is take the money and run. In the episodes involving lo Spagnolo and Anita, Gino again appears as a blank screen onto which they project their own desires.

In many respects, Gino is constructed by how others see him. This is best illustrated by the different ways in which he is seen by Giovanna and Bragana and how they interpret what they see as it suits them. Bragana sees Gino's tattered clothes and his muscular body as symptomatic of his status as a vagrant used to physical labour. For Giovanna, his physical vigour represents all that her husband lacks and he is immediately seen as an escape route. Bragana fails to see the threat Gino poses, and Giovanna fails to see that Gino cannot offer her the security she prizes more than anything. When, later in the film, Gino fails to live up to what lo Spagnolo sees in him the episode erupts into violence. Violence is in fact the end result of the failure to see the reality behind fantasy. Bragana and Giovanna both die violent deaths; the relationship between Gino and Giovanna had become violent in the wake of their mutual suspicion and resentment. That the problem of looking is an integral part of the film is suggested by the opening credit sequence shot from the front seat of the truck carrying Gino to the trattoria and accompanied by archetypally dramatic *film noir* music. Yet it is not Gino who is looking; he is hidden, asleep on the back. The significance of this shot emerges only late in the film when the police discover that the crime committed by Gino and Giovanna has been witnessed from the cab of a truck.

The suggestion that Gino is looked at yet never really seen is supported by the way the film is both shot and narrated. In the American version of the film, Frank (John Garfield) is also the film's narrator. His voice-over replicates the first person narrative of the novel. Everything is told and largely seen from his perspective. When we first see Cora (Lana Turner) it is from his point of view and the spectator shares his gaze as his eyes gradually move up her body to take in the effect of her statuesque and overwhelming glamour. This is almost an exact reversal of the parallel scene in *Ossessione*. At the beginning of the film, Gino is discovered hiding on the truck that pulls into Bragana's trattoria. In the exchange that follows between him, Bragana, and the truck drivers his face remains hidden. He enters the trattoria and the camera follows him from behind as far as the kitchen where Giovanna sits painting her nails. As she looks up in irritation and then desire, the camera angle changes and for the first time the spectator sees Gino sharing Giovanna's angle of vision. It is Gino, not Giovanna, whose body is the focus of the camera's gaze. Most often, it is his body that is lit in the scenes both with Giovanna and with lo Spagnolo. He tends to appear supine while the others (including the spectators) do the looking. This is clearly the case in the first bedroom scene with Giovanna where he sprawls languidly on the bed while she delineates her determination to alter a situation that has become untenable. Just as Gino does nothing to advance the plot, so too is he passive in front of the camera. Later when Gino is sharing a hotel room with lo Spagnolo, lo Spagnolo lights a match after the light has been switched out, the effect of which is to illuminate Gino's body. Gino's head is turned away from the camera; he is purely the object of the gaze. Throughout the film Girotti's torso and his torn vest are familiar sights and the camera lingers on them rather than on the body of the female star.

The prominence of Girotti's body poses a problem for critics. Some contend that it is simply a symptom of Visconti's homosexuality, and use the same argument to explain what they see as the rough treatment of Calamai. This view fails to pay due attention to the complexity and conventionality of how bodies are seen in the cinema, and is reductive in its assessment of how sexuality and artistic production might be linked. By inverting the spectator's expectations of what men and women usually look like on screen, Visconti successfully challenges commonplace ideas about gender. In particular he contests the very powerful ideals about gender roles and identity that circulated under fascism and found expression in Italian cinema in the 1930s and 1940s. He also, however, reveals something about how the technology of cinema encourages spectators to look at bodies in a certain way. It is in their effect on the spectator that Girotti and his vest are most disturbing for they constitute improper objects of desire in a medium that depends on the stability offered by the heterosexual, male gaze.

Ossessione is often viewed in terms of its contribution to how cinema developed after the war in Italy, yet spectators in the 1940s clearly could not see it in those terms, but they could appreciate how it differed from other films of the period. On one level Visconti's film works as a *film noir*, yet behind the melodrama the spectator can discern a cultural specificity that compels a historical reading. Visconti's film may not nowadays seem to be about fascism at all let alone to present an attack on it. However, *Ossessione* offered an alternative view of marriage and family life to the one familiar from fascist ideology, and also proposed a different sexual economy to that familiar from other films. This second point is important for it underlines the extent to which Visconti adapted cinematic conventions of the time. The values of American cinema and culture inhabited those of Italy under fascism, albeit always in concealed form. While directors in Italy had previously looked to the United States in order to imitate the models it offered, Visconti uses American culture as a malleable resource through which to articulate his own political critique. He transposes the darker, less optimistic face of the United States into an Italian context and shows the audience aspects of Italy that fascism pretended did not exist. Visconti's film re-works the cinematic forms of his time and as a consequence proposes new ways through which to represent the nation.

References

De Grazia, Victoria 1992: *How Fascism Ruled Women*. Berkeley, CA: University of California Press.
Gentile, Emilio 1996: *The Sacralization of Politics in Fascist Italy*. Translated by Keith Botsford. Cambridge, MA and London: Harvard University Press.
Hay, James 1987: *Popular Film Culture in Italy: The Passing of the Rex*. Bloomington, IN: Indiana University Press.
Landy, Marcia 1986: *Fascism in Film: The Italian Commercial Cinema, 1931–1943*. Princeton, NJ: Princeton University Press.
Wagstaff, Christopher 1984: 'The Italian Film Industry during the Fascist Regime'. In *The Italianist*, 4, 160–74.

Suggestions for Further Reading

Bacon, Henry 1998: *Visconti: Explorations of Vision and Decay*. Cambridge: Cambridge University Press.
Hay, James 1987: *Popular Film Culture in Italy: The Passing of the Rex*. Bloomington, IN: Indiana University Press.
Landy, Marcia 1986: *Fascism in Film: The Italian Commercial Cinema, 1931–1943*. Princeton, NJ: Princeton University Press.

Nowell Smith, Geoffrey 1967: *Luchino Visconti*. London: Secker and Warburg.
Overby, David (ed.) 1978: *Springtime in Italy: A Reader on Neo-Realism*. London: Talisman.
Sorlin, Pierre 1996: *Italian National Cinema, 1896–1996*. London and New York: Routledge.
Tonetti, Claretta 1987: *Luchino Visconti*. London: Columbus Books.
Wagstaff, Christopher 1984: 'The Italian Film Industry during the Fascist Regime'. In *The Italianist*, 4, 160–74.

Credits

Director	Luchino Visconti
Producer	Libero Solaroli
Production Company	Industrie Cinematografiche Italiane
Screenplay	Luchino Visconti. Mario Alicata, Giuseppe de Santis, Gianni Puccini
Director of Photography	Aldo Tonti, Domenico Scala
Editor	Mario Serandrei
Art Director	Gino Franzi
Music	Giuseppe Rosati

Cast

Clara Calamai	Giovanna
Massimo Girotti	Gino
Juan De Landa	Bragana
Dhia Cristiani	Anita
Elio Marcuzzo	Lo Spagnolo

Filmography

Ossessione (The Postman Always Rings Twice, 1942)
La terra trema [The Earth Trembles] (1948)
Bellissima (1951)
Senso (The Wanton Countess / Summer Storm, 1954)
Le notti bianche (White Nights / Sleepless Nights, 1957)
Rocco e i suoi fratelli (Rocco and his Brothers, 1960)
Il gattopardo (The Leopard, 1962)
Vaghe stelle dell'orsa (Sandra, 1964)
Lo straniero (The Outsider, 1967)
La caduta degli Dei (The Damned, 1969)
Morte a Venezia (Death in Venice, 1971)
Ludwig (1972)
Gruppo di famiglia in un interno (Conversation Piece, 1974)
L'innocente (The Innocent / The Intruder, 1976)

As co-director:

Siamo donne (We, Women, 1952)
Giorni di gloria [Days of Glory] (1945)
Boccaccio '70 (1962)
Le streghe (The Witches, 1966)

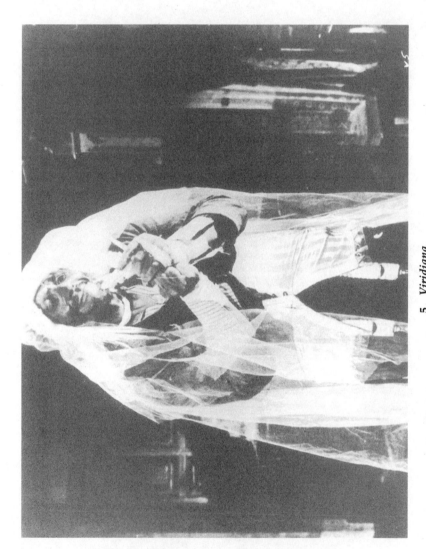

5 *Viridiana*

During the beggars' feast, the leper (Juan García Tienda) dresses in the bridal clothes of Don Jaime's dead wife and caresses a dead dove.

Viridiana

Annella McDermott

Derek Malcolm, the former film critic of the *Guardian*, chose *Viridiana* as one of the hundred great films of the twentieth century on the grounds that it 'caused the maximum annoyance to the type of people one is always glad to see offended' (*Guardian Supplement*, 1 April 1999, 12). It certainly gave great offence to the Franco government in Spain, where it was filmed in 1961 but promptly banned. It was, in fact, first released in New York in 1962, and was not seen in Spain until after the death of Franco in 1975, by which time it had been widely exhibited and was considered a classic, elsewhere in Europe and across the world. The film is a savage critique of the kind of right-wing Catholicism on which Franco's regime was based. The Spanish Civil War of 1936–9, one of the key historical events of the twentieth century – together with the Second World War, which it prefigured – began with a military uprising against the Republican government, and ended with the victory of right-wing authoritarian forces, led by Franco, who was to remain in power for the next thirty-six years. The Francoist state was anti-democratic, and opposed both to capitalism, which it considered materialist and decadent, and to communism. Basic freedoms were heavily curtailed; there were no political parties; all the media were subject to tight censorship; the Catholic Church exercised a great deal of influence, particularly through its privileged role in secondary education; laws had to conform to Catholic teaching, so that there was no divorce, for example, nor free access to contraception or abortion. Although Spain remained neutral during the Second World War, it was clear that the regime's sympathies lay with the fascist powers and, with their defeat, Spain found itself in an isolated position throughout the late 1940s and early 1950s.

Luis Buñuel, the director of *Viridiana*, was profoundly marked by the political events outlined above, which definitively altered his life and his directing career by forcing him into exile. Buñuel was born in 1900 into a wealthy middle-class family. His mother was a pious Catholic and Buñuel was educated until the age of eighteen by Jesuits. His early experience was of a highly traditional society, as he notes in his memoirs: 'In my own village of Calanda...the Middle Ages lasted until the First World War. It was a closed and isolated society, with clear and unchanging distinctions among the classes. The respectful subordination of the peasants to the big landowners was deeply rooted in tradition and seemed unshakeable' (Buñuel, 1984, 8). However, he moved for his University education to Madrid, where he lived from 1917 to 1925 in a college known for its liberal ideas, the *Residencia de estudiantes*, and met several other young men who would become radical figures in the intellectual life of Spain in the 1920s and early 1930s, particularly the poet Federico García Lorca and the painter Salvador Dalí. Buñuel developed an interest in film during a subsequent stay in France, and in 1929 he made a short film with Dalí, *Un chien andalou (An Andalusian Dog*, 1928), financed by Buñuel's mother.

This film, and a second film made in collaboration with Dalí, *L'âge d'or* (1930), are examples of surrealist cinema. Surrealism placed a high value on the products of the unconscious, as opposed to the conscious mind, giving great importance to intuition, dreams, trances, sleep-walking and other apparent manifestations of unconscious impulses, and being highly critical of the repression of these impulses by conventional morality, religion, or the institutions of the state. Buñuel writes with passion in his memoirs about the importance of his contact with surrealism, going so far as to say that it changed his life (Buñuel, 1984, 123).

Buñuel was invited by the Spanish Republican government in 1936 to work on their behalf in Paris, and he remained there until 1937, when he left for the United States. Like many intellectuals sympathetic to the Republic, Buñuel chose not to live in Francoist Spain, and he settled initially in the United States, then later in Mexico.

Spain's post-war isolation was attenuated by a Concordat signed with the Vatican in 1953, an agreement with the United States allowing the establishment of US military bases in Spain in 1955, and towards the end of the decade by a desire on the part of the regime itself to seek closer relations with the rest of Europe, which led to some flexibility in areas such as censorship in the arts. This explains why Buñuel, a prominent opponent of the regime, was able to take up an invitation from some young Spanish directors to shoot a film there in 1961.

Viridiana is a merciless attack on a certain kind of Roman Catholicism, one that expresses relative contempt for the needs of the body, as opposed to those of the spirit, and advocates the practice of charity as a remedy for poverty. Viridiana is an orphan, a novice in a convent, who shortly before taking her final vows is invited to visit her uncle, Don Jaime, whom she hardly knows, but who has paid for her education and maintenance and has provided the dowry which the families of wealthy aspirant nuns donated to the order which they would enter. Though reluctant to leave the convent, Viridiana is persuaded by her Mother Superior to agree to her uncle's request. From the moment of her arrival at his run-down estate, Viridiana's uncle shows a great interest in her, which is contrasted with the indifference, bordering on contempt, that she shows towards him. In the scene immediately preceding Viridiana's arrival there is a suggestion that Don Jaime is a sensualist, since he is shown gazing in pleasure at the legs of a little girl who is skipping with a rope he has given her. Viridiana, on the other hand, repeatedly shows distrust and fear of her own and other bodies.

As Viridiana and her uncle walk towards the house, he comments, to her evident displeasure, on her resemblance to his dead wife, her aunt. During

Viridiana's first night in his home, he is shown playing a piece of classical music on a small organ in his sitting-room, intercut with shots of the young woman undressing in her bedroom. Viridiana is played by a Mexican actress, Silvia Pinal, whose physical appearance is far removed from the classic dark Spanish type of beauty. She is blonde, pale and somewhat ethereal: as she rolls down her black stockings, we have a brightly-lit close-up of her long, smooth, white legs. The next shot shows Don Jaime, still playing his music, with a dreamy expression on his face. The maid, Ramona, who has peeped through Viridiana's keyhole, reports to Don Jaime that the young novice has prepared her bed on the floor, that she appears to have a crown of thorns in her suitcase, and is wearing a night-dress of very rough cloth; we then see Viridiana praying on her knees in her room, followed by a close-up of a cushion on which are laid the crown of thorns previously referred to, nails, a hammer and a sponge. For a Catholic, particularly a Spanish Catholic of the time, there was a perfectly acceptable, pious reason for the contemplation of these objects – to be reminded that Christ suffered on the Cross in order to redeem mankind (the hammer representing the one used to drive the nails into Christ's hands and the sponge being a reference to the sponge soaked in gall which was offered when Christ asked for water). However, for an audience distanced to some extent from this kind of religious practice, the bizarre appearance of these objects in a young woman's bedroom, and their juxtaposition with Viridiana's pale, vulnerable body, clearly carry the suggestion that Catholicism invites masochism by its insistence on repression and mortification of the body.

A related idea is suggested in a scene set on the morning following Viridiana's arrival, which begins with a close-up of a male farmworker's hand grasping a cow's teat, which has a comical resemblance to a flaccid penis. Viridiana is persuaded to try milking the cow, but she is clearly repelled by the feel of the teat in her hand and cannot milk effectively, even when the farmworker encourages her by clasping his hand around hers and urging her to pull hard at the teat and squeeze. Because the screenplay emphasises the fact that the farmhand is oblivious to the reason for Viridiana's squeamishness, it seems that Buñuel is suggesting that through Catholicism's attempts to suppress the practical realities of the body, perverse notions of transgression are introduced into otherwise innocent activities (Buñuel, 1969, 10).

The importance of surrealism to Buñuel's early film career has already been mentioned. Most commentators see its influence in this film also. Gwynne Edwards, for example, examines some statements by Buñuel about the lack of conscious planning of the film and concludes:

Buñuel's account of the film's birth and development is one which, stressing its natural and spontaneous evolution and his own instinctive feeling for certain associations, juxtapositions and contrasts, underlines the importance he has always given, in his life as well as in his art, to impulse and the expression of the unconscious freed from the constraints of reason and moral dictates.

To this extent *Viridiana* is as much a product of surrealism as *Un chien andalou* and *L'âge d'or.*   (Edwards, 145)

This refers, of course, to the creative process. In relation to the film itself, there are a number of sequences that could be considered surrealist. In the sleep-walking scene, Viridiana carries out an enigmatic series of actions, entering the sitting-room, throwing her knitting on the fire and putting ashes from the fire into her work-basket, which she then takes to Don Jaime's bedroom, where she sprinkles the ashes on the bed. When Don Jaime tells her of the incident the next day, Viridiana interprets it by recourse to religious symbolism: ashes, she says, mean penitence and death (and this does foreshadow later events in the film). However, an audience familiar with Freudian ideas will readily see the sleep-walking as a symptom of repression or guilt, and will probably interpret her actions to mean that she has some feelings with regard to her uncle, which she has consciously ignored, but which express themselves when her unconscious impulses take over in the state of somnambulism. Despite her orthodox interpretation of her actions, she appears to be embarrassed by her conduct while asleep.

Don Jaime's behaviour also displays some bizarre elements. He has kept his dead wife's bridal clothes in a chest, and we see him get these out and try them on – a white satin high-heeled shoe that he perches on the end of his own huge foot, and a corset which he wraps round his own body, this ceremony being lent an air of sublimity by the music of Beethoven's *Ninth Symphony* issuing from his gramophone. Later, he tells Viridiana that her aunt died in his arms of a heart attack, still wearing those clothes, on their wedding night, hence his desire to see Viridiana dress in them, which she reluctantly agrees to do. Don Jaime is a fetishist whose erotic attention has become focused on these items of clothing, and when he asks Viridiana to marry him, we take it that his principal incentive is her strong physical resemblance to her dead aunt, whence her ability to transport him back to his wedding night by dressing in the bridal clothes. He is so obsessed by this possibility that when Viridiana indignantly turns him down, he enlists the help of his servant Ramona to drug Viridiana so that he can prolong the illusion of having his wife back. There is a suggestion, too, of necrophilia, as we see him arrange the unconscious young woman into the image of a corpse, with hands crossed on her breast as though prepared for viewing and burial. The screenplay indicates that he 'begins to perfect his masterpiece' with 'an artist's meticulousness' (Buñuel, 1969, 30). However, Don Jaime's fetishism and necrophilia are not blamed on religion; they are the product of the particular circumstances of his wife's death and the sensuality that is part of his character, and the audience may well find his behaviour touching.

There is some ambiguity in Buñuel's attitude to sexual repression. The main theme of the film is that sexual repression is unnatural and produces frigidity, distance and even cruelty in human relationships. On the other hand, the use of music in connection with sexual yearning, in both the scene in which Don Jaime plays the organ, and the scene of his handling his dead wife's clothes, seems to allude to the theory of sublimation – that art is the product of a displacement of sexual energy into another activity, and may thus be viewed as a positive outcome arising from repression. Buñuel also mentions in his memoirs the role of prohibition as a stimulus:

> I've often wondered why Catholicism has such a horror of sexuality. To be sure, there are countless theological, historical and moral reasons; but it seems to me that in a rigidly hierarchical society, sex – which respects no barriers and obeys no laws – can at any moment become an agent of chaos. I suppose that's why some Church Fathers, Saint Thomas Aquinas amongst them, were so severe in their dealings with the disturbing aspects of the flesh.... Ironically, this implacable prohibition inspired a feeling of sin which for me was positively voluptuous.   (Buñuel, 1984, 14)

Don Jaime does not rape the unconscious Viridiana, although he is tempted to do so, and the next morning he initially pretends to her that he did, in order to try to prevent her from returning to her convent. When he sees the look of hatred on her face he confesses the truth, and hangs himself, presumably out of remorse, after she has left. However, before he does so he composes a document, which we will later realise is his will, in which he leaves his estate jointly to Viridiana and his illegitimate son Jorge. As he takes up his pen, he smiles and strokes his beard, a gesture which indicates he has thought of an amusing plan. We assume later that he realised that Viridiana would feel unable to take her vows when she learned of his suicide, and would come to live on the estate alongside Jorge. It is never made clear to us whether Don Jaime's pleasure in this prospect was malicious. His smile during the writing of the will may have been vengeful, or it may simply have indicated that he foresaw a positive outcome, as does Buñuel, to the enforced cohabitation of Viridiana and Jorge.

The film's critique of the practice of charity is mainly developed in the middle section, which deals with Viridiana withdrawing from the convent, and setting up a refuge for beggars on her dead uncle's estate. Buñuel's depiction of the beggars is resolutely unsentimental in that he rejects any idea that they are individuals who have been ennobled by poverty and suffering. They are sharply practical: when one of the women comments that Viridiana is a very good person, another woman replies: 'Very good but a bit of a simpleton' (Buñuel, 1969, 48). They are also cruel to each other, as shown by the blind beggar striking the bald one with his stick when the latter's intemperate language looks likely to jeopardize Viridiana's offer of charity. They show no charity towards the leper, as they call him, pretending to accept him while Viridiana is present but pulling a knife on him when she leaves, so that he has to go and sleep outside. He himself, while protesting to Viridiana that the sores on his arms are due to varicose veins, is evidently convinced that they are the result of a venereal disease, and he is accused by one of his companions of deliberately placing his arm in the holy water font in church with the aim of infecting others. Incidentally, the role of the leper is not played by an actor, but by a real beggar, and another of the beggars is played by a lottery-ticket seller. When Jorge, Viridiana, Ramona and the child have to go into town, leaving the beggars in charge of the house, the dialogue points up the brutality of the beggars' lives. The blind man urges Enedina to shut up her crying child, and she asks: 'You'd like me to kill them?', to receive the reply from another beggar: 'With the life that's ahead of them they'd be better off being sent to Paradise' (Buñuel, 1969, 84). At one point the blind man boasts of having turned in to the police a fellow-beggar who tried to cheat him out of his share of the day's takings. Sexual relationships among the beggars are portrayed as promiscuous and coarse.

It seems likely that Buñuel was a member of the Communist Party in the 1930s. John Baxter discusses the evidence in some detail and concludes that he was a Party member, probably from 1929 to at least 1945 (Baxter, 130–1). The depiction of the beggars in *Viridiana*, and the sceptical attitude the film displays towards charity as a response to poverty, have led many to see *Viridiana* as a communist film. Emilio G. Riera writes, for example: 'The beggars are monstrous because of their depraved profanity. Once and for all, Buñuel destroys the myth of purity cloaked in rags (which clearly identifies him with a Marxist line of thought)' (Riera, in Mellen, 222).

Buñuel clearly dislikes the paternalistic relationship charity establishes between donor and recipient. Viridiana is aware of the danger of spiritual pride inherent in her adoption of the beggars, as she shows by discouraging any compliments to the effect that she has the face of an angel. Yet she feels entitled to control the beggars' lives in return for her charity, separating the sexes and announcing that they are all to work (news which is greeted by a superb comic double-take from one of the beggars). There is a suggestion, too, that charity arises from a situation of privilege. Although Viridiana appears to have been virtually brought up in a convent, her manners are bourgeois. An example of this is the scene in which we see her hands in close-up, peeling the skin from an apple in one continuous strip, for in Spain, where fresh fruit is often served at the end of a meal, the ability to deal in a refined manner with skin and pips is a class marker. Unlike Viridiana, Moncho, the estate overseer, openly loathes and despises the beggars, and even Ramona's little girl, Rita, taunts the beggars with the fact that they are not to sleep in the house, but in the outbuildings, with the chickens. The beggars, for their part, despise Moncho because he is a servant. One beggar, told that in return for charity he must exercise self-restraint and humility, decides that he would rather take his chances elsewhere. He still asks for a handout, but only, as he remarks, because he is poor, that is to say, if he had the choice he would not submit to this indignity. The invasion of the house while the family is away demonstrates the naivety of Viridiana's assumption that the beggars will be content with a roof over their heads, plain food and hard work. On the contrary, they like lace tablecloths, porcelain, silver, roast lamb and good wine, just like everyone else, and help themselves to these luxuries at the first opportunity.

It is not, however, only Christian charity that is attacked in the film, but religious belief itself. One of the most famous scenes from the film is the freeze-frame when the beggars pose as though for a photograph. The composition of the shot imitates Leonardo's depiction of *The Last Supper*, with the blind man in the centre, like Christ, and the beggars grouped around him like the Apostles. The meaning of this parallel would seem to be that the goodness and altruism symbolised in the Last Supper are contradicted by the brutality and degradation of the lives of the destitute on earth. Depicting Christ as blind, a notion used again by Buñuel in his later film *La voie lactée* (*The Milky Way*, 1968), would seem to imply that there is an essential 'blindness' at the heart of Christian belief, which points up the principal theme of the film, Viridiana's awakening to reality from the dream or illusion of faith. The crucifix which conceals a knife-blade, found by Jorge among his dead uncle's possessions, seems to mock Christianity's claim to be a religion of peace. The beggars' orgy culminates in the leper's grotesque dance, dressed in Don Jaime's dead wife's corset and veil, during which he scatters feathers from the white dove we saw him capture earlier and which he has clearly killed. The importance of a white dove as a Christian icon hardly needs emphasising. Moreover, the dance is performed to the accompaniment of the Hallelujah Chorus from Handel's *Messiah*, a contrast which again appears to suggest that there is a radical incompatibility between the sublime beauty of religious music and the real behaviour of human beings, particularly those leading deprived lives.

It would be oversimplifying the film, however, to see it as providing a crude contrast between the religious impulse and reality, and forcing the audience to prefer the latter to the former. At one point, Buñuel uses a series of alternating shots of Viridiana and the beggars murmuring the Angelus under some almond trees, and workmen mixing cement, sawing planks, piling logs, and tipping stones out of a wheelbarrow. Clearly, the editing here aims to establish a contrast between Jorge's worldly practicality and Viridiana's adherence to ritual. For a Spanish audience, accustomed to a debate on tradition versus modernity that goes back to writers of the eighteenth and nineteenth centuries, the dry, dusty landscape of the neglected estate could easily be read as a metaphor for Spain itself, with Viridiana embodying archaic, obscurantist religious beliefs, and Jorge representing progressive modernity. Yet it is not entirely clear that the audience will find the scenes of construction more appealing than the prayers, murmured against a background of almond blossom. Moreover, although Viridiana strikes us in the first part of the film as cold and remote, this feeling vanishes in the second part, in which she is more relaxed and more appealing to the audience.

Jorge, in any case, suffers from his own form of blindness. He rescues a dog which has been tied to the back axle of a cart, but turns away and so misses the sight, clear to the audience, of another dog in exactly the same situation passing a few seconds later, illustrating the point he himself made earlier to Viridiana, that charity extended to individuals is a drop in the ocean compared with the numbers of the deprived and abused. Nevertheless, his pragmatic attitude to human motivation enables him to save Viridiana from being raped when they return to the house and interrupt the beggars' dinner, by bribing the leper to knock out her assailant. It is clear, too, that Viridiana knows that she was overcome and would have been raped if it had not been for Jorge. We understand that this experience brings her face to face with the reality of human sexual impulses and causes the veil of illusion to fall from her eyes, so that she subsequently seeks out Jorge, presumably to initiate a sexual relationship with him.

Jorge is handsome, energetic, full of curiosity, laid-back and tolerant in his attitudes (and he is played by Francisco Rabal, one of Spain's most popular and attractive actors). Yet some doubt has been cast over the character earlier in the film, in a scene where he and the servant Ramona end up making love in the attic and where Buñuel uses an uncharacteristic metaphorical montage, involving a cat leaping on a mouse, to suggest that he is rapacious. When Viridiana goes to his room, at the end of the film, he is listening to a record of a song with English-language lyrics whose banality constitutes an ironic comment on the accommodation to reality that will presumably take the place of Viridiana's religious philosophy: 'Shake, baby, shake, shake your cares away'. There is a certain sadness for the audience in watching defiant illusion giving way to a resigned acceptance of reality. Viewers more sensitised to feminist issues than Buñuel or his audience in the early 1960s may also feel uneasy with the notion of attempted rape as the agent of Viridiana's liberation, or wonder why facing reality has to involve a sexual relationship with a man, particularly Jorge. Celibacy born of fear or distrust of the body is clearly negative, but celibacy freely chosen is an option modern audiences might like to see offered to the former nun.

Viridiana was Spain's entry at the Cannes Film Festival in 1961. It won the Golden Palm but was subsequently attacked as blasphemous and sacrilegious and banned in Spain, thus creating the unusual situation of a country refusing to screen a film which had won for it the most prestigious international prize in cinema. A number of commentators argued that the use of the term 'blasphemous' was inappropriate, because the film was the work of an atheist. This was the view taken by Riera in the context of Buñuel's Marxism: 'Not once does this movie-maker deride or insult God, which would be tantamount to acknowledging His existence. Buñuel never discusses God. What he discusses is man's conception of God, thereby revealing the strange, unpredictable role that religion plays in the subconscious of his characters' (Riera, in Mellen, 220).

Some Catholic critics argued, even around the time the film was made, that Buñuel was attacking attitudes and practices that were no longer current. An article first published in 1962 cites the view of a progressive Catholic layman, Jean Carta:

Whether the spectator is Catholic or not, he will be hard put to recognize the social doctrine of the Church in the actions of [this illuminated creature].... It will be even harder if one is aware of the immense current of social Christianity which has come into being and daily grown stronger during the last several decades...in this movement, a spirit of charity without lucidity, without the value of a collective perspective, without political commitment, cannot suffice. The half-blind bigotry, the absence of common-sense which Buñuel attributes to...the devout Viridiana, reign still, perhaps, in certain sectors of the Spanish Church, the most archaic in Europe, but it certainly does not pertain to the militant church around us.... *Viridiana* comes too late to convince us.   (Seguin, in Mellen, 231)

In any case the attack on religion is unlikely to be a theme of major interest to the more secular audience, outside and inside Spain, of today. On the other hand, and perhaps rather unexpectedly, in the period since the 1960s, the sight of beggars, once confined to the 'backward' regions of Europe, has become commonplace in all our cities, and the concept of charity is once more a subject of debate.

Formally, *Viridiana* remains an intensely captivating film. Buñuel wrote the scenario himself, in collaboration with a young Spanish writer, Julio Alejandro. It is a highly literary script, reminiscent, for a Spanish audience, of the work of Spain's great nineteenth-century novelist Benito Pérez Galdós, both in its themes and in the rich, rather archaic, colloquial language given to the beggars. There are echoes too of the Spanish sixteenth- and seventeenth-century picaresque novel, in the depiction of the lives of beggars and tricksters; and Viridiana's awakening to reality from the illusion of religious belief is a modern reversal of a theme of awakening from delusion into belief that goes back to Spanish drama of the sixteenth and seventeenth centuries. Although these echoes are less evident to non-Spanish audiences, the latter will readily appreciate the pace and economy of the narration and, even through subtitling, the telling irony of much of the dialogue. The overall ironies of the theme are underlined by the repetition of visual details: the skipping-rope with the phallic wooden handles that we first see in the hands of Ramona's little girl, is the rope with which Don Jaime hangs himself, and is then used as a belt to hold up his trousers by the beggar who attempts to rape Viridiana. The shots of Ramona's legs and feet as she skips are echoed by Don Jaime's as he works the pedals of the harmonium, Viridiana's legs and feet as she rolls down her black stockings, Don Jaime's again as he hangs from the tree, and Jorge's as he bathes his feet in a basin after inspecting the estate on foot. Much of the film is visually very striking: the faces and bodies of the beggars, some of whom, as has been mentioned, were not professional actors; Don Jaime, and later the leper, dressed in the corset and veil of the dead bride; the flaming crown of thorns on the bonfire; the crucifix with its concealed knife-blade. These images have a power and originality undimmed by the years that have elapsed since the film was made.

References and Suggestions for Further Reading

Baxter, John 1994: *Buñuel*. London: Fourth Estate.

Buñuel, Luis 1984: *My Last Breath*. London: Fontana.

Buñuel Luis 1969: *Three Screenplays: Viridiana, The Exterminating Angel, Simon of the Desert*. New York: Grossman.

Carr, Raymond and Fusi, Juan Pablo 1981: *Spain: Dictatorship to Democracy*, 2nd edn. London: George Allen and Unwin.

Edwards, Gwynne 1982: *The Discreet Art of Luis Buñuel*. London: Marion Boyars.

Higginbotham, Virginia 1979: *Luis Buñuel*. Boston, MA: Twayne.

Mellen, Joan (ed.) 1978: *The World of Luis Buñuel*, New York. Oxford University Press.

Credits

Director	Luis Buñuel
Producer	Ricardo Muñoz Suay
Production Company	Gustavo Alatriste (Mexico) and Uninci Films 59 (Madrid)
Scenario	Luis Buñuel and Julio Alejandro
Director of Photography	José A. Agayo
Art Director	Francisco Canet
Editor	Pedro del Rey

Cast

Silvia Pinal	Viridiana
Fernando Rey	Don Jaime
Francisco Rabal	Jorge
Margarita Lozano	Ramona
Victoria Zinny	Lucía
Teresa Rabal	Rita
Juan García Tienda	Leper

Filmography

L'âge d'or (1928)
Un chien andalou (*An Andalusian Dog*, 1930)
Las Hurdes (*Land without Bread*, 1932)
Don Quintín, el amargao (*Embittered Don Quintín*, 1935)
La hija de Juan Simón [Juan Simón's Daughter] (1935)
¿Quién me quiere a mí? [Who loves me?] (1936)
España leal, en armas (*España 1936*, 1937)
Gran Casino (*Tampico*, 1946)
El gran calavera [The rake] (1949)
Los olvidados (*The Young and Damned*, 1950)

Susana (1950)

Una mujer sin amor (A Woman without Love, 1951)

La hija del engaño [Daughter of Deception] (1951)

Subida al cielo (Mexican Bus Ride, 1951)

Él (He, 1952)

El bruto (The Brute, 1952)

Las aventuras de Robinson Crusoe (Adventures of Robinson Crusoe, 1952)

La ilusión viaja en tranvía (The Runaway Streetcar, 1953)

Abismos de pasión (Wuthering Heights, 1953)

El río y la muerte (Death and the River, 1954)

Ensayo de un crimen (The Criminal Life of Archibaldo de la Cruz, 1955)

Celà s'appelle l'aurore [That is called the dawn] (1956)

La mort en ce jardin (Evil Eden, 1956)

Nazarín (1958)

La fièvre monte à El Pao [Fever mounts in El Pao] (1959)

La joven (The Young One, 1960)

Viridiana (1961)

El ángel exterminador (The Exterminating Angel, 1963)

Journal d'une femme de chambre (Diary of a Chambermaid, 1964)

Simón del desierto (Simon of the Desert, 1965)

Belle de jour (1967)

La voie lactée (The Milky Way, 1968)

Tristana (1970)

Le charme discret de la bourgeoisie (The Discreet Charm of the Bourgeoisie, 1972)

Le fantôme de la liberté (The Phantom of Liberty, 1974)

Cet obscur objet du désir (That Obscure Object of Desire, 1977)

6   *Alice in den Städten*

Framed? Alice (Yella Rottländer) takes a family snapshot of Winter (Rüdiger Vogler) in Holland at the beginning of their journey to search for her grandmother.

Alice in den Städten
(Alice in the Cities)
Stuart Taberner

'The old cinema is dead. We believe in the new' (in Elsaesser, 1989, 20–1). These words resonate at the close of the precociously self-confident manifesto signed by twenty-six up-and-coming West German film-makers at the 1962 Oberhausen Film Festival. The interlopers, who were inspired by the French New Wave, styled themselves as the 'Young German Cinema' and were exasperated by the way domestic theatres were dominated by Hollywood re-runs and the peculiarly German genre *Heimatfilme*, insipid depictions of sentimentalised rustic idylls. A decade later – once youth had mellowed into middle age – they would prefer to be known as the '*New* German Cinema'. Original signatories such as Alexander Kluge and Edgar Reitz had been joined by film-makers such as Werner Herzog, Rainer Werner Fassbinder, Margarethe von Trotta, and Wim Wenders. These film-makers gained international acclaim for their formal and thematic innovation and became leading intellectual figures in their own country.

Yet the story of the New German Cinema is a tale of glorious failure. In 1967 the *Board of Young German Film* was set up – partly in response to the clamouring of the Oberhausen directors – to pump-prime 'artistically worthwhile' projects. Semi-official support from the state and regional competitions furnished limited but indispensable funding for innovative film-making (although the parallel introduction of a tax on movie tickets favoured more commercial products, low-brow comedies, and soft porn). Making a virtue of necessity, directors transposed financial hardship into aesthetic gain. They exploited the unfinished appearance of their films in order to stress the open-endedness of the plot (and therefore of the social and political conditions they took as their themes) and to draw attention to the cinematographic process itself. Their films are often highly self-conscious and suspicious of the claims to omniscience made by Hollywood-inspired movies. Almost by definition, therefore, directors were celebrated for their creative input, but remained exiled in art-house theatres specialising in avant-garde 'European' pictures. In 1978, only 8 per cent of the West German film market was claimed by domestic production (Elsaesser, 1989, 36). It began to appear that the 'New German Cinema' was being kept alive by government subsidies, and, as such, had become a tool of the Federal Republic's foreign policy,

121

designed to demonstrate to sceptical outsiders the extent of West Germany's post-war commitment to liberal values, cultural variety, and the toleration of criticism.

Wim Wenders, one of the few West German directors to pass through film school, has also been one of a mere handful whose films have succeeded in appealing to audiences beyond those of art-house cinema. Two films in particular, *Paris, Texas* (1984) and *Wings of Desire* (1987), have charmed large audiences; others such as *Der amerikanische Freund* (*The American Friend*, 1977) and *Bis an Ende der Welt* (*Till the End of the World*, 1991) have attracted more modest attention, but none the less appear successful by the standards of European film. Along with fellow West German directors Volker Schlöndorff and Wolfgang Petersen, Wenders has been able to negotiate the move to Hollywood that is necessary for major international recognition, although he has consistently returned to work in his home country. In his association with American studios he also has followed in the path of earlier German directors such as F. W. Murnau and Fritz Lang. At the same time, Wenders's attitude towards Hollywood has been ambivalent. In *Im Lauf der Zeit* (*Kings of the Road*, 1976), one character complains 'the Americans have colonised our subconscious', while *Der Stand der Dinge* (*The State of Things*, 1982) delivers a biting satire on the suppression of directorial autonomy by movie moguls, reflecting Wenders's experience of making *Hammett* (1978–82) in partnership with Francis Ford Coppola.

This uncertainty regarding Hollywood reflects both the reaction of European avant-garde film-makers in general (from the 1920s onwards, and intensifying after 1945) to the dominance of American movies and a more specifically West German sensibility towards the influence of the United States upon the shaping of its institutions, values and culture following the establishment of the Federal Republic in 1949. Wenders's generation admired the Americans as the bringers of democracy and liberation from Hitler's national socialism. They aped the carefree informality, openness and exuberance of American culture, and embraced rock and roll, jazz, and Hollywood movies as the expression of a nation at peace with itself (in marked contrast to their own country's tortuous relationship to its own past, and present existence). Wenders has often spoken of listening to rock and roll as a teenager, and jukeboxes and popular culture feature as leitmotifs in his films, including music by the Rolling Stones, Jimi Hendrix, Bob Dylan, The Kinks, Roy Orbison, Chuck Berry, and many other British, but far more frequently American, recording artists. These are passions he shares with Peter Handke, the Austrian novelist with whom he has often collaborated – *Die Angst des Tormanns beim Elfmeter* (*The Goalkeeper's Fear of the Penalty*, 1972); *Falsche Bewegung* (*Wrong Movement*, 1975); *Wings of Desire* (1987).

By the mid-1960s, however, this inherited affection for the United States had become far more problematical. Politically, the United States had damaged its reputation as the bearer of democratic values through its deepening involvement in the Vietnam War, and as a result of the mistreatment of black Americans campaigning for civil rights in the southern states (this theme is intimated at the beginning of *Alice in den Städten* in images highlighting black social exclusion).

Culturally, film-makers, writers and intellectuals were becoming perturbed by the American permeation of West Germany's self-understanding, and by Hollywood's increasingly hegemonic claim. By the early 1980s Edgar Reitz even considered it necessary to introduce each part of his TV serialisation *Heimat* (*Home*, 1980–4) with the words 'made in Germany' (in English) in order to reclaim his vision of German history (in this case, the story of a small village from the end of the First World War into the 1980s) from its appropriation by American movies. West German film-makers were particularly conscious of the way in which Hollywood had been allowed to define images of the country's fascist past, a feeling reinforced by the German screening of the American TV series *Holocaust* in 1979, and felt that movie representations of jack-booted Nazis threatened to deprive Germans of any meaningful relationship with their history.

Personal and national identity are paramount in Wenders's *Alice in den Städten* (*Alice in the Cities*, 1974). The link between the two is established by images, photography, and film-making itself, although for much of the story this (literal) medium fails to function, engendering rootlessness, disorientation and alienation in the lead character Philip Winter (acoustically similar to Wenders, especially when pronounced by a Dutch voice speaking through a loudspeaker at Schipol airport in Amsterdam). *Alice in den Städten* is the narrative of multiple journeys, or searches. The film opens with Winter on America's Atlantic coast, apparently watching a jet flying from West to East, predicting his own physical and psychic voyage back to his European (more accurately, German) origins. His subsequent return to Europe is linked with his efforts to reinvest images with meaning following their reduction to one-dimensionality by the American culture industry. Winter's sense of his Germanness thus depends upon his reclaiming of images from Hollywood's grasp. More specifically, Winter turns to photographs to give meaning to his own existence and to insert himself into more tangible relationships with other people, as a substitute father (to Alice), and potentially at least, as a partner in a monogamous union with a woman. The theme of masculinity, so powerful in some of Wenders's other films (such as *Kings of the Road*; *The American Friend*; *Paris, Texas*, and *Wings of Desire*), is here linked to the American cowboy and road-movie genres. In *Alice*, therefore, Winter finally breaks with the model of male behaviour (heroic isolation, rootlessness, and the refusal of commitment) established by Hollywood through figures such as Humphrey Bogart, who was a popular role model for many West German men in the 1950s, and internalised by a generation of German males lacking any 'intact' personal or national identity.

In *Alice in den Städten*, America appears as uncompromisingly foreign. It is not the character of Philip Winter that alienates the viewer – actor Rüdiger Vogler's wry smiles and appealing interiority generate sympathy – but the unemotional landscapes, impersonal motels, and uninterrupted commercialism that dominate at the beginning of the film. Diegetic music – that is, music 'within' the film, this time from Winter's car radio – reveals the failure of American popular culture (rock and roll, folk and country music) to imbue this landscape with warmth and emotion. Winter becomes frustrated by the constant interference of commercials, the multiplication of stations which merely replicate the lack of diversity, and by the inanity of the presenters' chatter. The viewer is alternately identified with Winter through point-of-view camera angles and distanced from him by face-on shots inserting a third person narrative perspective. This technique may reflect the incongruity between the character and his environment. Subsequently, Winter stays in a motel, watches a TV advert for a Negro College fund juxta-posed with publicity for a town in the west, and is irritated by the way in which these marketing slots interrupt his viewing of the John Ford film *Young Mr Lincoln* (1939). The idealism of Ford's film, promoting America's initial liberal promise, has, it seems, been corrupted by commercialism. The adverts distort the American dream of the land of opportunity into a business proposition. In addition, this sequence anticipates Winter's inversion of the Hollywood fantasy of travelling west towards freedom when he later returns east to Europe to begin his rendering of another Ford film, *The Searchers* (1956). Before he finally leaves, however, he must pass through New York, where he is forced to admit to his editor that he has been unable to write the script to accompany the polaroids he has taken of America.

New York is a city that has been reduced to iconographic status. The images the film offers of the metropolis, in a series of long takes, are so familiar that they have become clichéd, representations of America that overwhelm reality and that refer only to their own commodity value. They short-circuit meaning and are empty of content. Shots of the Empire State Building, the Chrysler Building, the World Trade Center, and of Greyhound buses are void of emotionality and human reference. They suggest Winter's disillusionment with the compelling power of images once they have become stereotypes. At the beginning of the film, he complains that photographs 'never really show you what you saw'. Unlike Peter Handke's novel *Der kurze Brief zum langen Abschied* (*The Brief Letter upon a Lengthy Farewell*, 1972), to which the film partly responds, Wenders demonstrates the impossibility of 'knowing' America. The discrepancy between the hackneyed images of American life popularised by Hollywood and western popular culture and what Winter actually encounters in the United States distorts the country beyond all recognition. He protests to his editor that he is unable to write the script to his photo-journey through the United States because 'the story's about the things you see ... about signs and images'. The implication is clearly that he has not yet discovered a means of narrating these images, or making sense of them, in words, as a coherent story. Later, in conversation with an ex-girlfriend in New York, he acknowledges that he has lost his bearings, thereby confirming that the crisis he is experiencing with regard to images and icons has shattered his sense of personal identity. Yet her suggestion that he had lost direction long ago may imply that his recent sensitivity towards the deceptions of American culture in fact reflects his disappointment with the substitute lifestyle he had adopted in the absence of any self-confident *German* identity. The Peter Handke book lying on her table, *Wunschloses Unglück*

(1972), recalls this young novelist's efforts to trace his mother's experiences under national socialism, and his subsequent questioning of national identity. At the same time, Winter's ex-girlfriend also alludes to his taking of pictures as 'proof, proof that you still exist'. Photography, and by implication film-making, continues to offer the possibility of anchoring oneself. What Winter needs to do is to liberate his images from cliché, from their appropriation by Hollywood, and to infuse meaning into the snapshots that he constantly takes of his surroundings.

Winter's quest to reconnect meaning with images corresponds to Wenders's intentions in making the film. In keeping with the principle of *Autorenkino* (*auteur* cinema) that informed the work of the New German Cinema, *Alice* is a highly personal, subjective, and often autobiographical work. Winter's return to the heavily industrialised Ruhr area of West Germany, after the initial sequences in America, takes him back to Wenders's own past. The picture enacts Wenders's engagement with the United States, and mirrors his efforts to establish his identity as a film-maker, integrating Hollywood influences into a distinctively European heritage. *Alice* is littered with references to John Ford and Nicholas Ray, American directors close to Wenders's heart, the former for his vision of the integrative potential of film, the latter for his undermining of this wholesomeness (Ray in fact appears as a crook in Wenders's *Der amerikanische Freund*). John Ford's death is even acknowledged at the end of the film, in a newspaper obituary entitled 'Lost Worlds', an epithet that perhaps mirrors Wenders's perception of the mutation of a healthy tradition of American film-making into bland commercialism. Moreover, the cowboy genre refined by both Ford and Ray is adapted and transformed by the German film-maker to make it relevant to his own heritage. The road movie – the modern version of the cowboy story in which men roam *westwards* into the American wilderness to find themselves – is inverted. Winter travels *east* back to his European origins on a journey of self-discovery which takes the past as the starting point of identity, rather than a future in uncharted lands without history. American and German traditions fuse as the road movie becomes a *Bildungsroman*. Winter's automobile tour through the streets of West German cities is metamorphosed into a 'novel of self-development' in which the protagonist finally achieves maturity and social integration.

The allusion to the German *literary* heritage is significant, reflecting a typically European desire to raise the cultural status of film by association with the more prestigious medium. German films from the 1920s onwards have often had a distinctly 'literary feel', and from the 1960s onwards West German directors have often felt that it would be easier to attract state subsidies if they filmed classic works of fiction or otherwise blurred the lines between literature and film. More specifically, works of literature have been the inspiration for many of Wenders's films, including those by Peter Handke, and Nathaniel Hawthorne's *The Scarlet Letter*. The symbiosis of film and fiction sets images in a verbal context, replenishing the meaning they seem to lose when divorced from language. *Alice* attaches great significance to dialogue – a convention of nineteenth-century realist and naturalist novels – and especially to the discussion of pictures.

Wenders's debate with America does not only take place at the level of genre. The fabric of *Alice*, the way it is put together as a series of shots and sequences, also promotes a reconciliation of Hollywood conventions with European sensibilities. Establishing shots ensure that the viewer does not endure the deliberate disorientation typical of much European avant-garde cinema. Most of the dialogue sequences follow the Hollywood 'shot/reverse shot' pattern, stitching the viewer into the scene and creating the intimacy that Wenders requires if Winter is not simply to appear as a disaffected and unsympathetic outsider. The middle portion of the film, from Winter's arrival in Amsterdam to his abandonment of Alice at the police station, is highly conventional in its use of camera angles and cutting between scenes. Yet these tributes to Hollywood are blended with other techniques that establish an entirely different feel to the film than might be expected from an American director. Dissolves remove suspense, create a softer, more reflective focus, and erase the breaks between apparent oppositions. Winter's sojourn in America fades into his European odyssey, signalling the seamless merging of the two filmic traditions. Long takes and expansive panning shots perhaps repay a debt to Alfred Hitchcock, or Orson Welles, but they are endowed here with a new sensibility, especially in the last third of the film. The camera lingers nostalgically on antiquated houses soon to be demolished, and country landscapes encroached upon by industry. An obsession with social change and the erosion of familiarity underlines *Alice*'s European credentials.

If Wenders's aim is to marry America and Europe through cinematography, then Winter arrives at the same destination at the level of plot. The desire for rapprochement is present all along. Winter forgets to hand in his key for the American Skyway Motel and does not seem disconcerted when he happens across it back in Europe. After leaving Alice at the police station he attends a Chuck Berry concert and clearly enjoys experiencing American culture in a German context. On another occasion, he watches a young boy singing along to the rock and roll music playing on a jukebox and appears to feel an affinity. Yet the catalyst for his successful quest for greater self-awareness is Alice, the precocious child abandoned to Winter's reluctant care by her mother in New York. Alice reintroduces Winter to the passion for images from which he had become disconnected in America. She also inspires him once more to associate pictures with story-telling and thus to invest them with personal meaning. Finally, she helps him to resolve the crisis of male identity that derives, in part at least, from the rootlessness engendered by his inability to locate himself either in his German past or in the American present he had adopted as a substitute culture. The film closes with Winter's decision to travel with Alice to Munich, to share with her the views of the countryside outside their train, in an episode that signals his acceptance of the responsibility of the substitute father figure, his renewed pleasure in images, and his reintegration into the German landscape from which he had been alienated. The final scene points forward with Winter's decision to complete his story (we are not sure whether he means the script to his American photo-journey, or his travels with Alice). This resolution reverses his earlier insistence that the narration of images was impossible.

Alice in den Städten is not only about filmic representations – a self-reflexive excursus on cinematography and photography – it is also about its protagonist's self-image. Images become metaphors as Winter looks at himself in mirrors, unable to comprehend the person reflected there. The picture he receives from others reflects his adoption of the role of the libidinous predator in the company of the opposite sex. He appears to be attracted to Alice's mother and she fully expects him to want to sleep with her. The next day, of course, she abandons her daughter to his care in New York, thereby forcing him into a new role. The ex-girlfriend he visits in New York also feels it necessary to disabuse him of his certainty that he will be able to share a bed with her, despite his long absence and lack of communication. A woman in a bus on the way from Amsterdam to Germany smiles flirtatiously at him, probably responding to his initiation of eye contact, whilst Alice is left to play with another child at the back of the vehicle. Later, the woman at the open-air swimming pool he visits with Alice immediately understands his purpose in allowing the girl to engage in conversation with her. They spend the night together and Winter appears pleased by the implied lack of commitment. The next morning Alice disapproves and they leave the apartment before the woman wakes, in a scene that hints at her growing influence over his behaviour. His self-exculpatory remark that Alice had occupied the couch before he had been able to make his bed there appears defensive, patronising and devious in its attempt at concealment, and implicitly cedes her the right to comment on his actions.

Winter's disorientation throughout the first two-thirds of the film reflects his disaffection with the movies. He no longer empathises with the models of masculinity offered by Hollywood, and his playing of the male parts assigned to him appears correspondingly unconvincing. Alice prompts Winter to take an initial step towards self-knowledge when she induces him to narrate his anxiety – he admits that he is 'afraid of fear' – in their Dutch airport hotel at the beginning of their European trip, despite his insistence that he doesn't know any stories. Meaning is restored to images through story-telling, as the images of male identity that he has internalised from the movies are reworked into a tale of his own making. He improvises a parable of a boy who abandons his mother in the woods, crosses a river, comes across a man riding a horse, follows him to a road from the side of which he is picked up by a truck driver, only finally to arrive at the sea, where he is stricken by grief for the mother he had deserted. It is not difficult to interpret this sequence allegorically. Hauntingly nostalgic extra-diegetic music lifts the scene out of the flow of events unfolding within the linear narrative of the film, giving pause for reflection. Winter liberates himself from the stereotypes that previously determined his identity – his awareness of the clichés he lives by, but his inability to act otherwise – through his use of metaphor, imagery, and narration. The boy (clearly Winter) is initiated into masculinity via the archetypes of the cowboy figure and the road movie. The disavowal of the mother implies a repudiation of domesticity as the boy pursues the path of outsiderdom, heroic isolation, and freedom from obligation, mapped out by Hollywood. The rejection of the 'motherland' is intimated too, as the boy crosses the water in order to adopt new customs, leaving behind the woods (often associated with 'Germanness'), family, and community existence. America has colonised Winter's identity. The film promotes the idea that identity can be 'organic', that is, 'naturally' emerging from a national or, more often, regional affinity with a distinctive cultural heritage. The absence of an 'organic' concept of self consequently leaves Winter vulnerable to the images that threaten to engulf him.

At the same time, however, pictures and photographs offer the possibility of redemption. Soon after their arrival in Holland, Alice takes a polaroid picture of Winter, using his camera, and thereby turns his attempts to annex his environment through photography back on himself. He is forced to confront his own image and therefore his own confusion and disorientation. Significantly, Alice appears reflected in the shiny surface of the polaroid, looking over his shoulder, transforming Winter's representation of masculine detachment and self-isolation into a family portrait. Alice's presence 'completes' the picture, fills the gap, and gives it meaning as a transposition of intimacy, and of a human relationship. This meaning is formalised in a later scene when they pose together in a photobooth. Alice takes her lead from his expressions, alternately mock serious and comic, thus confirming her 'adoption' of him as a father figure. This sequence, in turn, provides the narrative solution to the episode in which Alice had asked the woman at the swimming pool whether she thought Winter was her father. On that occasion, he had betrayed the image that he and Alice had constructed of themselves, by exploiting the situation to seduce the woman. His response to Alice's implorings the next morning, however, signalled his growing awareness of the need to accept responsibility. Images regain a positive value in the subsequent photo-booth scene. Photographs create an identity – self-knowledge and mutual dependence – for Alice and Winter, institutionalising the father–daughter relationship that may not exist by virtue of blood ties, but which affection and their free choice substantiate.

Growing closer to Alice revives Winter's realisation that relationships with other people and an awareness of origins form an essential part of identity. He learns how to be a father to Alice and subsequently sets out to visit his own parents. His detour, symbolically, takes him across water, this time on a ferry, recalling the story he told Alice of crossing the river after having abandoned his mother, as well as duplicating his transatlantic passage to Germany from America. The entirety of Winter's journey through the Ruhr represents a pilgrimage back to his 'Germanness' and to the web of relationships that sustain it. Once again the role of images is vital. In an earlier scene, Alice had shown him a photograph of her grandmother's house and family snapshots, underscoring the concept that pictures can anchor identity. More generally, Winter chooses Oberhausen as the first town in which to search for Alice's grandmother. This pays a tribute to the original determination of signatories of the Oberhausen manifesto to create a national cinema. It also implies a healing of the wound exposed by the actions of the young directors who initiated the 'Young German Cinema'. The Oberhausen declaration was directed against 'Opas Kino', that is, against the film-making of their grandfathers, which they now pronounced dead. Significantly, fathers are missing from this formulation, reflecting a widespread feeling amongst Wenders's contemporaries that theirs was a 'fatherless' generation. War had robbed many of them of their real fathers. Complicity in national socialism, furthermore, had deprived them of role models and untainted artistic traditions. The alternative, it seemed, was to look to America for paternal influence and guidance.

All of the major themes of the film are united in the scene on the ferry. As Winter and Alice travel across the river, he aims his camera at a young woman with a small child. Alice appears in the background of the shot, completing, as usual, the family portrait. This time Winter's absence from the picture is legitimate. He takes on the role of father and photographer of a domestic outing. His perspective on a woman is, for the first time, entirely framed by children. The possibility of a monogamous relationship is implied, as is the resolution of his crisis of masculinity. The meaningfulness of images, moreover, is linked to human intimacy and this enables Winter to overcome the phobia of photography that had paralysed him in the United States. America, too, can be integrated into his newly established sense of identity. The woman is singing a song, an American rock and roll tune. Several words can be distinguished, including 'daughter' and 'son', evoking the theme of family relationships one last time, and juxtaposing this with the best of American culture – its non-conformist heritage rather than its commercialised mainstream – which is now seen as an integral part of a German identity rather than as a threat. Affection for America need not erase the individual's sense of self. Many influences, it seems, can co-exist and generate a fertile mix, both in film-making and in broad cultural terms.

Alice in den Städten embodies this fusion of cultures at all levels, in its plot, in its characterisation, and in the way it is shot. This is especially the case with regard to the pivotal relationship between Europe and America, and between the United States and Germany. More generally, the film shows that images can be filled with new meaning and spaces can be unlocked for new identities. Alice and Winter trace her grandmother's house with the help of a photograph, only to discover that the house is presently occupied by an Italian woman. In this case, pictures enforce an awareness of demographic change and invite the viewer to respond positively, if nostalgically. Later, we see shots of Turkish families. These images reflect the increasingly multicultural composition of West German society from the late 1950s, and particularly from the early 1970s, in a markedly reflective yet reassuringly unprejudiced fashion. *Alice* may be tinged with sentimentality – its lingering shots of pastoral scenes and its focus on old houses and new factories are evidence of this – but it also appears optimistic about social transformation, and refreshingly open to cultural diversity.

References and Suggestions for Further Reading

Elsaesser, Thomas 1981: 'A Retrospect on the New German Cinema'. In *German Life and Letters*, 41, 3.

Elsaesser, Thomas 1985: 'Germany's America: Wim Wenders and Peter Handke'. In Susan Hayward 1985: *European Cinema*, Birmingham: Aston University.

Elsaesser, Thomas 1989: *New German Cinema: A History*. London: Macmillan.

Kolker, Robert Philip and Beicken, Peter 1993: *The Films of Wim Wenders: Cinema as Vision and Desire*. Cambridge: Cambridge University Press.

Sandford, John 1980: *The New German Cinema*. New York: Da Capo.

Wenders, Wim 1991: *The Logic of Images: Essays and Conversations*. Translated by Michael Hofmann. London: Faber & Faber.

Wenders, Wim 1997: *The Act of Seeing: Texts and Conversations*. Translated by Michael Hofmann. London: Faber & Faber.

Credits

Director	Wim Wenders
Producer	Joachim von Mengershausen
Production Company	Filmverlag der Autoren
Screenplay	Wim Wenders
	Veit von Fürstenberg
Director of Photography	Robby Müller
Editors	Peter Przygodda
	Barbara von Weitershausen
Music	Can

Cast

Rüdiger Vogler	Philip Winter
Yella Rottländer	Alice van Damm
Lisa Kreuzer	Lisa van Damm
Edda Köchl	Edda
Didi Petrikat	Girl in bus
Ernst Böhm	Policeman
Sam Presti	Car salesman
Lois Moran	Airline assistant

Filmography

Summer in the City (1969–70)
Die Angst des Tormanns beim Elfmeter (*The Goalkeeper's Fear of the Penalty*, 1972)
Der scharlachrote Buchstabe (*The Scarlet Letter*, 1972)
Alice in den Städten (*Alice in the Cities*, 1973)

Falsche Bewegung (*False Movement*, 1975)
Im Lauf der Zeit (*Kings of the Road*, 1975)
Der amerikanische Freund (*The American Friend*, 1977)
Lightning over Water/Nick's Movie (1980)
Hammett (1982)
Der Stand der Dinge (*The State of Things*, 1982)
Paris, Texas (1984)
Tokyo Ga (1985)
Himmel uber Berlin (*Wings of Desire*, 1987)
Aufzeichnungen zu Kleidern und Städten (*Notebook on Clothes and Cities*, 1989)
Bis an Ende der Welt (*Till the End of the World*, 1991)
In weiter Ferne, so nah! (*Far Away, So Close*, 1993)
Arisha, der Bär und der steinerne Ring (*Arisha, the Bear and the Stone Ring*, 1994)
Lisbon Story (1995)
Lumière de Berlin (1996)
The End of Violence (1997)
Alfama (1997)

132

7 Carmen

The fight in the tobacco factory. Cristina (Cristina de Hoyos) taunts Carmen (Laura del Sol).

Carmen
Annella McDermott

Carmen is an excellent example of a particular kind of European film – intensely local, and displaying a preoccupation with ideas of national identity, yet appealing to a wider European and international audience. It is a dance film, a showcase for *ballet español*, a fusion of contemporary dance and flamenco. The main events in the film are the search for a principal dancer, followed by the rehearsals for a flamenco ballet based on the opera *Carmen*, by the French composer Bizet, itself based on the novel by Prosper Mérimée.

The opera is now one of the most popular in the classical repertoire, though it shocked audiences when it was first performed, with its portrayal of a free woman as the main character. Carmen is independent in an economic sense, since she works in a cigar-factory. She also claims the freedom to fall in and out of love as she chooses. In a quarrel, she stabs a fellow-worker and is arrested by José, whom she seduces into releasing her, thus sacrificing his army career. Despite her warning that love is a law unto itself, he is devastated when she leaves him for a bullfighter, and eventually kills her. In the film, the rehearsals of the ballet based on this opera are intercut with the story of an affair between Antonio, the director of the company, who is dancing the role of José in the ballet, and the dancer chosen for the role of Carmen. This 'real-life' relationship mirrors the relationship between the characters in the ballet, although the correspondence between the two levels of the film is not absolutely symmetrical: for example, in the 'real-life' story Antonio faces three rivals for Carmen's love, whereas in the ballet José has only one.

For a Spanish audience some of the meaning of the film derives from events in Spain in the years immediately preceding its making: the death of General Franco in 1975, the restoration of democracy and the monarchy after thirty-six years of dictatorship, Spain's re-application in 1980 for entry to what is now the European Union (Spain was finally admitted in 1986), and the election victory in 1982 of the PSOE, the Spanish Socialist Workers' Party. Spain had changed out of all recognition in the space of only a few years, and it was important to look again at national traditions and stereotypes in an attempt to decide which parts of the heritage were fake and which authentic, which parts had been contaminated by identification with the dictatorship, and which could be salvaged for the future.

Carmen dates from 1983, that is, the second year of the socialist government. During the Franco regime, Saura had been one of the leading exponents of a type of film that denounced the effect of authoritarian values and education on human psychology. His films of that period often had a strong autobiographical content, and they looked at middle-class Spaniards, in particular their family and personal relationships, in order to trace the effects of religious and social repression on behaviour. To overcome the problem of censorship, these films relied to a great extent on metaphor and allegory to make their points. The audience had to know how to read between the lines, interpret the allegory, and see its applicability to national political and social issues. For this reason, the films Saura made during the Franco years had difficulty finding an audience outside Spain, except among people particularly interested in Spain and Spanish politics. During those years, a standard judgement on Spanish films, Saura's amongst them, was that they were so preoccupied with Spanish issues, and were forced to deal with these issues in such an oblique fashion, that they did not travel well. With the transition to democracy, that particular subject-matter and that way of reading films were no longer relevant. This did not mean, however, that films ceased to have a specifically national character. Gwynne Edwards, in his preface to *Indecent Exposures*, a study of four Spanish directors, of whom Saura is one, insists that: 'the strength of Spanish cinema lies in its Spanishness: its concern with Spanish issues, its drawing on Spanish traditions, its essentially Spanish style' (Edwards, 10). What changed was not the national focus of films, but their accessibility to a wider audience.

Saura had always been very fond of music, which is a major feature even of his most political films. In the 1980s, he began a series of films about flamenco, an art form which is peculiar to Spain, and which embraces song, instrumental music, and dance. Naturally, the instrumental music and dance are the forms most likely to appeal to an international audience, since they involve no issue of spoken language. Saura has made five flamenco films to date. The first was *Bodas de Sangre* (*Blood Wedding,* 1981), filmed in black and white and purporting to show the dress rehearsal for a flamenco ballet based on a play by the poet and dramatist Federico García Lorca ('purporting to show', in that the ballet does not exist outside the film). *Carmen* is the second of these flamenco films. The third, *Love the Magician* (1986), like *Carmen*, is feature-length and in colour, a filmed version of a flamenco ballet by probably the best-known Spanish composer of the century, Manuel de Falla. All three films have been successful internationally, as well as in Spain. Saura has also made two documentaries on related topics: *Sevillanas* (1992), which illustrates the varieties of this particular dance form, and was made for EXPO 92 in Spain, and *Flamenco* (1995), which documents the main tendencies and exponents of flamenco music, song and dance.

The origins of flamenco are a matter of conjecture since there is a lack of documentation. It is generally considered to have originated in Andalusia, in southern Spain, though subsequent movement of workers from Andalusia to other parts of Spain has given flamenco a presence in other parts of the country. The type of scale used in the song, and certain movements used in the dance, suggest that it dates from the period of Muslim occupation of Andalusia, between the eighth and the fifteenth centuries, and is a mixture of Muslim, Jewish and Christian elements. It appears to have been taken up by the gypsies, who are said to be the descendants of groups of people who emigrated in successive waves from India from the eleventh century onwards, using two routes, one through Central Europe, the other via North Africa, settling in many places along these routes and reaching Spain probably in the fifteenth century. There is some controversy in Spain as to whether the gypsies should be considered a separate ethnic group from Andalusians in general. James Woodall, in his *In Search of the Firedance*, takes the view that the gypsies of Andalusia are a race apart, yet socially integrated. Nevertheless, he traces a history of persecution of the gypsies, from a law of 1499 to implement immediate banishment of gypsies without a certifiable occupation, through subsequent threats of forced labour in the galleys for those who remained vagabond, a prohibition on gypsies practising certain trades, prohibition of the use of the dress, name or language of gypsies, and laws denying the ancient custom of sanctuary in churches to gypsies, but ending with legislation in the late eighteenth century which removed legal obstacles to their plying any trade they wished, while requiring them to abjure their customs. Though integrated legally, gypsies nowadays live in what he describes as 'ghettos' and suffer from social discrimination (Woodall, 87). Despite the strong association of flamenco with gypsies, many of the leading exponents are non-gypsies. This is the case, for example, of the principal guitarist seen in the film, Paco de Lucía, who is considered one of Spain's best and most innovative flamenco guitar soloists.

There is some basis for considering flamenco a 'folk' form. It uses no system of notation for the style of singing and playing: like the dance, these styles are passed on by oral tradition, teaching and imitation (Paco de Lucía has never learned to read music). Saura's film emphasises the point that flamenco expression is not confined to performance: in the 'real life' layer of the film, Carmen invites Antonio to express his feelings for her by dancing a *farruca*, the key male solo dance in flamenco, and the birthday-party sequence shows flamenco being used spontaneously in celebration.

Needless to say, there is no necessary connection between flamenco and left-wing politics. Although the words of flamenco songs often reflect the history of persecution or discrimination outlined above, the protest is usually considered a-political. Indeed, a recent study by Timothy Mitchell, *Flamenco Deep Song*, accuses the form of expressing the misery of the singer, and the community he represented, in a way that allowed his listeners – the very people who were the cause of the suffering – to feel purged by pity from their burden of guilt (Mitchell, 107, 137). Mitchell, however, was speaking of a particular context in which flamenco song was performed – at private parties organised by members of Andalusia's elite landowning families. It does seem possible to argue that there is a connection between Saura's film and the coming to power of a socialist government in Spain after thirty-six years of dictatorship followed by eight years of the transition to democracy. The ballet that will emerge from the rehearsals is not, of course, a folk-form: it is choreographed, performed by dancers and instrumentalists who are mainly professionals, and is based on the 'high' art forms of literature and opera. However, one could readily see this ballet as a socialist project, since it combines these 'high' art forms with the popular art of a persecuted minority, one which includes Jewish and Muslim elements and therefore can carry notions of multiculturalism appropriate to the new, open and tolerant democracy. There is a history in Spain of attempts by leftist intellectuals to dignify flamenco, notably the festival of flamenco song organised in Granada in 1922 by García Lorca, who was killed by the rebel Nationalists in the first weeks of the Spanish Civil War, and the composer Manuel de Falla, who went into exile in Argentina at the end of the war. Saura can therefore be seen as re-initiating a project that had been interrupted by the Spanish Civil War and the dictatorship that followed.

It should be noted, however, that the Franco regime also promoted flamenco culture from a populist viewpoint, and Spanish film studios in the 1940s and 1950s produced a large number of musicals and melodramas set in Andalusia and using flamenco or flamenco-related music. Moreover, from the 1960s onwards Spain was keen to encourage tourism, which is a major earner of foreign currency, and flamenco dance was promoted as a spectacle suitable for tourist consumption. Saura alludes to this in the scene in the film where Carmen dances in a flamenco night-club full of Japanese tourists. While the dancers are performing, instead of remaining respectfully still, a waiter circulates, taking orders for drinks and delivering them to tables. The suggestion is that this is a commercial, soulless form of flamenco, in contrast to the flamenco seen in other parts of the film, which, it is implied, is more authentic.

Andalusia is one of the economically depressed regions of Spain, an area of high unemployment, from which large numbers of people had to emigrate, particularly in the 1950s and 1960s, either to more industrialised regions of Spain, such as Catalonia and the Basque country, or to other countries in Europe, especially France or Germany, to work in agriculture or industry. In all of these destinations, including the regions of northern Spain, they have experienced the discrimination and prejudice directed at those forced to emigrate to find work. It is thus ironic that a regional art from this neglected region has come to be seen as the typical manifestation of Spanishness, particularly since the nineteenth century, and particularly under the influence of French artists. Woodall has a chapter in his book entitled 'Andalusia Invented', in which he traces the origins of this process:

> In the twentieth century, many have been lured to Andalusia as it has represented the last refuge from the technological oppressions of modern life; in the nineteenth, for writers in particular, the region came to represent the embodiment of all the historical and cultural forces with which they felt their work needed to be infused, and which defined their imaginative universe. For the French Romantics, especially, Andalusia was what the Lake District

was for the first-generation English Romantics, with all the subsequent ste-reotyping effects the latter has had on Cumbria applying to Andalusia, and how it – Spain as whole – has forever been perceived. (Woodall, 121, 125)

Saura's film, then, is clearly in part an interrogation by Spaniards in the new democratic Spain of external, particularly French, images of their country over the last two centuries (Woodall emphasises the French role in the construction of such images). The pre-credit sequence in the film establishes that Antonio is the director of a dance company and that he is looking for a principal female dancer with particular qualities, which the available dancers lack. He arranges to make a trip on the following day to Seville, one of the key sites in the history of flamenco, to find a suitable dancer, explaining to his lead guitarist that none of the women he has seen so far is a convincing Carmen. With the pronunciation of the name, which is immediately redolent of a particular stereotype of Span-ishness, a chorus from Bizet's opera begins to be heard, sung in French, naturally, and the credits start to roll over a background of a set of drawings of typically Andalusian characters by the French artist Gustave Doré. At several points in the film, notably when Antonio first sees the girl who will dance Carmen, we hear voice-overs of Antonio reading from a Spanish translation of Mérimée's novel, and when he arranges for her to dance the part he gives her a copy of the novel, somewhat to her bemusement, saying that she is not obliged to read it, but will probably find it useful.

It is worth noting here that Spain's relationship with France over the last two hundred years or so has been a complex one. Although there was widespread popular resistance to the Napoleonic invasion of Spain in the early nineteenth century, and though *afrancesado*, meaning 'Frenchified', was used as a term of abuse, there was a current in liberal thought that admired the French and even welcomed Napoleon, in the belief that he would rescue Spain from the backwardness and obscurantism of feudal social institutions and clericalism. To some extent, Saura can be said to be following that current, in that the film is based on the premise that Mérimée, Bizet and Doré had, at the very least, something interesting to say on the subject of Spanishness. However, a signi-ficant sequence in this respect is the one following soon after the credits, in which Antonio is listening to a tape of an aria from the opera and tapping his fingers, clearly trying to work out how it can be choreographed. Paco de Lucía, the guitarist, listens intently for a few moments, tries a few notes on the guitar, then effortlessly transposes the aria into a flamenco rhythm. This sequence would appear to imply that Spain's elaboration of a new sense of identity does not require a wholesale repudiation of foreign images of Span-ishness: what is acceptable in those images can be appropriated, transformed and recycled for Spain's own purposes.

Some moments in the film acknowledge the existence of tawdry or kitsch versions of flamenco. The scene in the tourist *tablao*, or flamenco night-club, has already been mentioned. In the scene where Antonio dances alone in the studio in the middle of the night, after Carmen has got up, dressed and gone home, he is thinking about costumes for the ballet. He ponders the possibility of Carmen using a fan, veil, and high comb, calling it a cliché, but wondering whether that is really a valid reason for rejecting it. As he speaks, Carmen appears, a figment of his imagination, though presented realistically. As though to confirm his suggestion that something can be rescued from cliché, she looks stunningly beautiful in black dress, veil, comb and fan. On the other hand, at the birthday party, Carmen gets herself up in a deliberately tacky version of flamenco dress and make-up. In these scenes, the film seems to be exploring the possibility of rescuing an acceptable version of flamenco from grotesque distortions growing out of right-wing populism and the tourist industry.

Carmen is a multi-layered film which deliberately blurs the distinction between reality and film, just as it blurs within the film the distinction between 'real life' and performance. On one level, Antonio Gades, Paco de Lucía and Cristina de Hoyos, an older dancer who is denied the part of Carmen because of her age, play characters who are indistinguishable from themselves as real people, at least so far as their surface characteristics are concerned. Within the film, there are a further two layers: there is a level of 'real life' which is represented by the gypsy singers and musicians, the dancers in the intervals between rehearsals, Antonio and Carmen in their off-stage affair, and Carmen's husband in jail and on his release. The third layer consists of the scenes from the ballet, which we see in rehearsal. The situation is further complicated by the fact that the majority of the film is set in a rehearsal room, one entire wall of which is a mirror. We often see actions first of all in a mirror, though we may only realise that fact once the camera pulls back. There are therefore pervasive metaphors in the film of 'looking in a mirror' and 'seeing a reflection', which can easily be read to imply that the dancers are like Spaniards seeing themselves in the mirror of foreign (and national) stereotypes.

The boundaries between these levels of reality are deliberately violated on several occasions. A good example is the scene involving a poker game which develops into a confrontation between Antonio and a man whom we initially take to be Carmen's husband. The confrontation is expressed as dance, which surprises the audience, since there has been no previous indication that Carmen's husband was a dancer (he was in jail for drug-trafficking); we probably assume that he has been co-opted into the performance, though we are also encouraged to interpret the confrontation as taking place in 'real life' by the facial expressions of the onlookers, who seem concerned. After he falls to the ground, the tension is held for some time, until Carmen smiles, and says: 'That's long enough, surely,' whereupon her 'husband' is revealed to be a dancer wearing a wig, and we revise our understanding of the scene to conclude that the poker game and fight are part of the ballet, though it remains clear that Antonio is expressing, in this sequence from the ballet, his murderous feelings towards Carmen's husband. Similarly, the confrontation between Antonio and the dancer taking the role of the bullfighter raises a doubt in our minds as to whether what we are seeing is 'real life' or a scene from the ballet, or a product of Antonio's imagination. Even when Carmen is murdered by Antonio, we initially assume that the act is taking place in 'real life', though clearly echoing the murder in the opera, until the camera pulls back and shows us the other dancers, unconcerned, implying that the scene did not happen in the plane of 'real life', but is simply a projection of Antonio's violent jealousy. There is thus a second pervading metaphor in the film, that of performance, which invites us to reflect on the extent to which national identity may consist of the 'performance' of roles created partly by foreign observers and partly by national producers of culture with a social or political agenda of their own.

Another function of this blurring of levels is to draw attention to similarities between the passions expressed in the opera and those experienced by the dancers, particularly Antonio, in 'real life'. He may not kill Carmen, as José does in the opera, but there is no doubt that his jealousy is violent enough for him to want to do so. Saura appears to be asserting that the stereotype of the domineering and jealous Spanish male corresponds to reality and has persisted into the new Spain. As a recent study of Spanish film remarks, *Carmen* 'engage[s] critically with such issues as the destructive attitudes and behaviour prompted by Spanish *machismo* and traditional constructions of male pride, jealousy, honour, etc.' (Jordan and Morgan-Tamosunas, 29).

The Carmen story lends itself relatively well to updating, since the nineteenth-century character is already a woman who is economically independent of men, because of the availability of work in the tobacco factory. If anything, the modern-day Carmen is less objectively independent, since she wants the lead role in the ballet and is therefore dependent on Antonio's patronage. However, the film does not interest itself in this casting-couch aspect of the relationship between the two. Carmen is depicted as strong and self-confident. In the scene in her dressing-room at the flamenco night-club, she reassures Antonio that her agent will not be a problem, saying that when she makes her mind up, she tends to get what she wants, and adding that she is stronger than he might think. She surprises him by being the one who gets dressed and goes home after lovemaking, with hardly a word of explanation, and she rejects his attempt to impose notions of fidelity on her. This is not to say that the character is presented as a model of womanhood. Even the modern audience may find her intransigent and careless of others' feelings. Nevertheless, there is no suggestion in the film that Carmen bears any responsibility for the final act of violence. The emphasis is on Antonio, who is on the one hand a steadfast romantic who falls in love at first sight, and on the other an authoritarian figure, accustomed to moulding large groups of mainly female dancers to his vision, and who, finally, would prefer to kill a woman rather than have her resist his will. Parallel to the sexual politics, the Spanish audience would readily see an allusion in Antonio to the still-recent dictatorship, and in Carmen, to the new democracy.

So far there has been a concentration on the film's meaning in relation to Spanish history and identity. This should not blind us to the fact that there is also a documentary intention to the film. Saura clearly wants to illustrate the various elements in flamenco dance, and he can conveniently do this by using the convention of rehearsal, where there is a plausible reason for concentration on individual elements such as the sinuous movements of the arms and hands, the particular posture of head, neck, torso and waist, the use of castanets, the sounds produced by finger-clicking, rhythmic clapping, drumming with hands on tables, drumming with walking-sticks on the floor and drumming or stamping with the feet. Antonio's search for a dancer to play Carmen takes him to a flamenco dance academy in Seville, which again provides an opportunity for a fairly detailed study of certain movements. It also suggests the community-based nature of flamenco dance in that there are children, amateurs and professional dancers, all studying together. Although ideas of discipline and technique are present in these scenes, the main emphasis in the film falls on the notion of flamenco as an art-form that comes from the heart, and demands passion and sincerity. While there are many close-ups, particularly of feet, there is also masterly use of middle and long shot to illustrate posture, and fluid, sweeping movements of the camera to convey the speed and exhilaration, particularly of the ensemble dancing.

The film, then, can be seen as a celebration of flamenco. Yet it could be argued that marrying flamenco to contemporary dance introduces elements, such as complex narrative content, that are alien to flamenco, and perhaps betrays a fear that raw flamenco would not arouse the same enthusiasm in the audience. The spectator may also feel that the *machismo* being denounced in the film is in fact inherent in flamenco dance since the form appears to depend on fairly rigid notions of gender separation, with particular types of posture and movement considered appropriate to each gender. This raises the question of whether flamenco is an outdated form, enjoyment of which is essentially conditioned by nostalgia, or whether it can in some way be updated to accommodate new visions of gender.

Considerations of genre are relevant to this film. *Carmen* is considered, in the British market at least, as an 'art-house' film, but clearly there are elements of plot, characterisation, theme, and setting to connect the work to the genre of dance movies from Hollywood and elsewhere. The figure of the authoritarian dance director has a particular resonance in Spain because of its recent history of dictatorship, but his search for a dancer with particular qualities, which are hard to define in words, but which he will recognise immediately he sees them, and the obsessive quest for perfection which leads him to harry his dancers, are familiar to an audience that has seen Hollywood dance movies like Alan Parker's *Fame* (1980) or Richard Attenborough's *A Chorus Line* (1985). Similarly, the theme of dance as an art that depends as much on feeling and sincerity as on technique, is one that this film shares with Randal Kleiser's *Grease* (1978), Emile Ardolino's *Dirty Dancing* (1986), the Australian Baz Luhrmann's *Strictly Ballroom* (1992) or the Japanese Masayuki Suo's *Shall We Dance?* (1996). The film has attracted some criticism in Spain on account of its perceived commercialism, when contrasted with Saura's more politically committed films of the Franco era (Jordan and Morgan-Tamosunas, 28). Yet it could be argued that within the framework of an accessible genre film, Saura poses questions about gender, about regional and/or national identity, and about high and low art, that are of real concern to his audience, and are political in a wide sense.

References and Suggestions for Further Reading

D'Lugo, Marvin 1991: *The Films of Carlos Saura*. Princeton, NJ: Princeton University Press.

Edwards, Gwynne 1995: *Indecent Exposures: Buñuel, Saura, Erice & Almodóvar*. Marion Boyars: London & New York.

Fiddian, Robin W. and Evans, Peter W. 1988: *Challenges to Authority: Fiction and Film in Contemporary Spain*. London: Tamesis Books.

Hooper, John 1995: *The New Spaniards*. London: Penguin Books.

Jordan, Barry and Morgan-Tamosunas, Rikki 1998: *Contemporary Spanish Cinema*. Manchester: Manchester University Press.

Kinder, Marsha (ed.) 1997: *Refiguring Spain: Cinema, Media, Representation*. Durham, NC, and London: Duke University Press.

Mitchell, Timothy 1994: *Flamenco Deep Song in Text*. New Haven, CT: Yale University Press.

Washabaugh, William 1996: *Flamenco: Passion, Politics and Popular Culture*. Oxford and Washington, DC: Berg.

Woodall, James 1992: *In Search of the Firedance: Spain through Flamenco*. London: Sinclair-Stevenson.

Credits

Director	Carlos Saura
Producer	Emiliano Piedra
Production Company	Emiliano Piedra
Scenario	Carlos Saura and Antonio Gades
Editor	Pedro del Rey
Director of Photography	Teo Escamillo
Art Director	Felix Murcia
Music	Georges Bizet, Paco de Lucía

Cast

Antonio Gades	Antonio
Laura del Sol	Carmen
Cristina de Hoyos	Cristina

Paco de Lucía   Paco
Juan Antonio Jiménez   Juan/Husband

Filmography

Los golfos (*The Hooligans*, 1959)
Llanto por un bandido [Lament for a bandit] (1963)
La caza (*The Hunt*, 1965)
Peppermint frappé (1967)
Stress es tres, tres [Stress is three, three] (1967)
La madriguera (*The Honeycomb*, 1969)
El jardín de las delicias (*The Garden of Delights*, 1970)
Ana y los lobos (*Anna and the Wolves*, 1972)
La prima Angélica (*Cousin Angelica*, 1974)
Cría cuervos (*Raise Ravens*, 1975)
Elisa, vida mía (*Elisa, My Love*, 1977)
Los ojos vendados (*Blindfolded Eyes*, 1978)
Mamá cumple 100 años (*Mama Turns a Hundred*, 1979)
De prisa, de prisa (*Faster, Faster / Hurry, Hurry / Fast, Fast*, 1981)
Bodas de sangre (*Blood Wedding*, 1981)
Dulces horas (*Sweet Yesterdays / Sweet Hours*, 1982)
Antonieta (1982)
Carmen (1983)
Los zancos (*The Stilts*, 1984)
El amor brujo (*Love the Magician / A Love Bewitched*, 1986)
El Dorado (*Eldorado*, 1988)
La noche oscura (*The Dark Night*, 1989)
¡Ay, Carmela! (1990)
Sevillanas (*Carlos Saura's Sevillanas*, 1992)
Dispara (*Outrage*, 1993)
Flamenco (*Carlos Saura's Flamenco*, 1995)
Taxi (1996)
Pajarico (*Little Bird*, 1996)
Tango (1997)

144

8 *Good Morning Babilonia*
In the film's final sequence the brothers Nicola (Vincent Spano) and Andrea (Joaquim de Almeida) stage and record their deaths for the camera.

Good Morning Babilonia

Derek Duncan

The extraordinary commercial and critical success outside Italy of *La vita è bella* (*Life is Beautiful*, 1997), Roberto Benigni's romantic comedy about the Holocaust, marks the culmination of a decade in which Italian cinema has re-established itself on the international scene. Films such as Giuseppe Tornatore's *Nuovo Cinema Paradiso* (*Cinema Paradiso*, 1987) and Gabriele Salvatores's *Mediterraneo* (1992) won Oscars for Best Foreign Film, and the established stars Sophia Loren and Marcello Mastroianni received similar Lifetime Achievement awards. This was not the first time, however, that Italian cinema had attracted world acclaim. Previously the type of Italian films to attract attention abroad had been strictly art-house, yet the films successfully exported since the late 1980s appeal to a broader market. They do not, therefore, represent a continuation of the experimental tradition of Italian cinema best known through the neo-realist cinema of the immediate post-war era, and the work of innovative film-makers such as Antonioni and Fellini in the 1960s and 1970s. Their appeal is more middlebrow, attracting an audience closer to the mainstream. This chapter will look at *Good Morning Babilonia* (*Good Morning Babylon*, 1987), an early example of this more recent trend in Italian film-making. Typically, these films are elegantly crafted, slow moving, spectacular epics. Set sometime in the recent past, they recall a lost Italy that nevertheless is in the compass of living memory. They are sentimental, occasionally humorous, films about men and masculinity, and their historical dimension is largely the backdrop for the exploration of intimate, but never sexualised, relationships between the male protagonists. In every respect *La vita è bella* fits firmly into this category. While some have hailed Benigni's treatment of the Holocaust as startlingly original, it is perhaps more accurate to see his film as characteristic, or indeed imitative, of this strand in contemporary Italian film production in terms of its aesthetic values, its thematic concerns, and crucially its marketability.

Good Morning Babilonia, directed by Paolo and Vittorio Taviani, is not the most successful, nor the best, of these Italian films but serves usefully as a compendium of their cinematic values. Set in the early part of the twentieth century, it relates the story of two brothers who leave Italy to make their fortune in the United States. They are able to utilise their traditional stonemasonry skills in the burgeoning Hollywood film industry, and although they die (in each other's arms) fighting in the First World War, they manage to film their deaths, providing a permanent record for posterity. The film was a joint production venture securing finance from France and the United States as well as from RAI, the Italian state television company (Sorlin, 162–4). Its cast included internationally known stars such as Greta Scacchi and Charles Dance. Only in the opening section set in Italy is Italian used; when the brothers are in America they speak in (accented) English. Such factors indicate that the film was created and marketed very much with an international audience in mind. In its content, however, the film is decidedly Italian, tackling the very complex issue of Italian national identity in the 1980s through an exploration of the immigrant experience earlier in the century. The journey from Italy to the United States is not solely a geographical one for it brings to the fore a number of contradictory elements that complicate what it might mean to be Italian, or indeed to become American. The experience of immigration involves clashes of language and culture and asks questions about the possible continuity of historical experience. The film sets up a dialogue between cultures that is enacted through the personal stories of the two brothers set against a period of momentous social, political, and artistic change.

One possible way of approaching films such as *Good Morning Babilonia* is through the admittedly contested category of 'heritage cinema' that has been applied to other film cultures of the period. Andrew Higson's discussion of British heritage cinema offers a useful starting point from which to consider similar films made in Italy although there are inevitably crucial differences between the two contexts (Higson, 232–49). Higson admits that there are difficulties in trying to define what constitutes a 'heritage' film. The term seems most obviously applicable to films such as the Merchant Ivory romantic epics *A Room with a View* (1985) or *Howards End* (1992). These films, both based on classic novels by E. M. Forster, look back to a glorious Edwardian past in which the upper middle classes of England appear to be enjoying the last days of a reassuring social stability. The aesthetic qualities of these films play an enormous part in diverting the spectator's attention from a narrative that has the potential to challenge such reassuring fictions. He notes that the preference in many of these films for long and medium shots rather than close-ups, and a slow-paced narrative not held together by tight editing, contributes to the creation of what he calls a 'restrained aesthetic of display' (234). The past appears solely as spectacle. They are, Higson suggests, 'intimate epics of national identity played out in a historical context' (233). The past offers at least the illusion of a better way of life; nostalgia functions as a form of indirect critique of the present.

Higson's argument cannot be transplanted wholesale into the Italian context. Although the Merchant Ivory films were well received in Italy, attracting the kind of audience they might have had in the UK, 'somewhere between the art-house and the mainstream', whatever nostalgia they displayed was for England not Italy. Nevertheless, in films such as *Mediterraneo*, it is possible to see elements of a similar aesthetic at play although the historical setting is clearly and necessarily different. The film's visual dimension is stronger than its narrative, which serves largely to motivate the lingering camera-work. The concept of a group of Italian soldiers setting up an idyllic community on a Greek island where they had landed as invaders offers a very benign statement on Italian national identity. Set in the Second World War, the narrative, however, longs for a more distant past as the values embodied by the soldiers are those of a lost pre-industrial age. The film's unfettered nostalgia is exemplified by its dedication to 'all those who are running away'.

Just as *Mediterraneo* avoids the trauma of the Second World War, *Good Morning Babilonia* barely investigates the upheavals of mass emigration that Italy experienced round the turn of the century. The film's historical dimension is supplied rather by cinema itself; its own historical development and its role in preserving/constructing historical memory. History and cinema, visual spectacle and political critique, have been constant preoccupations of the Taviani Brothers since their directorial debut with *Un uomo da bruciare* (*A Man for Burning*, 1962). In the early years of their career this project was informed by a Marxist perspective, yet although their sense of ideological commitment has since diminished (most notably in their 1996 adaptation of Goethe's *Elective Affinities*), their interest in exploring the past through the medium of film has remained. *Good Morning Babilonia* is their most self-conscious exploration of cinema's historical role and is also a commentary on the historical development of cinema.

Hollywood has not always dominated world cinema. Only in the 1920s did it become such a powerful force, building the robust studio system whose financial might attracted many of the most talented actors, directors and technicians from Europe. Until then, however, Italian film-makers had enjoyed world renown particularly for their grandiose historical epics. In 1915, when production was at its height, well over 500 films were made in Italy, while the rapidity of the industry's decline in the face of American competition is demonstrated by the fact that by 1930 only seven films are estimated to have been made there. Fascism's determination to halt the influx of films from the US stemmed largely from economic factors, and through the regulation of imports and the provision of financial subsidy succeeded in revitalising the Italian film sector. After the Second World War, however, the influence of the US on the economic, political and artistic life of Italy reasserted itself dramatically and has been a source of anxiety for both left-wing parties and the Catholic right ever since (Wagstaff, 89–116). In cultural terms these anxieties tend to focus on what is seen as the commodification of mass culture. From this perspective, cultural products are marketed and sold like any other; they are intended neither to educate, edify, nor induce intellectual contemplation, but simply to entertain. As an enormously popular form of mass entertainment, cinema has been the focus of much of this debate. Since the war American finance has had a critical effect on the development of film production in Italy, particularly the case in terms of distribution and marketing.

Italian audiences, like many others in Europe, have enjoyed a film culture that is American in origin rather than indigenous. Italy itself was a favoured location for American directors so that in the post-war period Italians often saw themselves represented on the screen through foreign eyes. On another level, Italian film-makers and actors adopted American styles of film-making and acting; Italian stars were often marketed as imitations of existing American idols. To the dismay of many, American values were purveyed as social norms, and were seen as the unwelcome agents of social change; the relative degree of autonomy granted to modern women is one example. Yet it is too simplistic to see American culture as a product imprinted on the Italian psyche in a direct manner. American culture as experienced in Italy was transformed and made into something else, mediated by the distinctive Italian context. An interesting example of this in the field of cinema is the practice of dubbing all foreign-language films. This has meant that while Italian audiences saw American stars, what they heard were Italian voices, which transformed the American landscape into something much closer to home and created a product that was neither purely American nor purely Italian but rather a hybrid mixture of the two.

The term 'hybridity' is one often used in current cultural debates on identity to refer to the unpredictable fusions that occur when cultures meet; what results is not a dilution but rather a dynamic mix of contrasting elements that is never assimilated, always remaining productively different. Such hybridity, however, challenges the attempt to write its history, for it is precisely a history of change and discontinuity that constitutes it. Nevertheless, identities and cultures often seek to affirm themselves through the creation of a history even if this history is largely the result of an imaginative reworking of the past rather than its scrupulous documentation. In *Good Morning Babilonia*, the Taviani Brothers attempt to piece together such a past, bringing together two apparently irre-concilable cultures and finding a way of giving them a common history. This they achieve through historicising the medium of cinema itself.

The film opens with a scene of astonishing luminosity, and indeed, the play of light and shade is one of the central motifs of the film. A group of workmen are completing the restoration of the façade of a Tuscan Romanesque cathedral. The canvas sheets are taken away to reveal the shining white stone and the intricacy with which the craftsmen have deployed their skills. Only one section remains covered where two of the workmen are putting the finishing touches to the figure of a white elephant seen in close-up. The workmen are Andrea and Nicola Bonanno, the youngest sons of the master-craftsman directing the restoration work. They work in the family business along with their five older brothers but are the most talented, and consequently favoured by their father. After his eulogy to the stonemason's art, praising the combination of the hands working with the imagination in a tradition that stretches back to the Middle Ages, the next scene sees the family seated around a large dinner table for what should be a celebration for the completion of the work. The father, however, announces the bankruptcy of the family business. At odds with their older brothers, Andrea and Nicola determine to buy back the firm. They leave for the United States, vowing to return only when they have made enough money to carry on the family tradition. Having received their father's blessing they set off.

The opening section of the film introduces most of the elements that will be developed later in the film. Most notably, it makes clear that it is a film about men; no women appear at all in the early part of the film. The skill passed on from father to son is part of a solely masculine tradition of craftsmanship. The names of the characters are significant in establishing this. Nicola Pisano was a thirteenth-century Tuscan sculptor whose most famous work is the extraordinarily intricate pulpit decorated with scenes from the life of Christ in the baptistery in Pisa. In the following century, the unrelated Andrea Pisano was responsible for sculpting the bronze doors on the baptistery in neighbouring Florence, the design of which he completed after having studied the baptistery doors in Pisa, which had been made some hundred and fifty years before by the sculptor Bonanno. Bonanno is the family name of the Tavianis' Tuscan craftsmen. Nicola and Andrea are considered to be two of the great masters of Tuscan art, bringing to sculpture the qualities Giotto brought to painting. The brothers are consequently situated directly in this illustrious Tuscan tradition, the various nuances of which the Tavianis exploit in the course of the film. A less subtle reference later in the film makes them the descendants of Michelangelo and Leonardo da Vinci, the great artists of the Italian Renaissance.

Although at this stage no mention is made of the cinema, a comparison is already being set up between the father and the American film director D. W. Griffith, who appears later in the film. Both are responsible for co-ordinating the work of skilled technicians and for producing great public art. Bonanno's request for a chair from which to contemplate the completed restoration, and the staged theatricality of the way in which the scene is shot, prepare the spectator for the parallel made more explicit later on. Similarly, the dinner scene in which the patriarch addresses his dependants anticipates a later scene in which the father and Griffith meet when the boys marry. The figure of the elephant and the form of the Romanesque church recur throughout the film as images that structure the narrative, providing a sense of continuity that transcends the limits of time and place. When the brothers first catch sight of America through the porthole of their ship, what they see is a stylised Manhattan sky-line whose glittering lights transport them back to childhood and a vision of the Christmas tree and its promise of future delight. The sense of place is constituted through imagination and longing. The representation of the United States as a land of opportunity is of course clichéd and will inevitably be revealed as false; the brothers will not make their fortune nor return home to live happily ever after. Nevertheless, the foregrounding of the fantasy through which America is imagined allows the Tavianis to explore the ways in which cultural representations, or ideas, vie with social and economic realities. The film goes on to examine the consequences of this myth of America but in doing so demonstrates that Italy is also a mythical place. It is this process of imagining place that the film recounts and shows.

For the two brothers the move from one culture to another causes the fracturing of their identities. The dream of America is short-lived as these skilled craftsmen are forced to earn a living as swineherds. Their struggle to speak English is a sign of their struggle to adapt to their new environment. By chance they encounter a group of Italian workmen on their way to San Francisco to work on the Italian pavilion at the World Exposition in 1915. They first of all hear them singing a piece from Verdi's *La forza del destino* and through the music are nostalgically transported to Italy. Music is often used in the film to evoke Italy, and the operatic tradition of Verdi and Rossini heard in America suggests the potent influence of Italian culture on the other side of the Atlantic. The Italian pavilion is a dazzling success and it is here that the American director D. W. Griffith sees the epic Italian film *Cabiria* (1914). He is so impressed by the quality of the craftsmanship displayed in it that he decides to employ the Italian workmen on the set of his new film. The brothers, who had only worked as day-labourers on the film, try to pass themselves off as foremen. They are caught out and accused of being shiftless liars, fulfilling the American stereotype of Italians. When they first meet Edna and Mabel, the girls they eventually marry, they are dismissed as losers because of their nationality yet they, too, pander to another stereotype by playing the part of romantic Latin lovers. The brothers are themselves trapped by America's own myth of Italy.

The brothers' identity is constructed largely through their work and the recognition of their skills. Eventually, they attract the attention of the famous director by building a model of an elephant for his film *Intolerance* (1916). The Tavianis probably overstate the impact of the Italian film on Griffith. Nevertheless, *Cabiria* was important in the history of cinema, noted especially for the grandiosity of its sets, and its development of the tracking shot. Griffith acknowledges his debt to Pastrone, the director of *Cabiria*, who used a model of a black elephant in his own historical epic. On one level this is an example of film quoting film as one director pays homage to another (a feature also of the Tavianis' work), but it also recalls the elephant carved by the brothers on the façade of the cathedral at the beginning of the film. By successfully redeploying their skills the brothers are able not only to ensure their livelihood in the present but also to effect a reconciliation between cultures and between eras through the continuity provided by their technical abilities. A historical narrative is made possible through the hands and the imaginations of the brothers.

The Tavianis are not interested simply in creating a narrative of historical continuity but seek to pay their own homage and acknowledge their own debt to the early cinema and to their own craft as film-makers. Much of the film's long middle section set in Hollywood serves only to recall the excitement of an era when film-making technique was still being honed. A greater dependency on natural light meant that shooting often took place in the open air, or was harnessed by crudely improvised means, as in the dance scene where Edna and Mabel are awakened by the sun's rays. A number of scenes simply recall the genres of the early cinema: the historical epic, the slapstick comedy, the exotic melodrama are revisited purely for the pleasure of their spectacle. The importance of cinema as a growing cultural phenomenon is reflected in the feverish questioning of Griffith by reporters anxious to know how he will respond to the challenge laid down by *Cabiria*; and the riots outside the cinema after the first screening of the anti-war *Intolerance* underline the role of cinema as a purveyor of ideas and an opinion maker.

Yet the Tavianis' view of the early cinema is not just nostalgic, for they also draw attention to the role of cinema in recording and preserving history for future generations. This theme is first introduced elliptically. Griffith is only able to see the elephant made by Andrea and Nicola because it was captured on film; their model having been destroyed by jealous rivals. This anticipates the film's conclusion where Nicola, having joined the Italian army to fight in the First World War, and nicknamed Hollywood, is given the task of regimental cameraman. By an extraordinary coincidence he bumps into Andrea on the battlefield. Both mortally wounded, they manage to record their deaths for their sons. As they raise their hands in blessing against the background of a Romanesque church, the spectator is transported back to other blessings, other churches seen earlier in the film. The act of filming allows the narrative both to return to the past and to be projected forward into the future. The imagery allows it to be circular and linear at the same time.

This sense of continuity stretches across both time and space. It is closely bound up with the film's representation of masculinity. The brothers' sense of identity is dependent largely on the recognition of their craft, which has been handed down from their ancestors. Their skill is an amalgam of creation and preservation; through it the cathedrals of the Middle Ages and the celluloid film of the twentieth century become historical archives. There is no place for women in this tradition just as there is very little place for them in this film. The conquest of Edna and Mabel is part of the brothers' process of integration into the United States; love changes Nicola to Nickie, for example. The romantic plot is an important element in negotiating cultural difference and the passage from a traditional to a modern way of life. As well as being exceptionally beautiful, Edna and Mabel are indelibly modern. Sexually liberated career girls, they embody the sense of opportunity and freedom from tradition that defined the myth of America. Their sexual liberation is, however, also part of the film's spectacle, as they undress for their lovers, and for the spectator, in a woodland setting that underlines the film's nostalgic pastoral longing. The narrative destiny of the girls is therefore at odds with their representation as independent women but entirely consonant with their passive eroticism. They cannot remain lovers but must become wives and then mothers in order to ensure the continuity of the male line. It is no coincidence that both women give birth to sons.

The death of Edna provokes a crisis in the film's construction of masculinity. Nicola refuses to bring up the baby alone, appearing therefore to refuse the patriarchal mantle. It is this crisis that brings him to return to his origins by enlisting in the Italian army (Andrea fights for the United States). Yet, the rejection of his son is motivated by the fact that his wife's death has made him unequal to his brother. Their relationship had been premised on their equality and the bond that this created protected them from the rivalry of their older brothers and the envy of their competitors in Hollywood. This doubling is also fundamental to the relationship between Bonanno and Griffith. Their meeting at the marriage of the brothers constitutes the film's central scene. The tableau takes place on the set constructed by Griffith for *Intolerance*, reconstructed by the Tavianis for *Good Morning Babilonia* and, like the rest of the film, shot in Tuscany. Placed at either end of a long table the patriarchs face up to each other like gunfighters. Their encounter, in which the urbane Griffith exchanges fire with the defiant Bonanno, concludes in an act of mutual recognition that confers their authority on the sense of continuity through change set up by the brothers. Women have no place in this exchange; their role as onlookers confirming their place in the masculine chain of reproduction. It is men who both make and maintain historical tradition.

One of the consequences of this mode of gender representation is that the challenges of modernity and cultural displacement are met and overcome by a reassertion of traditional values. These are asserted even in the final scene when the fairy tale's apparently tragic conclusion is salvaged by an ironic smile to the camera and to posterity. The film struggles with two contrasting ideas of time; the timeless mode characteristic of the fable, and linear time in which history is made. It is through the representation of space that this conflict is most apparent. The image of Italy created by the film is that of the tourist fantasy; the Tuscan farmhouse, the cathedral façade, the sun-drenched landscape evoke a sense of history that stands outside time. The United States does not, however, represent a historicised counter to this; brief glimpses of the metropolis and modernity give way to the fantastic space of Hollywood or the countryside. When modern space is represented (the hospital or the architect's office) it is a hostile environment threatening to the brothers. This may go some way to explaining the reference in the film's title to the biblical city of Babylon with its dual connotations of exile and sinfulness.

Good Morning Babilonia proposes a comforting historical model at odds with that suggested by the Tavianis' earlier films. *Padre padrone* (*Father, Master*, 1977) is a study in generational conflict set in rural Sardinia and is also a narrative detailing the transition from pre-industrial to modern society. Rural life is portrayed as harsh and unforgiving and patriarchy as brutal and oppressive; there is no anticipation of the bucolic idyll central to *Good Morning Babilonia*. Similarly, in *La notte di San Lorenzo* (*The Night of the Shooting Stars*, 1982) the Tavianis look back at the unresolvable conflict that splits a small Tuscan village during the Second World War; again there is no mechanism through which to render the past a more habitable place than the present even when viewed through the lens of fantasy and memory. Although both films share many of the production values of the later one, most notably the lingering camera-work on the natural landscape, their aesthetic dimension never displaces the historical enquiry of the narrative. However, it might also be added that their analysis is limited to the issue of conflict within a given society and culture, and does not address the perhaps more difficult questions involving exchange between cultures. In *Good Morning Babilonia* the Tavianis attempt to explore cultural and historical difference through the personal experience of two immigrants. It is an attempt to understand how such differences are inhabited and made sense of by those in the midst of the process of transition. The fairy-tale structure of the film and the sentimental emphasis of the narrative combine with the film's aesthetic to conceal the underlying political, social, and economic realities that motivate events. Yet what this reveals is the extent to which myth-making and the construction of specific histories form part of how cultural change is negotiated by those involved. The centrality of cinema as a cultural institution in the film is an essential element of this, for the Tavianis show how crucial the medium has been to the process of cultural interpretation and the construction of historical memory in the twentieth century.

It may be possible to relate the phenomenon of the Italian heritage film to broad social changes taking place in Italy during this period. The political consensus established after the setting up of the Italian Republic after the war had been broken in the 1970s and new political formations, most obviously those led by the media tycoon Silvio Berlusconi, were in the process of creating new alliances with unpredictable consequences. The divide between the prosperous north and the still impoverished south had fostered a climate of separatism and racist intolerance. The arrival, in large numbers, of economic migrants from Africa and Asia also forced Italy to reconsider its status as a First World power and to deal for the first time with questions of racial difference. The diminishing authority of the Catholic Church, and the rise of social movements, most notably feminism, in the wake of 1968, contributed to the reshaping and reconceptualisation of what it might mean to be Italian. To draw attention to these broad changes in Italian society is not simply to attempt to explain films such as *Good Morning Babilonia* or *Nuovo Cinema Paradiso* as merely the products of such change, but rather to indicate the hidden historical moment from which they look back.

Tentatively, it might be suggested that in Italian heritage cinema of the 1980s the longing for Edwardian England is replaced by a longing for a pre-industrial rural society which in the Italian imagination harbours similar connotations of national stability and integrity. Ultimately, however, what the Italian versions of heritage cinema may nostalgically yearn for is less the idealised picture of a pastoral nation than a form of masculine identity that stands outside history and society but, paradoxically, is seen as its motivator, and its agent of preservation and continuity.

References

Baranski, Zygmunt G. and Lumley, Robert (eds) 1990: *Culture and Conflict in Post-War Italy: Essays on Mass and Popular Culture*. London: Macmillan.

Duggan, Christopher and Wagstaff, Christopher (eds) 1995: *Italy in the Cold War: Politics, Culture and Society, 1948–58.* Oxford: Berg.

Higson, Andrew 1996: 'The Heritage Film and British Cinema'. In Andrew Higson (ed.), *Dissolving Views: Key Writings on British Cinema.* London: Cassell.

Sorlin, Pierre 1996: *Italian National Cinema, 1896–1996.* London: Routledge.

Wagstaff, Christopher 1995: 'Italy and the Post-War Cinema Market'. In Duggan and Wagstaff 1995: *Italy in the Cold War: Politics, Culture and Society, 1948–58.* Oxford: Berg.

Suggestions for Further Reading

Ferrucci, Riccardo and Patrizia Turini (eds) 1995: *Paolo & Vittorio Taviani: La poesia del paesaggio.* Rome: Gremese Editore.

Forgács, David 1990: *Italian Culture in the Industrial Era, 1880–1980: Cultural Industries, Politics and the Public.* Manchester: Manchester University Press.

Malavolti, Francesca and Katia Ugolini (eds) 1994: *L'utopia, la poesia, il silenzio. Il cinema dei fratelli Taviani.* Rovigo: Tipografia la grafica.

Sorlin, Pierre 1996: *Italian National Cinema, 1896–1996.* London: Routledge.

Taviani, Paolo 1987: *Good Morning Babilonia.* London: Faber.

Wagstaff, Christopher 1996: 'Cinema'. In David Forgács and Robert Lumley (eds): *Italian Cultural Studies.* Oxford: Oxford University Press. 216–32.

Credits

Directors	Paolo and Vittorio Taviani
Producer	Giuliani G. de Negri
Production Company	Filmtre/MK2 Productions/Pressman Film Corporation, in association with RAI, Films A2
Screenplay	Paolo and Vittorio Taviani
Director of Photography	Giuseppe Lanci
Editor	Roberto Perpignani
Art Director	Gianni Sbarra
Music	Nicola Piovani

Cast

Vincent Spano	Nicola
Joaquim de Almeida	Andrea
Greta Scacchi	Edna
Désirée Baker	Mabel
Omero Antonutti	Bonanno
Charles Dance	D. W. Griffith

Filmography

Un uomo da bruciare (*A Man for Burning*, 1962)
Fuorilegge del matrimonio [Outlaws of matrimony] (1963)
Sovversivi (*The Subversives*, 1967)
Putiferio va alla guerra (*The Magic Bird*, 1968)
Sotto il segno dello scorpione (*Under the Sign of Scorpio*, 1968)
San Michele aveva un gallo (*Saint Michael had a Rooster*, 1971)
Allonsanfan (1974)
Padre, padrone (*Father, Master*, 1977)
Il prato (*The Meadow*, 1979)
La notte di San Lorenzo (*The Night of the Shooting Stars*, 1981)
Kaos (*Chaos*, 1984)
Good Morning Babilonia (*Good Morning Babylon*, 1987)
Il sole anche di notte (*The Sun also Shines at Night*, 1990)
Fiorile (1993)
Affinità elettive (*Chosen Affinities*, 1996)
Tu ridi (*You Laugh*, 1998)

9   *Das Versprechen*

Sophie glimpses West Berlin for the first time, her expression full of anticipation or apprehension.

Das Versprechen (*The Promise*)
Stuart Taberner

9th November 1989 is etched onto the German national consciousness as the day on which the Berlin Wall fell. Televised images of the euphoria experienced by the inhabitants of this divided city, of their seemingly infinite delight and disbelief, provoked unprecedented sympathy worldwide for a people long respected for the economic success and political stability of the two states in which recent history had determined that they should live, but for whom few outsiders had been able to muster any real affection. The Wall had been erected on 13 August 1961 by the communist rulers of the German Democratic Republic (GDR), ostensibly to 'protect' their East German population against the 'imperialism' of the capitalist west. Berlin thus embodied the global division into two competing power blocs after the Second World War. The collapse of the Wall thirty-eight years after its construction inaugurated the final chapter in the Cold War following the 'velvet revolutions' that had swept across eastern Europe at the decade's end, and a new beginning for Germany, which was unified almost a year later on 3 October 1990.

Epochal events in national history seem to demand an appropriate response in national culture. Almost before the ink was dry on the treaty constituting their new state, Germans were clamouring for *the* novel, *the* drama, *the* work of art that would encapsulate their sensation of being present at the making of history. People needed to work through collective experience and to make sense of a forty-year period that appeared exceptional, even abnormal, from their new perspective. One art form above all may be particularly suited to this task. A film can foreshorten a lengthy chronology, its images can capture monumental events succinctly, provoking 'unmediated' emotional responses, and the medium's popularity means that a director may reach the entire nation. It is not surprising, therefore, that the release of Margarethe von Trotta's *Das Versprechen* (*The Promise*) in 1994 was eagerly awaited by a public impatient to see their experiences reflected back to themselves.

With its use of voice-over narration and documentary material in its intro-ductory scenes, and its frequent recourse to imposing extra-diegetic music, von Trotta's film claims to be an authoritative response to the momentous occurrences it depicts. Yet *Das Versprechen* is just as much about the early 1990s, the time of its production, as about 1989, or even the long years of the Wall's existence. Contemporary affairs are investigated in equal measure with recent history. The film closes with an image of its female protagonist, Sophie, standing on a bridge linking East and West Berlin, surrounded by revellers celebrating the opening of the border. She is gazing at her former lover Konrad, who had remained in the east when Sophie escaped, separated from her by the Wall. Sophie contemplates Konrad (west inspects east), yet her expression reveals little elation, rather an uncanny failure to recognise someone who should be so well known to her. She makes no attempt to approach him, leaving the film's conclusion ambiguous. East and West Germans, a family riven for more than forty years (since the founding of the two states in 1949, and all the more so after the building of the Wall in 1961), are unsure whether they will get on once reunited, and still less confident that they will like one another, or have anything in common after such a long period apart. Indeed, the 'family' metaphor is used extensively in the film. Sophie flees west, but wants her mother to know that she still loves her. Konrad is also alienated, from his father, by his scepticism towards the East German state that his father helped to create. Sophie, on the other hand, blames her stepfather for the suicide in police custody of her real father, implying that an 'authentic' GDR patrimony has been supplanted by an unscrupulous successor. Later, Konrad concedes to Sophie that 'our break-up didn't kill me', much as she contemplated whether their cohabitation in Prague in 1968 would succeed: 'I don't know. We've never lived together'. In both cases, East and West Germans admit that family ties have loosened and that it is not certain that the grand reunion will flourish. The symbolism of the bridge (one of many images of bridges and trains in the film) may be an empty gesture as Germans continue to be divided by the 'Wall in the head' – an expression that has become shorthand for the many misunderstandings between *Ossis* and *Wessis* – by different value systems, cultural codes, and economic prospects. In a sense, therefore, the film suggests the failure of unification, and reveals the promise that stands as its title to be one that has been neither kept, nor fulfilled. Its final scene denies the classic cinematic pleasure of closure and refuses to deliver the happy ending that the audience might have expected.

More particularly, the film expresses the disappointment of the left–liberal social, political and intellectual consensus that had dominated West Germany's cultural sphere since the late 1960s, most often in implied, sometimes even explicit opposition to the conservative politicians who had ruled the country for much of its short existence. The attitudes of the writers, dramatists, and film-makers whose beliefs had been shaped by their participation in the student revolts of 1968 had always been ambiguous on the question of German division. On the one hand, they insisted that the carving up of the nation was just punishment for their parents' complicity in Hitler's madness. At the same time, they were critical of their own state, of the conservative nature of society and politics in West Germany, its materialism, unexpunged racism, social divisiveness, and inequality. They looked to East Germany, therefore, to realise their ideal of a fairer society, free of capitalism and of the dominance of one social class over another. In their minds the German Democratic Republic had always offered a potential utopia – in *theory*, at least – to be contrasted with the seeming corruption of their own state, which appeared to many of them as latently fascist, indeed barely reformed after national socialism. Intellectuals had been particularly disturbed by the ease with which ex-members of the Nazi party had risen to high positions in the West German economy and government. Yet the collapse of East Germany in 1989, followed by countless revelations of neighbours spying on one another, propitious political conversions, supposed dissidents collaborating with the state secret services, and ubiquitous social disintegration finally revealed the emptiness of the promise that the GDR had long embodied for West German intellectuals. They could no longer believe that the country's geriatric totalitarian leadership had been an aberration, the corruption of a dream that had none the less remained alive within the population as a whole, and which ordinary East Germans would rush to accomplish once they were free to do so, in 1989/90, and a whole range of writers, intellectuals and film-makers, including Margarethe von Trotta and Wim Wenders, were forced to look again at their previous attitudes towards both East and West Germany.

The realisation that they had been wrong to trust in the GDR's ability to reform itself and fulfil its potential led to a crisis of confidence amongst the mainly left-leaning West German cultural aristocracy that had held sway since the late 1960s. This was compounded by their powerlessness to resist the march towards unification between November 1989 and October 1990. They were forced to acknowledge that – far from desiring to introduce 'true' socialism in the GDR – the majority of East Germans, as proved by elections and demonstrations, wanted only to join West Germany as quickly as possible in order to enjoy a standard of living of which they had only been able to dream previously. The call with which the revolution in the GDR had started, 'We are *the* people' – interpreted by West German intellectuals as the demand of ordinary East Germans for self-determination, democracy, and social justice – had given way to the more insistent, and rapacious, 'We are *one* people'. Access to the affluence taken for granted by West Germans had become the major impetus for unification.

This condemnation of *eastern* materialism features strongly in *Das Versprechen*. The young East Germans who escape to the west with Sophie shortly after the building of the Wall in 1961 are portrayed as acquisitive. They joke about Sophie's aunt, asking whether she lives in a villa, and about her uncle, demanding to know if he owns a castle. On emerging from the sewage system into West Berlin, one of the youths exclaims: 'I love Fords', thereby embracing American-style consumerism from the moment he arrives. Even Sophie is seen to partake in the fashions and comforts of the west, especially in later years, when her sophistication is contrasted with the 'impoverishment' of Konrad's life in the east. In a memorable scene, shortly after her arrival in West Berlin, Sophie is pictured at a fashion show with the ruins of the church built in memory of the Emperor Wilhelm in the background. This places her on the Kurfursten-damm, West Berlin's most elegant shopping street, and allegorises the links between West German consumerism, West Berlin landmarks, the repression of Hitler's war, and even the First World War (Kaiser Wilhelm's war). More frequently, however, the film engages with questions of complicity, conformity, and opposition in the GDR, interrogating Konrad about the compromises he makes with the regime in order to pursue his career and personal happiness. The attention paid to Konrad in fact highlights the film's lack of balance in its almost exclusive focus on the East. *Das Versprechen* thus serves a dual purpose: education about East Germany, and condemnation of those in the GDR who failed to reform a corrupt communism. Significantly, perhaps, von Trotta's production was partially funded by the Ministry of the Interior of Helmut Kohl's conservative government – that is, a government that was against both the GDR and the dominance of the intellectual left in West German culture.

One of those who played a major role in the conceptualisation of *Das Versprechen* as co-writer was Peter Schneider, an established author and critic of West Germany's social and political conservatism since the 1960s. Schneider's novel *Der Mauerspringer* (*The Wall Jumper*, 1982) had attracted much attention for its vision of a shared German culture, and more particularly for its suggestion that the imagination might occupy the (literal) no-man's land between the ideological positions of the two states. The border zone of the Berlin Wall where Schneider's characters meet on their fantastical journeys from east to west and west to east creates a realm where the potential inherent in both Germanies – distorted by the Cold War – might be realised, if only in fiction. In 1990, however, Schneider was forced to concede that even this might be too much to ask. In a collection of essays published in that year, the author outlines the need for those on the West German left (including himself) to recognise the folly of their identification with the aims and ideals of what they mistakenly saw as the 'real' GDR, that is, 'true' socialism, equality, and solidarity as opposed to the corruption of the leadership.

Schneider's participation as a writer in the making of *Das Versprechen* is reflected in the fact that its 'message' is conveyed in the dialogue and narrative progression. The participation of Margarethe von Trotta is perhaps more puzzling. Von Trotta's interest in recent German history had been apparent in almost all of her previous work, and she has often commented that she cannot imagine making a film that does not bear directly upon the situation in Germany. Likewise, her concern with the fate of liberal values, the humanist heritage of the Lutheran Church, and her anti-fascist and pro-peace agenda are as evident in *Das Versprechen* as in her previous work, as is her concentration upon the family as a microcosm of society. Yet, above all, von Trotta is a feminist film-maker, who has been concerned more with the oppression of women than with German division. She has been at the forefront of 'women's film' (an ambiguous but perhaps inevitable term) in West Germany since the emergence of the feminist movement in the early 1970s gave it its initial impetus. Women directors focused on abortion, patriarchy, and female identity, often favoured a documentary style, and engaged with issues of spectatorship (who is looking at whom, and the question of audience). A creator of more conventionally narrative cinema than other women directors, von Trotta soon established herself as a leading feminist film-maker in a country in which the existence of television stations interested in social themes and film subsidies had brought more women into film production than anywhere else in the world.

The fact that *Das Versprechen* does not focus on matters of particular relevance to women, in contrast to von Trotta's earlier films, may mirror the transformation of West Germany's film culture in the early 1990s. Once again, therefore, *Das Versprechen* reflects upon the historical circumstances of its own production. In the 1970s, various types of 'women's film' (as befits the ambiguity of the term) had emerged in response to the feminist movement and to the perception that women (who had previously made up the majority of audiences) were no longer going to the cinema. Hence, at the same time as innovative film-makers such as von Trotta, Helma Sanders-Brahms, and Helke Sander were exploring female identity in an avant-garde fashion in their films, male directors such as Rainer Werner Fassbinder and Alexander Kluge were responding to the demand for female autonomy by scripting women protagonists. Hollywood, more cynically, aimed to appeal directly to a potential female audience in movies such as Scorsese's *Alice Doesn't Live Here Anymore* (1974), in which a woman escapes male domination and begins a new life.

By the 1990s, however, the market for women's cinema had changed. A decline in interest in both 'highbrow' women's films and the Hollywood variant of the genre had coincided with the emergence of a 'post-feminist' sensibility. At the same time, German culture has undergone a 'normalisation' since 1989, that is, it has become more similar to the patterns in force across the western world. Unification, and the arrival of a new generation of writers, artists, and film-makers, has led to the substitution of the 'traditional' themes of West German culture – the national socialist past, German identity, and the divided nation – for the issues that dominate the 1990s in other western countries. In common with film culture elsewhere in Europe and America, German films, and especially those by female directors, have been examining the legacy of feminism, and redefining it in the context of a wider debate on gender and sexuality. Romantic comedies for 'thirty-somethings' have scored incredible successes in a way that would have been improbable only a few years earlier. Sönke Wortmann's *Der bewegte Mann* (*Maybe ... Maybe Not*, 1994) thus features a man, thrown out by his girlfriend after an affair, who finds refuge in the gay scene as a straight object of desire. Gender and sexuality confusion follow with comic alacrity until the woman takes him back, creating new ground rules for the relationship, reuniting men and women, and conceding her need for his love. This need for male affection is also central to Katja von Garnier's *Abgeschminkt!* (*Makin' Up!*, 1993), as the tomboy protagonist reconciles her desire for independence with her attraction for a partner who combines a 'fundamental' masculinity with a 'new man' attitude towards women.

In the context of these developments in German film, *Das Versprechen*, with its focus on history and the theme of national identity, seems to belong to a pre-1989 cultural paradigm. Von Trotta avoids the issue of gender relations almost entirely, perhaps in acknowledgement of changed market conditions, perhaps because it is not central to her theme of divided Germany. Yet another aspect of the film's production reveals a rather more astute understanding of the transformation of the film scene. *Das Versprechen* is a German–French–Swiss co-production filmed in the Berlin Babelsberg studios (ironically the former home of the East German DEFA film company). This internationalisation reflects the increasing trend towards co-operation between European television stations with a more 'art-house' and less obviously commercial remit, such as Channel Four Films, or Canal Plus, with European financial assistance. This has raised questions about the extent to which films made in Europe can still be divided into 'national cinemas', even as it has enabled European directors to compete with Hollywood. The scale of *Das Versprechen*, as well as the conventionality of its cinematography and plot (a standard, perhaps even trivial love story), may imply a new confidence in European film's ability to survive alongside its American rivals.

Das Versprechen discloses its debt to America not only in its wholesale adoption of Hollywood film techniques (such as the fact that at key moments the camera imitates the conventional Hollywood romantic two-shot), but also in its recognition of the centrality of the United States to European culture, particularly in West Germany. The 'Americanisation' of the western part of the country is integrated into the film's theme of the divided nation. Sophie's son Alexander lives with his mother in West Berlin, separated from his father Konrad by the Wall. He is thoroughly 'American', and is typically seen wearing a baseball cap turned backwards on his head along with a bomber jacket. He emerges as sophisticated and cosmopolitan, especially in contrast with his half-sister, who lives with their father in East Berlin. The theme of national identity, or its absence, is implied by Alexander's appearance and attitudes. The fact that he is indistinguishable from American youths of his age suggests the saturation of West German identity by American popular culture.

West German society is criticised for its materialism, consumerism, and superficiality, traits that are believed to have derived from the wholesale adoption of American values. On its few excursions to West Berlin, the film is determined to insinuate the social disintegration, anomie, and inequality typically associated with American-style capitalism. When Konrad visits Alexander in West Berlin, for example, the symptoms of urban decay are obvious. They walk past youths stripping down an abandoned car, and Alexander appears unsurprised by what is clearly an everyday occurrence in his district. Konrad's brother-in-law Harald is later expelled from the GDR by the authorities (a favoured means of exporting 'awkward characters') and deposited in the Zoologischer Garten railway station, a West Berlin location in which drug-pushers, beggars, and prostitutes infamously gather. Harald is overwhelmed by the depravity of the west and effectively commits suicide by attempting to recross the border illegally. His bewildered reaction highlights the relative absence of 'western' social ills in East Germany, partly as a consequence of generous welfare provision (concealing problems such as structural unemployment and homelessness through subsidies), and partly resulting from the authorities' ruthlessness in stamping out criminality.

To a large extent Sophie embodies the unease felt by the makers of *Das Versprechen*, and by the intellectual left in general, with regard to West Germany as a capitalist state within the economic, military, and political system of the west. Unlike her fellow escapees from the GDR, she never feels entirely at home in West Germany. She represents the intellectual conscience of the divided nation, made uncomfortable by the superficiality of the west, but shocked by the denial of freedom in the east. Her reluctance to celebrate the opening of the Wall suggests her disillusionment with the materialism that came to dominate the drive towards unification in 1989/1990 and her regret at the missed opportunities made manifest by the failure of East German socialism. This sense of rootlessness is expressed on a number of occasions during the film, most notably when Sophie responds to questions about her departure from the GDR with the revealing words: 'I left but I don't really know if I got anywhere', and later with distinctly lukewarm enthusiasm, in Prague in 1968, to an enquiry from a Czech friend as to whether she is from West Germany: 'I lived there'.

During her stay in Czechoslovakia in 1968, Sophie admits that she has never felt at home in the west. The Prague Spring, in fact, is given great prominence in the film, reflecting the profound impression it made upon intellectuals in both East and West Germany. The efforts of Alexander Dubcek's reformist government to liberalise Czech politics, to achieve a degree of independence from the Soviet Union, and to steer a 'third way' between capitalism and communism – summed up in the rallying call 'socialism with a human face' – generated immense sympathy amongst those West German intellectuals who disapproved of their own country's reliance on the United States, and who were disappointed by the GDR's failure to realise its utopian potential. Many East German intellectuals also watched developments in Prague with passionate interest, hoping that the example might spread to the GDR. For Sophie and Konrad, however, the Prague Spring is but a brief interlude, time snatched together on neutral territory in a place where they might both feel at home. The film's images of the arrival of Soviet tanks in the dead of night and of courageous, yet futile, Czech resistance possess an almost ritual quality. The rumble of the tanks' engines shatters window panes, protesters are beaten off by heavily armed Soviet troops, and western press photographs are used by the authorities to identify the 'culprits'. The fact that the film is able to offer no new images of Prague in 1968 may suggest the collective trauma of those intellectuals in east and west whose hopes were destroyed by the crushing of the Czech experiment. The failure of the Prague Spring remains a stumbling block in the psyche of the left that cannot be overcome nor revisioned in aesthetic terms other than those that have dominated since the events themselves.

The outcome of 1968 marked a turning point in the history of the GDR. In *Das Versprechen* East German troops are rumoured to be part of the Soviet force. Intellectuals in both parts of Germany were horrified by the apparent complicity of German infantry in the demolition of Czechoslovakia less than thirty years after Hitler's brutal conquest (in fact no GDR soldiers were directly involved in the Soviet invasion, but this was not clear at the time). For East Germans in particular, the failure of the Prague Spring made it painfully clear that reform was impossible in their own country. The choice was stark, therefore, between conformity and opposition. Yet this could never be an easy decision. Konrad's professor, mentor, and friend, signs the denunciation of the Prague Spring that is required of him by the East German authorities, thereby compromising his earlier commitment to improving the communist state from within. Individual history, the fact that he chose the GDR over what he saw as the resurgence of fascism in the West after 1945, means that Konrad's boss is emotionally linked with the GDR, despite its imperfections: 'I'm part of this fucked up country'. Biographical ties, idealism, and personal identification made it difficult for many East German intellectuals to cross over into direct opposition.

Notwithstanding the effort required to overcome previous identification with the founding ideals of the GDR, von Trotta's film interrogates its East German protagonists as to the motives for their continued conformity after the crushing of the Prague experiment in 1968. By implication it also asks whether West German intellectuals were naive in their refusal to abandon their utopian vision of the 'other GDR', that is, of the resistance offered by supposedly 'ordinary' East Germans to the state in their pursuit of 'true' socialism. In doing this, the film also addresses the key post-unification debate on the question of whether GDR socialism can be compared to national socialism. This is a vital issue. If East Germany and the Nazi state can be equated, then the failure to resist GDR totalitarianism constitutes a 'second guilt', a repeated dereliction of the moral imperative to oppose evil. As Konrad says to his professor: 'It's because of people like you that tanks decide'. East Germany, moreover, drew much of its legitimacy, and even its appeal, from the claim that it alone represented the anti-fascist tradition in German history. Many of the film's East German characters defend their state, and its occasional excesses, as the only alternative to West Germany, which is seen as the successor state to Hitler's Third Reich. Konrad's father, for example, initially justifies the building of the Berlin Wall as a necessary evil if the communist cause is to counter the threat posed by a 'fascist' West German state. Later in the film, Konrad's secret police chaperone, Müller, claims that he joined the security services because he was so incensed by Nazi barbarism as exposed in early East German didactic films.

Müller represents the distortion of the anti-fascist ideals that underpinned the founding of the GDR into the reality of intrusive state surveillance and social control. Yet the analogy between East Germany and the Hitler regime is most pointed at Konrad's trial for refusing to add his name to the condemnation of the Prague Spring already signed by his professor. His father is refused entry to the courtroom and comments bitterly that even under Hitler his own parents had been allowed to attend his hearing. The implicit analogy, suggested by a member of the founding generation of the GDR, a victim of fascism for whom the new state had initially represented the redemption of Germany's Nazi past, almost goes unnoticed by the official on duty: 'well, we no longer live in the … did you say "Nazi days?" ' The hesitation perhaps implies that the comparison is less scandalous than it might at first appear. The point is well made for an audience accustomed to self-recrimination for their national socialist past. Here is another legacy that must be confronted in an ongoing investigation of an apparent historical propensity for acquiescence and complicity.

Shortly after Konrad's trial, his father dies, a broken man, disaffected from the state he had helped to create, and urging his son to flee west to be with Sophie and the child that she had conceived in Prague. The fact that the possibility even exists for Konrad to attend a congress in Stockholm (where he plans to abscond with Sophie) raises questions, however, about the extent to which he has sacrificed the principled stand he took with regard to the Prague Spring, for the sake of personal gain. It is clear that he must have signed the denunciation of the Czech experiment required of him, or otherwise compromised with the state, in order to get permission to travel in the west, since this was a privilege reserved only for the most trusted servants of the regime. In many ways, Konrad's duplicity here merely confirms his ambivalent attitude towards the state from the very beginning. At the start of the film he stumbles whilst trying to tie his shoelaces and is left behind by Sophie and their friends who escape through the drainage system from East into West Berlin. He subsequently fastens them on the orders of the party official who interrogates him. Konrad's son Alexander unwittingly alludes to the 'shoelace motif' much later when standing with his father near the East Berlin manhole through which Sophie had escaped. Alexander jokes about escaping and kneels down to tie his father's laces.

Throughout the film, in fact, doubts are raised as to whether Konrad was ever committed to leaving the GDR. He accepts promotions, adjusts to the limited possibilities that are open to him in order to realise his scientific talent, and consistently gives in to the state's efforts to coerce him into conformity by threatening to deny Alexander permission to enter the country. Konrad's single act of rebellion when he strikes Müller has less to do with resistance to an oppressive regime than with his inability to contain any longer the frustration that has been accumulating within him for years. The uprising of 1989, embodied by Konrad's explosion of anger, is thus dismissed as a rather uncharacteristic – and belated – gesture of almost immature defiance by an otherwise passive GDR population. Konrad may be reading a book entitled *Das neue Denken* (*The New Thinking*), but he has insufficient presence of mind to grasp that a neighbour's cry that the wall has come down refers to the Berlin Wall.

Margarethe von Trotta's *Das Versprechen* responds to contemporary concerns on a number of levels. It belongs to a pre-1989 pattern in its final reckoning with the themes that traditionally dominated cultural practice in West Germany – national socialism, German identity, and national division – but which, since unification, have gradually given way to the issues of sexuality and personal identity that have shaped the postmodern 1990s throughout the western world. In its recognition of the internationalisation of European film-making, however, it also embodies the transformation of the film market. More specifically, *Das Versprechen* addresses the debates that have been raging in the new Germany about the nation's most recent past. It alludes to the questions of whether GDR socialism can be equated with Hitler's Germany, whether left-wing intellectuals in the west were naive to cling on to their idealistic assessment of the GDR's ability to realise its potential, and whether ordinary East German citizens were complicit for too long in tolerating an oppressive state. The film implies that there is always a choice, and that the majority of people decide for personal security rather than moral integrity.

In an intentional echo of the controversy surrounding court cases brought against former GDR border guards who had carried out the state's shoot-to-kill policy, Konrad is shown early in the film practising bayoneting techniques in preparation for his own service at the Berlin Wall. Another soldier refuses to countenance the murder of fellow citizens desiring to escape and is dismissed. Konrad, on the other hand, continues with his training, perhaps hesitantly, but none the less certain this is the only way to achieve his ambitions of university education and a career as a scientist. Unlike his sister, whose activities as a protestant pastor bring her into constant conflict with the state (and with the Church authorities, who were keen not to antagonise a regime that tolerated religion only with the greatest reluctance), Konrad remains in the country not because of any idealistic notion of transforming socialism, but because he is comfortable there. Ultimately, he is 'at home'. We may imagine that he, unlike his sister, will prosper in the new Germany. The church groups, grassroots political organisations, and various pressure groups that had fought so courageously against their own hierarchies and the state to bring about the amelioration of the GDR, disappeared after 1989, rendered insignificant by the numbers of people favouring affluence over meaningful political change. The determination of Konrad's sister to make a difference in East Germany is mocked by the masses crossing the bridge to the west. For the overwhelming majority the consumerist paradise on earth proved to be preferable to the heavenly promise that the protestant pastor, along with fellow intellectuals in east and west, had hoped the GDR might help to realise.

References and Suggestions for Further Reading

Knight, Julia 1992: *Women and the New German Cinema*. London: Verso.

Elsaesser, Thomas 1987: 'Public Bodies and Divided Selves: German Women Film-makers in the 80s'. In *Monthly Film Bulletin*, December.

Elsaesser, Thomas 1988: 'A Retrospect on the New German Cinema'. In *German Life and Letters*, 41, 3.

Elsaesser, Thomas 1989: *New German Cinema: A History*. London: Macmillan.

Fulbrook, Mary 1991: *Germany: The Divided Nation*. London: Fontana.
Fulbrook, Mary 1995: *Anatomy of a Dictatorship: Inside the GDR, 1949–89*. Oxford: Oxford University Press.
Sandford, John 1980: *The New German Cinema*. New York: Da Capo.
Schneider, Peter 1992: *The German Comedy: Scenes of Life after the Wall*. London: I. B. Tauris.

Credits

Director	Margarethe von Trotta
Producer	Eberhard Kunkersdorf
Production Company	Bioskop-Film, Munich; Odessa Films; J. M. H. Productions, Lausanne; Westdeutscher Rundfunk; Babelsberg Studios; Canal Plus; Centre National de la Cinématographie; Fonds Eurimages du Conseil de l'Europe; Bundesministerium des Innern
Scenario	Margarethe von Trotta, Peter Schneider
Editor	Suzanne Baron
Director of Photography	Franz Rath
Art Director	Martin Dostal
Music	Jürgen Knieper

Cast

Meret Becker	Sophie 1
Corinna Harfouch	Sophie 2
Anian Zollner	Konrad 1
August Zirner	Konrad 2
Susann Ugé	Barbara 1
Eva Mattes	Barbara 2
Pierre Besson	Harald 1
Hans Kremer	Harald 2
Christian Herschmann	Alexander 1
Jörg Meister	Alexander 2
Otto Sander	Lorenz
Udo Kroschwald	Müller 1
Hask Bohm	Müller 2
Tina Engel	Sophie's aunt
Jean-Yves	Gaultier Gérard
Dieter Mann	Konrad's father
Ulrike Krumbiegel	Elisabeth

Filmography

Das zweite Erwachen des Christa Klages (*The Second Awakening of Christa Klages*, 1977)
Schwestern oder Die Balance des Glücks (*Sisters or The Balance of Happiness*, 1979)

Die bleierne Zeit (*The German Sisters*, 1981)
Heller Wahn (*Friends and Husbands*, 1982)
Rosa Luxemburg (1981)
Drei Schwestern (*Three Sisters*, 1988)
Rückkehr (*Africana / Return*, 1990)
Il lungo Silenzio (*The Long Silence*, 1993)
Die Frauen in der Rosenstrasse (1994)
Mit 50 Küssen Manner Anders (1998)

10 *La haine*
Vinz (Vincent Cassel), Saïd (Saïd Taghmaoui), and Hubert (Hubert Koundé) try to get into Astérix's flat.

La haine

Jill Forbes

Since its initial screening at the Cannes Film festival in 1995 where it was awarded the director's prize, *La haine* has become a cult movie inside and outside France, attracting large audiences and generating websites and electronic discussion groups – a success which is based on its ability to appeal to widely different audiences. Its subject-matter is parochial, but it addresses all those who live in large, cosmopolitan conurbations; it appeals to generational solidarity beyond distinctions of race, gender or nationality; it refers to the traditions of French cinema and culture and depicts a social context which is French, but its citation of American filmic and musical material gives it an international dimension. It is a highly wrought and meticulously planned work of art, but it looks like a television current affairs or documentary programme. Like Godard's *A bout de souffle* or Blier's *Les valseuses*, *La haine* is a *zeitgeist* film which sums up the mood and preoccupations of a particular time and place, but in a way that is internationally appealing.

The film depicts twenty-four hours in the life of three unemployed young men, Vinz, Saïd and Hubert – a Jew, a Beur (child of North African immigrants) and a Black – who live on a housing estate called the Cité des Muguets (lilies of the valley) and who hang out together. It is distantly inspired by events in April 1993 when the seventeen-year-old Makomé (Mako) M'Bowole from Zaire died in custody, allegedly as a result of police brutality. In *La haine* the fictional Abdel Ichaha is in a coma in hospital because of a police blunder (*bavure*) and the inhabitants of the Cité have protested by rioting, causing a great deal of damage to property and totally destroying the gym where Hubert used to train.

La haine is divided into segments, each representing roughly two hours, by digital time-checks flashed onto a black screen. These are accompanied by a ticking sound, as though the film were a countdown to an explosion, which builds up dramatic tension and creates a powerful teleological movement. As in so much French newspaper and television reporting of 'les quartiers chauds' (problem districts), the Cité is presented as a powder keg made up of a lethal mixture of drugs, unemployment, racism and police brutality. At the beginning of the film we see the image of a Molotov cocktail hurled at a globe and breaking into flames, prefiguring the lethal outburst of violence at the end. The image is given an allegorical dimension by a parable, heard first in voice-over at the beginning, and repeated twice, about a man who jumps from a fifty-storey block of flats and who, as he falls, repeats to himself 'so far so good', with the punchline 'what's

171

important isn't the fall but the landing'. What propels *La haine* is the irony and creative tension which derive from this contrast between the film's structural purposefulness and the aimlessness of the protagonists' lives, between the inevitability of the explosion of violence and the friends' essential innocence and naivety.

The unemployment, racial tension and rioting in several large cities, which contributed to the rise of the extreme-right National Front in France in the 1980s, provide the film's social backdrop. Under electoral and media pressure from the Front, the right-wing government of the late 1980s tried to enact new nationality laws which particularly targeted Beurs like Saïd and required them to 'prove' that they were worthy of being French. This gave rise to a national debate about citizenship, integration and multiculturalism which set the French tradition of 'universalism' (whereby immigrants are seamlessly incorporated into the national community through an education system which does not recognise ethnic, religious or racial diversity) against a 'multiculturalist' tradition, seen as originating in America. The three protagonists were all born and brought up in France but because they all belong to minority religious or ethnic groups, it would be customary to refer to them as 'immigrés' even though they are not technically 'immigrants' at all. Though they reject the cultures associated with their families – Vinz's grandmother complains about him not attending synagogue – they have not been integrated into the national community in a way that community accepts. Their language is 'verlan', a kind of backslang that has become the fashionable dialect of young people, rather than the standard French heard on the television, and their values are those of homosocial, cross-race, generational solidarity. Whatever the public rhetoric about universal values, these young men are excluded from the national community by unemployment and poverty and by their geographical relegation to a housing development outside the narrowly defined boundaries of central Paris.

La haine seizes brilliantly on a metaphor which is a commonplace in French novels and films about the city, and re-interprets it for the 1990s. From the nineteenth century onwards many writers, such as Baudelaire whose blown-up image adorns a wall of the Cité, embroidered on the distinction beween Paris and the surrounding area, known as the 'zone', which was supposedly populated by gangs of criminals and prostitutes, and was richly invested with imaginative possibilities. One was that the bourgeois inhabitants of Paris could visit the outlying areas as tourists in search of visual or sexual thrills; another was that the denizens of the outlying districts, the 'zonards', might invade the city and cause havoc of one kind or another. This notion was exploited by many of the French reviewers of the film who described how hordes of young people from 'la banlieue' were swarming into Paris to see themselves represented on screen. Axiomatic to this convention was the idea that the rules and codes of conduct of one area did not apply and, indeed, were often inverted in the other, just as the 'verlan' used in the Cité inverts standard French; and this can be seen in the films of Marcel Carné or Jacques Becker which are the distant ancestors of *La haine*. *La haine* uses the relationship of inversion between the city and its outlying districts as a structuring trope and combines literary and filmic convention with contemporary social discourse that is itself influenced by such clichés. The latter are evident in the gallery owner's comment on the friends' behaviour as the 'malaise des banlieues' ('housing estate' sickness) as well as in the stream of slogans and proverbs the friends cite, with some irony, to pass the time before they can go home. In this way, the friends' trip into Paris and their adventures in the city, which occupy most of the second half of the film, combine social comment on the difference between the values of the *banlieue* and those of the metropolis, a critique of the exclusion of one group from the centre of culture and civilisation, a critique of that civilisation, and a calculated evocation of artistic conventions which are based on the distinction between Paris and the zone. *La haine* succeeds in espousing the values of the outlying districts, keeping the viewer's sympathies firmly with the three friends, even when they are shown behaving badly, whilst at the same time transforming their adventures into spectacle and entertainment for bourgeois consumption by the use of recognisable conventions of French literature and cinema.

The credit sequences are a telescopic montage of most of the themes and techniques in the film. We see a Molotov cocktail thrown onto a blue globe which explodes in flames that change from colour to black and white, marking a transition from the high-gloss world of the advertising hoarding where the globe originates (as we discover later in the film), to the gritty reality of documentary film-making. A man in overalls with his back to the camera shouts to a distant line of armed police that the workers' only weapon is stones. Shots of CRS riot police fitting metal screens over the windows of their vehicles alternate with footage of demonstrators in central Paris. We then see the police lined up in riot gear, confronting young people dancing in the streets. Gradually the images of confrontation become more violent: the police fire tear-gas grenades and flares; the demonstrators overturn and set fire to a car, break the windows of shops, hurl stones at the CRS. Finally we see the neon sign of a shopping centre illuminated by a conflagration. The Bob Marley song *Burnin' and Lootin'* is dubbed over these images, replacing the original soundtracks attached to the footage, and it is not until the end of the sequence that sound and image finally coincide when we see glass being broken and hear it as well. As the song ceases, a female newsreader's voice reports the riots in the Cité and we cut to her face on the TV screen. We realise that this montage is a brief history of urban protest which has taken us from the relatively peaceful student demonstrations of May 1968, through the hippy street parties of the early 1970s, to the gradual importing into France of race hatred and police brutality – it is implied, from America. One poster reads 'Don't forget the police kill'; another 'Remember Mako'. The sounds of violence and what the Marley song calls 'the music of the ghetto' come together to underline and problematise the coincidence of art and reality.

The use of the newsreader is an economical way of informing the viewer about what is happening and it also introduces a major theme of the film, which is the power of the media. The friends depend on television to know what is going on in their community, and hope to see themselves 'making the news'. Vinz tries to watch the news when in Darty's store, as does Hubert when he calls in at home, and it is while they are sprawled in front of a giant, silent TV screen, waiting for the first train to take them home, that they learn from a newsflash that Abdel has died. But in the Cité communications are distinctly low-tech, the televisions don't work properly and when Saïd wants to get in touch with Vinz he shouts up to an open window. In Paris, on the other hand, Astérix's flat is entered via a high-tech intercom and video screen and all the hoardings and screens in the metropolis convey their messages with smooth efficiency, exacerbating the sense that the Cité is dispossessed. The film criticises the patronising approach of much television reporting of 'la banlieue' and the way television seeks to sensationalise confrontations between the police and young people. Thus the friends accuse a TV crew, who are too frightened or too lazy to get out of their van, of treating them like animals in the safari park at Thoiry, dangerous beasts to be looked at from the safety of a car. At the same time, they long to see themselves on television because it is a form of legitimation, a confirmation that they exist for the world outside.

In this society it appears that people are constantly being filmed. This can be for security reasons (Astérix's flat), for comic effect (Saïd's brother's virtually incomprehensible story about the candid camera), or because of an almost prurient curiosity about how the other half live (the TV crew). At various points the film asks who owns images, how images relate to reality, and how they take on symbolic significance. Vinz mimics Travis Bickle, the hero of Scorsese's *Taxi Driver*, leading the audience to wonder if he will adopt Bickle's gun-crazy persona. Hubert's image as a boxer appears on a poster for a match, perhaps recalling that of De Niro in Scorsese's *Raging Bull*, but its implied violence is at odds with Hubert's reflective, sober and essentially non-violent character. Abdel, who is, ironically, the only member of the community to achieve the legitimation of television, has ceased to be real and has become an image on countless TV screens and a symbol of police brutality.

In general in the film, the media transform reality into theatrical spectacle. They dramatise events such as the riots, or the loss of the policeman's gun, which turns into a suspense narrative that requires a tragic dénouement. Theatricality is emphasised by the three-part structure of the film, which might be thought to emulate the protasis, epitasis and catastrophe of Greek or Racinian tragedy. Television transforms the Cité into an entertainment in which people do not act naturally but perform predetermined roles which inevitably lead to a final, tragic shoot-out.

Against this we are given glimpses of more spontaneous or authentic creativity in the apparently irrelevant story told by Grunwalski in the toilet, or the various forms of expressive activity open to the friends. Vinz is an actor and dancer, or would like to be; Hubert is a sportsman; Saïd is an artist who embodies the anarchic spirit of the Situationists by spraying graffiti on a police van or altering the message on a billboard. By leaving his mark in this way and changing the slogan from 'the world is yours' to 'the world is ours', Saïd is momentarily able to repossess the public sphere which is otherwise regulated by strenuous but pointless efforts to dominate the people by physical or ideological means.

An immediately striking aspect of *La haine* is the very minor role women play in the film. The central characters are male, the police are almost all male, the children hanging around the estate are male and almost all the people encountered in Paris are men. Women are referred to with a combination of exaggerated respect and contempt, and put in only brief appearances as sisters, mothers and grandmothers. Hubert, Vinz and Saïd discuss women so as to valorise their masculinity, but in practice they are bossed around and often intimidated by their female relations in a manner which underlines their disempowerment. Vinz, for example, is verbally abused by his sister, and is scared of his grandmother's reaction when he brings red peppers rather than green ones back from the shop. Likewise Hubert's mother asserts her dominance of the domestic space by chasing him from the kitchen. On their rare appearances outside the home, young women, in pairs or in groups, are not impressed or intimidated by the boys' aggressiveness. Saïd is teased by his sister and her friends as he tries to police her sexuality, while his attempt to chat up two girls in the art gallery in Paris falls extremely flat since they had expected an intellectual rather than a sexual approach.

The virtual elimination of women from the action emphasises the fact that space in the Cité des Muguets is divided on gender lines. The exterior belongs to the men, who compete to dominate the available space: the roof where the barbecue takes place is a prized vantage point which the young men, the security guards and the plainclothes police all fight to control with a degree of primitive territoriality; the walkways and piazzas are places where Vinz, Hub, Saïd and their contemporaries wander freely, as do the male children. The interiors are dominated by women, who are shown in the stereotypically female pursuits of cooking and sewing. The women uphold traditional moral, educational and social practices reflected in child-rearing (Hubert's mother is pregnant), domestic labour, and religion (Vinz's grandmother's attachment to synagogue), which are all the domain of the females on this estate.

Spatial relations are initially disrupted by the riot. Saïd puzzles over how a car managed to get inside the gym, transforming the interior into an exterior. Surreal moments, such as Vinz's vision of a cow, or the literal flight of fancy over the rooftops which is apparently induced by a sound-mix of rap and Edith Piaf, turn into acute disorientation when the trio arrive in Paris. Their sense of dislocation on arrival is underscored, for the audience, by a shot that combines a dolly-in and a zoom out, flattening the perspective and distorting the relationship of the planes of the image. Such spatial *dépaysement* is echoed in the polite behaviour of the Paris policeman who, to Saïd's astonishment, treats him respectfully.

In Paris the friends find that they cannot map gender onto space as they can, for the most part, in the Cité. The simple and easily understood spatial relations in the first part of the film gradually turn into a metaphor for exclusion as the friends attempt to enter various spaces and find either that their presence is not acceptable, or that the space is not decipherable, or that the spaces become prisons of one kind or another. The Astérix episode is a case in point. 'Astérix' is an ironically assumed French identity (Astérix the Gaul); he does not own the apartment, he has borrowed it; his gestures and body language are aggressive not because he is male but because he is on drugs, and his sexual preferences are ambiguous since it is implied that he is attracted to Saïd. The loin cloth he is wearing also contributes to the uncertainty about whether this space is inside (female) or outside (male). One of the girls in the gallery is a Beur but she has more in common with the gallery owner than with Saïd; another is sporting an extravagant decolleté which, like Astérix's clothes, creates confusion about interior and exterior space and which Saïd misreads as an invitation to seduction. This confusion is compounded by the gallery owner, who is not only precious in speech and manner but also sides with the girls instead of with Vinz, Hub and Saïd, as male solidarity ought to have dictated. Other spaces are equally difficult to decode. The shopping mall is half interior and half exterior (unlike the shop on the estate in which Vinz does not feel at home and which the queue of women codes as interior); the hospital is an interior which the friends cannot penetrate, while the police station is an interior that they enter literally at their peril. Sometimes only violence will force a way inside, as when Vinz sees, or imagines he sees, a Black trying to shoot his way into a nightclub. The culmination of this confusion is the way Paris itself becomes a prison. By deliberately holding Hub and Saïd too long in custody the police make the friends miss the last train home, with the result, as Said puts it in another graphic inversion, that they are 'enfermés dehors' ('locked in outside').

   Just as the music is a montage of reggae and French rap, so the cast of characters in *La haine* provides a *métissage*, or mixing, which derives from a complex set of references to both French and American film traditions. The threesome is a dramatic device used in films as various as Truffaut's *Jules et Jim* (1961), Blier's *Les valseuses* (*Making It*, 1974) and in the more farcical *Tenue de soirée* (*Evening Dress*, 1986) or Balasko's *Gazon maudit* (*French Twist*, 1995) to explore heterosexual rivalry and homosocial attraction. *La haine* differs from such films in having no 'love interest', but it shares this characteristic with many French films of the 1990s which centre on friendships among young people, women as well as men, but are not based on the heterosexual romance which was the staple of New Wave films about young people in the late 1950s and early 1960s or the homosexual version that became popular in the 1970s and 1980s. The French vogue for films about men can be traced back to the 1970s, but the friendship and solidarity that links Vinz, Hubert and Saïd is more directly reminiscent of American buddy movies and gangster films.

   In some respects, therefore, *La haine* appears to have an answer to French intellectuals such as Pierre Bourdieu or Alain Finkielkraut who denounce multiculturalism as a form of American imperialism, appearing to consider it an attempt to dilute the principles on which French republicanism is based. The giant TV screen which announces that Abdel has died defaults to an image of the old France associated with the traditional 'blue, white, red' tricolour and the slogan 'liberté, égalité, fraternité'. It is a motto Vinz, Hub and Saïd quote ironically when hanging out in the shopping mall, and their trio is clearly meant to exemplify a 'new tricolour' of 'black, blanc, beur' – one that was on display in France's victorious 1998 World Cup team – an ideal *métissage* which might be France's response to the multicultural challenge.

On the other hand, the film also shows that young people – or at least young people from this social background – are profoundly influenced by American culture, even in details such as how they cut their hair. The police gun Vinz acquires is compared to the gun in Donner's *Lethal Weapon* (1987) while the final Mexican stand-off parodies Tarantino's *Reservoir Dogs* (1992) which, itself, parodies shoot-outs in innumerable gangster films and westerns. In interviews about the film the director has stated that in Brian de Palma's *Scarface*, Al Pacino as the 'guy who comes from the ghetto, is stuffed full of drugs, and who dies a violent death but only after he has reached the top' (Rémy, 23) serves as a powerful role model. Indeed, the billboard slogan 'the world is yours', altered by Saïd to 'ours', is a quotation from *Scarface*. According to Kassovitz, *Scarface* is one of the few films people like those in the Cité des Muguets will have seen, and they believe it depicts reality in the United States. Tales of American gangsters are as compelling, and have the same degree of reality, as other narratives, like Hubert's story about the man falling from a block of flats, or Saïd's brother's tale about the candid camera. More worryingly, perhaps, the specifically European shaggy dog story about deportation told by the elderly Jew encountered in the public lavatories in Paris, whom Kassovitz said he modelled on his own grandfather, is seen as 'pointless'.

But above all, *La haine* is influenced by Martin Scorsese. Vincent Cassel's febrile performance and obsession with guns inevitably recalls Robert de Niro as Johnny Boy in *Mean Streets*, while De Niro/Travis Bickle's solipsistic 'Are you talking to me?' routine enacted in front of a mirror in *Taxi Driver* is mimicked by Vinz. Scorsese's semi-indulgent, semi-critical attitude towards the Italian immigrant community and his invention of autobiographical personae for De Niro are echoed in Vinz's attitude towards his immigrant background and the way in which Vinz, actor and Jew, is cast as a representation of Kassovitz (who himself plays the skinhead). Indeed, Kassovitz has said that *Mean Streets* is the film he would most like to have made. As influential as the detail of characters and settings, is Scorsese's aesthetic – the brilliance with which he combines the realistic and the poetic, the rational and the irrational, the everyday and the fantastic, not least in the soundtracks of his films which are extraordinary montages of music, dialogue and street noises. Like Scorsese, Kassovitz contrives to achieve a synthesis of traditions of urban film-making so as to combine the documentary/realist representations familiar from television with the poetic representations of the city in French films from the 1930s onwards. Thus the gag about turning off the lights on the Eiffel Tower is lifted, inter alia, from Eric Rochant's *Un monde sans pitié* (1989). But one of the most powerful intertexts, perhaps, is Marcel Carné's *Le jour se lève* (1939) with which *La haine* shares a 24-hour time frame, opened and closed by an explosion or gunshot, a setting in the outlying districts of the city, and a powerful tragic teleology. And just as its star, Jean Gabin, served as the symbol of the French working man in the 1930s, so Vinz, Hubert and Saïd collectively embody the dispossessed of the 1990s.

La haine rapidly became a media phenomenon in a way that might appear ironic for a film which criticises the media's tendency to turn any spectacle, however gruesome or violent, into entertainment. Its success depended on extremely skilful marketing and its release was accompanied by various tie-ins. For the bourgeois audience there was an exhibition of production photographs and an accompanying book by Gilles Favier and Mathieu Kassovitz entitled *Jusqu'ici tout va bien* (so far so good). For the younger audience there was a CD of the soundtrack which combined reggae performers like Marley with rap music from French bands like NTM. For film buffs there was a video edition of the 'director's cut', about thirty minutes longer than the version released on screen. And when it was released in the United States, the subtitles deliberately drew comparisons with race violence in America, referring, for example, to 'Rodney King'. In this way, Kassovitz ensured that a film about the difficulty of crossing boundaries owed its success to its ability to cross such national and generational divisions.

However, in France there was another dimension to its success. By forgoing the romantic plot and the attractive young actresses, like Emmanuelle Béart, Julie Delpy or Sophie Marceau, who are usually central to the international sales of French films, and by deliberately making its actors appear ugly – even Vincent Cassel, who plays the romantic lead in other films such as Mimouni's *L'Appartement* (1996) – the film gained credibility as a slice of life and as a warning shot, a 'pavé dans la mare' (hence the image of the exploding Molotov cocktail). Kassovitz's criticism of police brutality is serious, especially when it is set alongside the relative triviality of the friends' misdemeanours. It is true that they try to steal a car, but it turns out that none of them knows how to drive. It is true that they steal a credit card but they cannnot find a taxi driver who will let them use it to take them back home. *La haine* takes a strongly opposing view to Bertrand Tavernier's contemporaneous *L 627* (1992) which attempted to depict the police as heroes in the struggle against drug-related, immigrant-perpetrated crime. By slightly modifying the opening parable from 'it's the story of a man' to 'it's the story of a society', the lines with which the film closes, and by ending the film with the sound of an explosion over a black screen as Saïd shuts his eyes in terrified anticipation, Kassovitz appears to wish his film to convey the message that a generation of essentially decent young people is being forced into violent and murderous action by a society that is unwilling or unable to acknowledge their predicament. In this way he seems to suggest that the role models offered by American cinema, in the characters played by actors such as Al Pacino, Robert de Niro or Spike Lee, are likely to move out of the realm of art and enter that of real life.

Reference

Rémy, Vincent 1995: 'Entretien avec Mathieu Kassovitz'. In *Télérama*, 31 May, 19–24.

Suggestions for Further Reading

Alexander, Karen 1995: 'La haine'. In *Vertigo*, Autumn/Winter, 45–46.

Bourguignon, Thomas and Tobin, Yann 1995: 'Entretien avec Mathieu Kassovitz'. In *Positif*, 412, 8–13. Translated in Ciment, Michel and Herpe, Noël 1999: *Projections 9: French Film-makers on Film-making*. London: Faber, 183–93.

Chambers, Ross 1999: 'Interesting Circumstances: Queerness, Cruising and the Parasocial (Thoughts on and around Kassovitz's *La haine*)'. Unpublished article.

Darke, Chris 1995: '*La haine*'. In *Sight and Sound*, November, 221.

Favier, Gilles and Kassovitz, Mathieu 1995: *Jusqu'ici tout va bien: Scénario et photographies autour du film* 'La haine'. Arles: Actes Sud.

Rémy, Vincent 1995: 'Entretien avec Mathieu Kassovitz'. In *Télérama*, 31 May, 19–24.

Trémois, Claude-Marie 1997: *Les Enfants de la liberté*. Paris: Éditions du Seuil.

Credits

Director	Mathieu Kassovitz
Producer	Christophe Rossignon
Production Company	Les Productions Lazennec
Screenplay	Mathieu Kassovitz
Director of Photography	Pierre Aim
Editors	Mathieu Kassovitz Scott Stevenson
Art Director	Giuseppe Ponturo
Music	Bob Marley, Tony Joe White, Roger Troutman, Expression Direkt, Cut Killer, Etan Massuri, Solo, The Beastie Boys and others.

Cast

Vincent Cassel	Vinz
Hubert Koundé	Hubert
Saïd Taghmaoui	Saïd
François Levantal	Astérix
Peter Kassovitz	Gallery Patron
Vincent Lindon	Drunk Man
Mathieu Kassovitz	Skinhead

Filmography

Cauchemar blanc (1991)
Assassins (1992)
Métisse (*Café au lait*/*Blended*, 1993)
La haine (*Hate*, 1995)
Assassin(s) (1997)

11   Trainspotting

'Hollywood come in please. . . your time is up'. *Trainspotting* at odds with Scottish heritage.

Trainspotting

Sarah Street

Trainspotting was released in New York in July 1996, ten months after its UK première. It took $262,000 on its opening weekend and continued to attract audiences, earning $12 million at the US box office after eight weeks. By Hollywood standards this is not a large sum – in seven weeks Roland Emmerich's *Independence Day* (1996) grossed $285 million – but *Trainspotting*'s career abroad exceeded expectations, it 'travelled' well, receiving excellent reviews and high-profile publicity in Europe and the USA. As a low-budget, parochial film which certainly did not exemplify the conventional virtues and values of Britain, utilising broad Scottish accents (some dubbing was necessary for American release) and dealing with risqué subject-matter, it would, at first sight, appear to be destined for short theatrical domestic release followed by a video career. John Hill has argued that:

> [T]he most interesting type of British cinema, and the one which is most worthy of support, differs from the type which is often hoped for – a British cinema capable of competing with Hollywood and exemplifying the virtues and values of Britain. A different conception of British cinema recognises that its economic ambitions will have to be more modest. However, its cultural ambitions can, and should, be correspondingly more ambitious: the provision of diverse and challenging representations adequate to the complexities of contemporary Britain.   (Hill, 18–19)

This chapter will consider *Trainspotting* as an example of the sort of cinema John Hill would like to be considered as 'British' and discuss the reasons for its success at home *and* abroad. It will argue that the film is representative of contemporary hybrid forms associated with generic fluidity and cinematic 'flow' which are conducive to exportation while at the same time retaining an acute sense of national identity.

Registered as British, *Trainspotting* falls into the category of British films that seek to challenge dominant notions of 'Britishness'. As Hill points out, this does not disqualify them from being British, it simply locates them within a dissident, but significant, tradition. By this I am referring to 'oppositional' films such as those directed by Derek Jarman which, as I have argued elsewhere (Street, 181–4), subvert the iconography of 'Britishness', such as can be seen, for example, in archive film of the Second World War, by placing it in a more

contemporary context. Similarly, one of *Trainspotting*'s most recurrent strategies is to take a particular image or idea, and subvert it by suggesting an
alternative scenario by visual or aural counterpoint. This technique originates
in the theories and practice of classic Soviet montage and is assisted by the
film's energetic pace, verve and wit. It is this quality, combined with the particular subject-matter, which renders *Trainspotting* both British *and* exportable,
for it operates within a tradition of British films which appeal to European and
American audiences.

Indeed, *Trainspotting* is a film which contains a sense of national specificity
'without being either nationalist or attached to homogenising myths of
national identity' (Hill, 16). In an interview, the producer Andrew MacDonald
argued that although it is set primarily in Scotland it is nevertheless 'British' in
the sense that it appeals south of the border with its context of life in the
Thatcherite 1980s: 'We set out to create a world that could be anywhere –
pubs, estates and dole offices' (*Premiere*, 61). The film could well have been set
in any major British city and the drug culture it describes transcends national
boundaries. The film contains observations about being Scottish in the 'United'
Kingdom, or, as Renton puts it, living as 'the lowest of the low' in a 'colonised'
country; but, as will be suggested below, the film's strategy of counterpoint
and refusal to conform to generic fixity works to broaden rather than limit its
address.

One compelling aspect of the film is its narrative and the degree to which it
breaks with conventional closure. Will Self's review of *Trainspotting* criticises the
film for adopting a linear narrative which, he argues, is littered with incidents
that lose their pathos by selling-out to neat comic pay-offs (the examples he
gives are the 'worst toilet in Scotland' incident when Renton dives down the
toilet to recover opium suppositories which he has evacuated, and Tommy's
funeral). On first examination the narrative would indeed appear to be linear
– it introduces us to Renton and his friends; charts Renton's attempts to get
'clean'; the subsequent resumption of his heroin habit, court appearance and
overdose; his resolution to 'find something new' after seeing Tommy in a state
of HIV-infected degradation; his move to London; Tommy's funeral and
Renton's involvement in a lucrative drugs deal with Sick Boy, Begbie and
Spud which takes them back to London; and Renton making off with the
money at the end. Yet the narrative works in a more complicated way than
this brief outline would suggest, and as a more detailed analysis shows, contains
room for ambiguity and a refusal of closure on several occasions.

This strategy is signalled from the arresting opening sequence of the film,
when the main characters run down a street, being chased by police. The
opening serves as a signal for the film's style and content: we are simultaneously being introduced to the characters, prepared for a later story event and
at the same time exposed to the film's major technique of counterpoint
between and within the visual and aural. The visual style is of stasis and dis-
ruption: the first shot is a low camera angle showing shoppers walking slowly,

viewed from behind. Renton runs into the frame with the camera in the same position and the next series of shots alternate between medium and long shots of Renton and Spud from the front. The sequence follows their dash through the crowds until Renton's path is halted by a car coming around a corner, when he tumbles across its bonnet as it halts to avoid hitting him. This gives time for a brief pause as Renton looks directly at the camera and his introductory caption appears in freeze-frame: 'Renton'. Far from being a strictly linear opening, this comes from the middle rather than the beginning of Renton's story. We see the same shot of him on the car bonnet later on in the film, just before the courtroom scene and his overdose. While we are seeing this fast-paced, urgent sequence we also hear Renton's voice-over: 'Choose life, choose a job, choose a career, choose a family, choose a fucking big television, choose washing machines, cars, compact disc players and electrical tin openers.' The soundtrack plays 'Lust for Life' (Iggy Pop), creating a pulsating beat which matches the images and establishes a contrast with Renton's sardonic, ironic listing of consumer purchases that are supposed to be essential for modern living.

The rest of this opening sequence is divided between two locations – Renton's room where he has just 'shot up' heroin, and the introduction of his friends on a football pitch. As with the introduction of Renton, each of the main characters in the film is singled out by freeze-frame with his name in caption, reminiscent of the opening sequence of the 1960s cult television series *The Monkees* and utilising devices like the jump-cut in reference to Richard Lester's Beatles film *A Hard Day's Night* (1964), which was a world-wide success. These two locations are in stark contrast: while we see Renton alone, smoking, his movements slow and the camera static (first in medium shot and then a long shot), the voice-over invites us to 'Choose good health, low cholesterol and dental insurance. Choose fixed interest mortgage repayments, choose a starter home, choose your friends' (at which point we cut to a shot of his friends, gathered in goal as for a football-team photograph). The football scenes are quick, jaunty and fun but as Renton is hit on the head by a football we hear him again say 'choose life', and we revert to shots of Renton at home. He falls to the floor and the camera follows his body slowly, at a low-angle. The sequence makes clear that he *didn't* 'choose life' but instead opted for drugs: 'who needs reasons when you've got heroin'. In just a few minutes the film-makers have managed to convey some essentials about *Trainspotting*: that image and dialogue are often at odds with one another (the incongruity of the running figures and Renton's catalogue of consumer durables); that the main characters in the film are five young males; and, via voice-over, that Renton is the central character.

Renton's agency as a central character is crucial in ensuring that the audience maintains a more intimate relationship with him than with the other characters. This is in contrast to the Irvine Welsh novel on which the film is based, which permits a variety of characters to have a direct 'voice'. The film is, in many ways, *Renton's* story, from drug addiction to lucky break and upward mobility in London. Possessing the voice-over usually endows a film character with a degree of control over the narrative, often encouraging us to see things from her/his point of view. Renton acts as our mentor, our guide through his world of addiction and theft. The comic, ironic spin on his voice-overs, however, also single him out to us as more intelligent, more street-wise and, eventually, more successful than his friends. At the end of *Trainspotting*, when Renton has stolen the money, he explains in voice-over that Sick Boy would have done the same and that the violent Begbie deserved to be swindled. We see him leave some of the money for Spud to recover, thereby making us appreciate the gesture and accept the theft more readily.

Although voice-over and image can sometimes be in conflict with each other, on most occasions Renton has the last word, as in the scene when Tommy (not yet a heroin addict) wants them all to go for a walk when they visit the Scottish hills. Tommy has gone on ahead and calls to the others to join him. The shots of him with the hills in the background are much brighter, with sunshine and billowing clouds, than the reverse images of his friends, each of them reluctant to take to the hills. The landscape behind them is dark, the sky is cloudy, linking them with a bleaker, more dangerous Scotland than the one that appears in holiday brochures. For a moment it seems as if Tommy's more idyllic background will persist in the memory, but when he calls to them, 'Doesn't it make you proud to be Scottish?' Renton delivers a classic riposte which undermines Tommy's (and our) enthusiasm: 'It's shite being Scottish, we're the lowest of the low, the scum of the fucking earth, most wretched, miserable, servile, pathetic trash that was ever shagged into civilisation. Some people hate the English – I don't – they're just wankers. We, on the other hand, are colonised by wankers – can't even find a decent culture to be colonised by. We're ruled by effete arseholes. It's a shite state to be in Tommy and all the fresh air in the world won't make any difference.'

The above sequence typifies the film's attitude towards conventionality – it cocks a snook at accepted notions of representation – in this case of the Scottish tourist industry – and replaces them with a dissident view. When an unwary American tourist asks to use the pub toilet at the start of the Edinburgh Festival, Begbie leads the troupe of angry Scottish friends in pursuit, with the intention of beating him up. Again, this is a blatant rejection of an established element of Scottish heritage. The film also critiques the genre of American films which perpetuate stereotypical notions of Scottish heritage, including Vincente Minnelli's *Brigadoon* (1954) and Mel Gibson's *Braveheart* (1995).

As a film not just about national identity, or feeling estranged from a sense of traditional nationalism, *Trainspotting* dares to draw attention to itself by refusing the realist cinematic traditions which one would have expected to spawn a film about drug culture in the 1980s. Instead of delivering a didactic message against drug-taking, *Trainspotting* claims to know what it is like to be an addict, avoiding a heavy-handed 'message' approach which would undoubtedly have alienated many cinemagoers, and instead daring to represent some of the pleasures of heroin, particularly in the scenes of ecstatic release experienced by Renton when the drug is first administered. The avoidance of didacticism is a major strategy utilised by the film-makers even though, ironically, the audience is encouraged to admire Renton's ability to rise above the mundane, conquer his addiction and, in Thatcherite fashion, apply himself to money-making in London and be the major beneficiary of the drugs deal at the end of the film. As the credits roll we are tempted to speculate: has he swapped one dubious way of life for another?

The inclusion of surrealist, fantastical elements enables *Trainspotting* to deal with issues and scenes that would have been particularly harrowing in more conventional realist form (even if there is a risk, in so doing, of trivialising the incidents). Thus the scene when Renton dives into the toilet to recover the suppositories begins in realist fashion as we see him put his hand down the bowl, desperately trying to avoid retching at the same time. The surrealism begins when his whole body disappears down the toilet, emerging into an underwater location in which he appears to be diving for pearls on the bed of the sea. Combining realism with this imaginative conclusion to the scene serves the purpose of conveying both the desperation of the drug addict and something of his elation when the drugs have been recovered. To Renton they are like valuable pearls and there are clearly no lengths to which he would not go in order to retrieve his lost treasure. Far from trivialising the incident the scene achieves an impressionist conclusion by encouraging the audience to understand Renton's psyche and how his quest for drugs blinds him to the revulsion we experience from a more realist perspective.

The use of music also serves as effective counterpoint. In the sequence after Renton has been given a suspended prison sentence for theft on condition that he undergoes a monitored detoxification programme, the pressures build up as he craves a 'hit' of heroin. He visits 'Mother Superior' for a fix 'to get me through this long day'. After a comic scene between the two in which they role-play a rich customer and a waiter, Renton lies back in relief once the drug has been administered, much as we have seen him react before in an ecstatic haze of pleasure when the heroin kicks in. We hear the beginning of Lou Reed's *Perfect Day* and in a break with realism we see Renton disappear through the floor. The languid tones and lyrics of the song continue as background to this serene moment but we gradually realise that he has, in fact, overdosed and is rapidly descending into a coma. 'Mother Superior' drags him out to an empty street where a taxi rushes him to hospital. The song then becomes completely ironic as what started out as a scene in which Renton's desperation, depression and loneliness is 'cured' by heroin, ends up as a nightmare of near-death, anything but a perfect day.

Trainspotting's stylistic break from realism facilitated its export, and the rest of this chapter will discuss how the film's success was in part due to its marketing and reception by reviewers, many of whom debated the film's relationship with previous traditions of British cinema. Reviews commented particularly on the celebrated, unexpected surrealism of the 'toilet' scene, creating an expectation of sensationalism – British films do not normally do this sort of thing. Many American reviews pointed out that the film was a far cry from the films of Mike Leigh or Ken Loach, instead comparing it with previous 'cult' successes like Stanley Kubrick's *A Clockwork Orange* (1971) and the films of Scorsese and Tarantino. It is somewhat ironic that these last comparisons go some way towards explaining its success in America, although this should not imply that it was not appreciated as a British film. It was understood primarily in terms of its relation to British cultural icons. References to The Beatles encouraged its 'cult' status: the Internet Movie Database website, for example, compiled a list of 'trivia' points which occur within the film, including reference to a scene where store detectives chase Renton down a street that is reminiscent of a scene in *A Hard Day's Night* where the Beatles are pursued by fans, and a scene towards the end of *Trainspotting* in which the four friends cross a road in similar fashion to the front sleeve shot of The Beatles on their album *Abbey Road*. The film's focus on the men's friendship and involvement in counter-culture is reminiscent of the way the Beatles are pitted against the Establish-ment in *A Hard Day's Night*, particularly in both films' use of 'in-joke' humour as a discourse which is reflective of, in their different contexts, their appeal to the youth market. As a result of Sick-Boy's obsession, the film also contains many references to James Bond films, another example of its preoccupation with British cultural icons from the 1960s.

Filmic intertexts are also referenced when Renton arrives in London. Boyle creates an ironic montage of 'famous signposts/sights' which are reminiscent of British 'Swinging London' films of the 1960s, in which the capital was repres-ented, in films such as John Schlesinger's *Billy Liar!* (1963) or Richard Lester's *The Knack* (1965), as an escape from small-town life, parochialism and stasis. As in many of these earlier films, the city in *Trainspotting* is depicted as ruthless, in the midst of the 1980s boom, with Renton working at a property agency, saving his money and living in a squalid bed-sit. Despite the film's energy the prognosis is bleak: the only way out is to make money but what you should spend it on is unclear. Renton's suggestions – drugs, 'life', or consumer durables – are not presented in a positive light. The only scenes of 'ordinary' life in the film come across as stultifying, and in the case of Begbie's alternative of addiction to alcohol, violent and dangerous. The scenes of the four friends in London at the end of the film serve as a reminder of Britain's regional diversity as they struggle to profit from their big deal, appearing as strangers to the London drug-dealing scene, amateurs in a world of organised crime.

Contrary to accepted opinion, the British films which have done best in the USA are not pale imitations of Hollywood epics, 'international' films that are devoid of national identity. Rather, they are precisely those, like the Ealing comedies or the satirical, surreal Monty Python films, which do engage with 'Britishness' in an intriguing way. From this perspective it is not at all surprising that *Trainspotting* should have been so well received outside the UK, and most of the American reviews placed it in the tradition of slightly surrealistic, satirical humour, particularly in relation to its noted resemblances to *A Hard Day's Night*. What would appear to be a paradox – a 'small', parochial British film breaking out of the domestic market – is not, therefore, an exception. It is the result of an intriguing combination of a fresh look at national identity with an arresting cinematic visual style which delivers that much sought-after quality: world-wide critical recognition *and* box-office success.

Along with a refusal to conform to expectations of British social realism, *Trainspotting* is also difficult to locate in generic terms. While this can often have the effect of producing a confused, unfocused impression of a film prior to release, it can, if handled astutely, maximise interest. Reviewers found it hard to place in terms of genre, alternating between discussing its comic merits, its 'cult' status, links with 'Britpop' music, intertextual relations with *A Hard Day's Night* – 'the boys shoot up and fall down in pleasure, and sometimes they jump about Edinburgh, chasing down streets like The Beatles in *A Hard Day's Night*, romping in and out of bars or just sitting around making preposterous jokes' (*New York*, 12 August 1996) – and comparing it to *A Clockwork Orange*, Scorsese and Tarantino films, and to the loosely-defined genre of 'drug' films including Abel Ferrara's *Bad Lieutenant* (1992), Ulrich Edel's *Christiane F* (1981) and David Cronenberg's *Naked Lunch* (1991). In many senses, *Trainspotting* is all these things. As an example of the contemporary hybrid film its negation of fixity allows discussion to involve the production team, the stars, the themes, the style and soundtrack in a fluid, intertextual fashion. One feature most reviewers agreed on, however, was the film's ability to communicate energy: 'There's no escaping its bluster and commotion... Even when there is nothing to it but noise and colour, it still has swagger and style, and it feels very rowdy' (*Première*, March 1996). The art direction, by Tracey Gallacher, is excellent, making it a visual spectacle that contains many qualities of contemporary European and American independent/art house movies, for example Jean-Pierre Jeunet's and Marc Caro's *Delicatessen* (1991) or the Coen brothers' *Barton Fink* (1991). Much of *Trainspotting* was shot in a large disused cigarette factory in which thirty of the fifty locations were built. The camera was often at a low angle to create a sense of space and the colours of the rooms were blues, oranges, reds and purples, similar to the bold stylistic approach that had been adopted for *Shallow Grave* (1994).

Steve Neale (1990) has observed the inherent mutability of generic film forms and the importance of a film's publicity campaign in creating a climate of expectation in the potential audience's mind before they see the film. In the case of *Trainspotting*, the 'narrative image' was rather a 'stylistic image' that relied on visual spectacle, the charisma of the performers, and the 'event' of the soundtrack release. This would appear to take the film back to the realms of the 'cinema of attractions', a phrase used by Tom Gunning (1986) to describe early cinema's appeal to the senses as a display of technological artistry which drew the spectator in for its own sake rather than as an adjunct to narrative.

These many qualities were evident from *Trainspotting*'s marketing campaign (by Polygram in the UK and Miramax in the USA), which in turn influenced reviews. This aspect of the film's success was crucial, enhancing its status as a 'must-see' film and pitching it at the youth, 'cult' market with the assistance of a distinctive 'Britpop' soundtrack. From this perspective, people were familiar with the *idea* of *Trainspotting* before the film's release, especially if they had read Welsh's novel, first published in 1993. In February 1996 the British press was full of comment about the novel and the forthcoming film. The production team and cast, particularly Ewan McGregor, who was a familiar name as one of the main actors in Danny Boyle's earlier film *Shallow Grave* (1995), were available for interview and contributed to a precise and well-organised publicity campaign which heightened audience expectation for a film that was different, hip and visual. The posters, produced by design company Stylo Rouge, were distinctive in their singling out of the characters in monochrome, with orange type which was influenced by the wording on drug packages and British Rail signs. The production team's previous success with the stylish *Shallow Grave* served to augment anticipation of another new and exciting British cinematic experience. The poster which declared 'Hollywood come in please ... your time is up' characterised the film's brazen and confident attitude in no uncertain terms.

Although the seriousness of heroin addiction was also discussed, some reviewers took exception to the apparent contradiction between the energy and pace of the film's style and its deathly subject-matter:

> The film is governed by the sort of indiscriminate regard for the Spunky Spirit of Renegade Youth that you usually only find in building societies worried about their image, or television executives worried about their age. Imagine *Mean Streets* re-made by Janet Street-Porter and you're halfway there. Add some street poetry ('It wasn't just the baby that died that day ... '), the likes of which you won't have heard since the last Hanif Kureishi effort, and some finger-snapping editing, the likes of which you won't have seen since the TSB last got hungry for young money, and you have *Trainspotting*: the film about drugs that likes to say 'YES!' (Shone)

> I'd have hated to be a using heroin addict in London over the past week. In fact I'd hate to be a using heroin addict at all and anywhere. But this past week in London, I would've been subjected to a continual taunt from hoardings advertising the listings magazine *Time Out*, and by extension, the film, *Trainspotting*. The taunt is a line from the film extolling the virtues of the hit of heroin: 'Take the best orgasm you've ever had, multiply it by a thousand, and you'll still be nowhere close.' (Self)

Indeed, it is this aspect of the film which attracted most controversial comment – the possibility that the sequences of ecstatic relief when a heroin-filled needle is inserted into the vein might not be cancelled out by their binary opposites, the sequences showing the agonies of 'cold turkey'. As an example of the contemporary hybrid film, *Trainspotting* delivered its promise of excitement, colour, wit and energy. In cinematic terms, the refusal to allow conventional realist representations of drug addiction to dominate the film opened it to a wider audience at the risk of trivialising the subject of heroin addiction. As has been argued, however, the film's open-ended narrative events and strategies of visual and aural ironic counterpoint achieve a sense of complexity which would have been impossible from a more overtly didactic perspective. Indeed, *Trainspotting* chose cinematic 'life' as a means of producing 'diverse and challenging representations adequate to the complexities of contemporary Britain' (Hill, 19). On the strength of *Trainspotting*, the Boyle–Hodge–MacDonald team managed to obtain finance for a subsequent project, *A Life Less Ordinary* (1997), although it did not attract the same degree of critical acclaim or box-office success, while the film also established Ewan McGregor as a major British film star who went on to work in a variety of films including Peter Greenaway's *The Pillow Book* (1996), Mark Herman's *The Rise and Fall of Little Voice* (1998) and George Lucas's *Star Wars (Episode 1)* (1999). Probably the closest generic inheritors of *Trainspotting* were Kevin Allen's *Twin Town* (1997) and Guy Ritchie's *Lock, Stock & Two Smoking Barrels* (1998), films which displayed similarly inventive formal structures, lively cinematographic styles, wit, pace and verve. Above all, the legacy of *Trainspotting* has been a greater tolerance of cinematic difference and the opening up of new perspectives on national identity(ies) for world markets.

References

Gunning, Tom 1986: 'The Cinema of Attractions: Early Film, its Spectators and the Avant-Garde'. In *Wide Angle*, 8, 3–4.

Hill, John 1992: 'The Issue of National Cinema and British Film Production'. In Duncan Petrie (ed.), *New Questions of British Cinema*. London: British Film Institute.

MacDonald, Andrew 1996: 'It's Such a Perfect Day'. In *Premiere UK*, March.

Neale, Steve 1990: 'Questions of Genre'. In *Screen*, 31, 1.

Self, Will 1996: 'Trainspotting'. In *Observer Preview*, 11–17 February.

Shone, Tom 1996: 'Trainspotting'. In *Sunday Times*, 25 February.

Street, Sarah 1997: *British National Cinema*. London: Routledge.

Suggestions for Further Reading

Caughie, John 1990: 'Representing Scotland: New Questions for Scottish Cinema'. In E. Dick (ed.), *From Limelight to Satellite*. London: British Film Institute/Scottish Film Council.

Petrie, Duncan 1996: 'British Cinema: The Search for Identity'. In Geoffrey Nowell-Smith (ed.), *Oxford History of World Cinema*. Oxford: Oxford University Press.

Credits

Director	Danny Boyle
Producer	Andrew MacDonald
Production Company	A Figment Film in association with Noel Gay Motion Picture Company Ltd for Channel Four
Screenplay	John Hodge, based on Irvine Welsh's novel
Director of Photography	Brian Tufano
Editor	Masahiro Hirakubo
Production Designer	Kave Quinn
Art Direction	Tracey Gallacher
Music	No original music

Cast

Ewan McGregor	Renton
Ewen Bremner	Spud
Johnny Lee Miller	Sick Boy
Kevin McKidd	Tommy
Robert Carlyle	Begbie
Kelly Macdonald	Diane

Filmography

Shallow Grave (1995)
Trainspotting (1996)
A Life Less Ordinary (1997)
The Beach (2000)

12 *The Barber of Siberia*
McCracken (Richard Harris) in front of his invention, the Barber of Siberia.

Sibirskii tsiriul'nik
(The Barber of Siberia)
Birgit Beumers

While the first Russian film discussed in this book, *The Battleship Potemkin* (1926), ranks among the world's best films, *The Barber of Siberia* (*Sibirskii tsiriul'nik*, 1998) is one of the most expensive feature films ever made outside Hollywood ($49 million). While Eisenstein had a hand-painted red flag in his film, emphasising the triumphant spirit of the Revolution and turning its success forward in time, Mikhalkov turned time backwards by having the red stars, symbol of Soviet power, removed from the Kremlin towers to allow for the film's setting in pre-Revolutionary Russia. While Eisenstein constructed Soviet history, Mikhalkov remembers Russia's past values with nostalgia. The temporal axes of the two films are thus diametrically opposed, although both film-makers look towards the future in their reassessment of the past. They represent in their spirit the beginning and the end of the Soviet era, and of a century of film-making.

The Barber of Siberia is a rare film in its combination of English and Russian dialogue, its production history, its use of star actors from Russia, the USA and the UK, but, above all, because of the director's aim to provide a model of direction and to offer moral guidance to an audience at a time when the mainstream of Russian film-makers portray the bleakness, the abyss and the degeneration surrounding them. Mikhalkov's *The Barber of Siberia* shapes the values of the future by telling a story about Russia's past, which elevates the traditions of the east above those of the west, tells a fairy tale without a happy ending, and stands in both form and content aloof from Hollywood expectations.

It is more than surprising that such a film should come from a country like Russia, shaken by economic crises and trying to define its national identity after the collapse of the Soviet Union. The Soviet film industry had been state-controlled and state-managed, so that film-makers could work almost independently of audience taste, but were subjected instead to ideological control. The industry almost collapsed after 1991 when the country entered the free market which forced producers to raise money in a system that offered no tax incentives to investors in the arts. To make the situation worse, the cinema infrastructure was outdated and video piracy undermined any chance of recouping production costs. Mikhalkov's successful collaboration on earlier film projects with the French producer Michel Seydoux secured him a business partner for the project who could raise two-thirds of the funds. The film is a co-production between TriTe (Russia) and Camera One (France), shot at the Barrandov studios in Prague, in Moscow, Kostroma and Nizhny Novgorod (Russia), and in Portugal.

The film brings together stars from American and British cinema, as well as from Russia's film and theatre scene. Julia Ormond plays Jane Callaghan, while Richard Harris is cast as the eccentric inventor McCracken. Oleg Menshikov, a major star of Russian cinema who has become known internationally since *Utomlennye solntsem* (*Burnt by the Sun*), plays Andrei Tolstoi, and Alexei Petrenko, Elem Klimov's Rasputin in *Agonia* (*Agony*), stars as Radlov. The director of the film, Nikita Mikhalkov, plays Tsar Alexander III, the 'father' of Russia, which is a significant choice because the pre-publicity and release of the film coincided with Mikhalkov's real-life political interests in the run-up for the next presidential elections, and amidst ongoing speculation about his candidature. Mikhalkov's daughter Anna plays Dunia, his son Artem plays the cadet Buturlin, and his daughter Nadia (the little girl Nadia of *Burnt by the Sun*) appears in an episode at the fair. Almost the entire Mikhalkov family features in the film, continuing the director's preoccupation with the themes of fatherhood and family which have been evident in almost all of his films.

The film is shot almost equally in English and Russian. While Jane and McCracken speak only English and Tolstoi converses with them in English, the rest of the dialogue is in Russian. Jane's narrative through her letters to Andrew is also in English, with a voice-over for the Russian version narrated by the film's director. The title of the film echoes that of Rossini's opera *The Barber of Seville*, which is also concerned with money as a motivation for people's actions, and with role-play to achieve a set goal, two key themes which dominate Jane's actions. The choice of the name Tolstoi for the male protagonist will, of course, suggest to international audiences a parallel to the ninteenth-century writer Lev Tolstoi, whose novel *Anna Karenina* Jane is reading on the train. Tolstoi was also the name of the Minister of Interior Affairs under Alexander II. Mikhalkov's approach to dialogue, casting and story-line make the film viable for an international market. Russian habits are unfamiliar to Jane, a foreigner to the country, and through her they are explained in an unpatronising form to an international audience, a strategy which does not necessitate special editing of the film for its international release.

Nikita Mikhalkov is the son of Sergei Mikhalkov, a writer of children's stories, plays, and of the text of the Soviet national anthem (1943). Mikhalkov's elder brother, Andrei Konchalovsky, is also a film-maker who left for Hollywood in the 1980s. Nikita Mikhalkov began his career as an actor before completing his studies as a film director, and he rose to international fame with the Italian co-production *Dark Eyes* (1987) and the Oscar-winning *Burnt by the Sun* (1994). He occupies many influential positions in Russian cultural politics: in 1990 he became adviser to the Prime Minister on cultural issues, and in 1993 he was elected president of the Russian Fund for Culture. Since 1989 he has run his own production company, TriTe, which also has a publishing arm that has published archival material relating to Russian history.

In December 1997 Mikhalkov was elected chairman of the Film-makers' Union in a vote of trust. In his speech to the Congress of the Union in May 1998, Mikhalkov proposed the creation of an extra-budgetary fund to support the film industry, to be created from fees collected from licensing video retail, which would then be invested in the reconstruction of cinemas, the production of new films, and the renovation and maintenance of the Union's properties, significantly suggesting forms of assistance based on those within other European film industries rather than looking to Hollywood as a model. In his speech, Mikhalkov argued strongly that the task of a national Russian cinema should be to instil hope in the cinema audience by re-creating the myth of a Russian national hero in order to regain a spirit of patriotism that had bonded the Soviet Union in the past, a spirit which Mikhalkov believes to exist in contemporary America, encouraged by the Hollywood 'myth' factory. Thus for Mikhalkov, cinema is capable of projecting a lost sense of national identity, inspiring the people to have hope in the future while the political reality is void of any direction or ideology. The means by which this can be achieved, he argues, are by encouraging the growth of a financially sound film industry and by producing popular films which inculcate a coherent sense of national identity. Using the example of the US film industry, whose success, he suggests, lies in the creation of positive heroes with whom the American nation identifies, Mikhalkov neglects the fact that America is also proud of its industry because it makes $3.5 billion profit per year.

The evolution of the script for *The Barber of Siberia* spans the period of belief in the reform of the political system under Gorbachev, the collapse of the Soviet Union, and the emergence of the new Russia. The script was written in 1987–8, published in Russia in 1992–3, and filmed between 1995 and 1997. Because of the economic crisis that hit Russia in August 1998, *The Barber of Siberia* could not be launched in ten Siberian cities before its Moscow première, as had been anticipated, but it was eventually premiered in lavish style in the Kremlin Palace of Congresses on 20 February 1999, the first film to be premiered there in over twenty years.

The publicity campaign around the film was carefully co-ordinated. Banners and posters were positioned all over central Moscow, and a new brand of vodka, 'Russian Standard', was launched as well as a new perfume range, 'Cadet No. 1' and 'Cadet No. 3'. Mikhalkov appeared for over a week on almost all television shows, with several channels screening retrospectives of his films, and the première brought together Moscow's VIPs and beau-monde in the Kremlin Palace of Congresses, specially fitted with a Dolby Stereo Surround system and a new projection screen for this purpose. Moreover, the campaign connected Mikhalkov's role in the film to his political programme, which gave rise to speculations about his candidature during the forthcoming presidential elections. The linking of art and politics, however, together with the media hype around the film, drove journalists to review the film in negative terms as a political manifesto rather than as an artistic product. The nationalist ideas of the film-maker had been a thorn in the flesh of most journalists, if not since Mikhalkov's takeover of the Film-makers' Union, then certainly after his failed attempt to position the director of his studio in the vacant ministerial chair at Goskino, the State Committee for Cinematography.

The Barber of Siberia tells the story of Jane Callaghan, an American woman who travels to Russia in 1885 in order to assist the Irish-American inventor Douglas McCracken in securing funding for his machine, the 'barber', which is designed to chop down the Siberian forests. McCracken has run out of funding and, under pressure from his creditors, has hired Jane to charm General Radlov, the head of the Military Academy, in order to gain through him the support of Grand Duke Alexei. Jane achieves this task by pretending to be McCracken's daughter and flirting with the self-conscious and vain General who proposes to her. In her business-oriented approach to life Jane offers her ability to charm for hire, and sells her body when necessary, since she was abused in her childhood by her stepfather and was forced to fend for herself at an early age. Then she meets the cadet Andrei Tolstoi, who falls in love with her. As a cadet, Tolstoi has very high moral values: he defends his feelings for Jane in a duel, he humiliates himself when he proposes to Jane in front of the General, and he is prepared to sacrifice his career for Jane. She, on the other hand, continues her intrigues in which Radlov plays a key role, in order to fulfil her contract and get the papers which McCracken needs to be signed by the Grand Duke. Unwilling to sacrifice her scheme for the sake of love, she spends a day with the General at a Shrovetide fair and encourages him to drink, seeking to compromise him. When he sees Jane flirting with the General in the theatre just after she has spent the night with him, Tolstoi attacks his rival with a violin bow during a performance of *The Marriage of Figaro* in which Tolstoi is singing the part of Figaro. The production by the Military Academy is taking place in the presence of the Grand Duke, and Radlov swiftly accuses Tolstoi of an attempt upon the Grand Duke's life. Thus Radlov secures promotion for himself by 'preventing a terrorist act'. Tolstoi is found guilty and sent to a prison camp in Siberia, without ever attempting to defend his actions.

Ten years later, Jane has married McCracken so that her son (Tolstoi's child) will have a father. On the occasion of the launch of McCracken's 'barber' Jane travels to Siberia. As the machine begins the massive destruction of the Siberian *taiga*, Jane finds the house where Tolstoi, who now earns a living as a barber, lives with his wife Dunia (formerly a maid in the Tolstois' house in Moscow) and their children. Jane then leaves Russia.

The love story of Jane and Andrei Tolstoi is embedded in a narration by Jane, who, in 1905, writes a letter to her son, Andrew, a recruit at a US military base. Time and again, we see her writing the letter, while her voice reads parts of it, and we see Andrew at the US base, as stubborn as his father and upholding values and principles which he defends with his life. A key example of this is when he stands up for his veneration of Mozart by refusing to repeat a phrase denigrating the composer. Rather than do this he wears a gas mask for more than twenty-four hours because he refuses to repeat commander O'Leary's remark, 'I don't give a shit about Mozart'. Finally, when Andrew's endurance wins out, O'Leary accepts that 'Mozart is a great composer'. As the commander is shouting this phrase across the barracks, Jane drives up in a car to visit her son and she shows the commander a portrait of Andrew's father, the former Russian cadet Tolstoi, suggesting that Andrew's Russian roots explain his behaviour.

The film's narrative stretches over twenty years. Each part (Jane's retrospective narrative, the episode at the US military base, and the love story) develops chronologically, and the three story lines are joined up at the end. The way Tolstoi behaved towards Jane parallels the stubborn insistence upon principle displayed by the recruit Andrew. The Jane who reflects on the past does so with hindsight, but is still unable fully to understand Russia, underscoring the notion that Russia cannot be grasped by reason alone. Jane and McCracken represent a world that is largely deprived of any spiritual ideals, while the Russian cadets are endowed with a sense of honour and love for the Fatherland. The western characters acknowledge only success in business or the achievement of goals, while most of the Russian characters surrender to a fatalistic vision of their life, accepting suffering and solitude.

Almost all the characters lack a happy family life. Jane comes from a broken family: her father died, her mother remarried, and she was abused by her stepfather who then left her mother. She was never loved by her mother, and was destroyed by her stepfather; she has nothing to believe in, nothing to live for, and has never experienced love. She has abandoned herself, reduced herself to selling her services, physical or social. When she spends the night with Tolstoi she realises his devotion to her; yet she continues to play her game in order to fulfil her contract, for her financial benefit. Jane is gambling, thinking she can both fulfil her contract and achieve happiness with Tolstoi, but the stakes are too high. She never really understands Tolstoi's pride and honour; instead, she interprets his behaviour as that of an immature boy. Their relationship does not come across as one endowed with love. The love-scene happens offscreen and remains unconvincing, with a lack of genuine emotion between the characters. Tolstoi's family too is broken: his mother has an affair with his uncle. Both the military men in the film, the General and the Captain, are bachelors. Love fails on a human level across all classes of society: neither Jane's nor Andrei's families were happy, and even the Tsar would have had no children if things had gone the way his wife, the Empress Maria Fedorovna (Dagmar of Denmark), had wished. The only love acceptable for a military man is the love of the Tsar, and when Tolstoi places Jane above the Tsar he betrays the 'Father' of the nation.

Tolstoi and the cadets have high moral values and are bonded by a comradeship that transcends the boundaries of everyday life: the cadets Polievsky and Tolstoi fight a duel, but later it is Polievsky who fetches Jane so that she can visit Tolstoi in hospital after the duel, and who summons her to the railway station when Tolstoi is sent to Siberia. Set in a time when ideals were high, the film also displays the cadets' absolute belief in the Tsar, while their encounter with him strengthens their love for the Tsar as their father. Their captain, Mokin, often assumes the role of a father-figure when he covers up for some of the cadets' adventures. Both Captain Mokin and Commander O'Leary at the US military base are strict, but they are ready to listen to their cadets. Both are ultimately concerned with more than discipline and are ready to admit when they have been wrong, and to defend 'their' soldiers. In this way, despite its discipline, life in the military is endowed with human concern and the military is idealised. The Tsar is the ideal father, and the only person worthy of love. In the absence of intact family life and genuine father-figures, the military community replaces the family, while the Tsar substitutes for the father who is also represented on a lower level by the military commanders. In Mikhalkov's vision the whole of Russian society is transformed into one large family with a patriarch at its head.

Tolstoi seems confused in his behaviour and his words. While he serves and loves the Tsar he allows a terrorist to escape. He also confuses his love for the Tsar with his love for Jane and defends a woman who is a liar. The director's intended portrayal of a positive hero is hampered by the naivety of the young cadet, who is easily fooled, shows a high level of human compassion and who follows ideals unquestioningly. Tolstoi's personality is not suited to the discipline required for a military career but his acceptance of his sentence is indicative of his sincerity because he accepts his imprisonment and exile as the price to be paid for following a false ideal.

The love intrigue in the film draws a subtle distinction between the passion and foolishness of Tolstoi and Jane, and the love displayed by Dunia, who shares her remaining money and follows Tolstoi to Siberia. Jane seduces Tolstoi in his moment of weakness, when the naive, inexperienced, but devoted cadet faints. Jane discovers that love is possible for her, despite all her negative experiences in the past; yet she destroys their relationship, sullying the pure feeling of the cadet, Tolstoi, with her intrigues. The film uses a historical setting for this romantic plot, with a positive hero to transport the moral values of the past into the present. Even Jane can, and will, find her place in life and follow the path which everybody must find for themselves. High moral values, ideals and principles may have a price, but they will triumph: Mozart *is* a great composer. Andrew is the spitting image of his father, with the same principled outlook on life.

The film is set in the Russia of Tsar Alexander III (ruled 1881–94), a world into which an American woman and an Irish-American inventor intrude. The reactionary and nationalist Tsar Alexander III is portrayed as a benevolent ruler who loves children and takes his son Mikhail on horseback to the parade. The Tsar is endowed with human rather than god-like traits, covering Mikhail's mouth when the boy wants to shout a second greeting to induce a reply from the cadets, a game he would like to play. As the cadets stand to attention, the camera captures a sparrow at the cadets' feet and closes up on the small creature. Mikhalkov never neglects the small at the expense of the grand. The Tsar is thus presented as an ideal father, for his child as well as for the nation. Such a portrayal is important in the light of the absence of a father-figure in so many contemporary Russian films of the post-Soviet period, such as Sergei Bodrov's *Kavkazskii plennik* (*The Prisoner of the Mountains*, 1996), in which soldiers no longer know what they are fighting and dying for.

In the publicity leaflet for the film, Mikhalkov wrote: 'I hope that our film will help the spectator to feel again pride in the genuine merit of his Fatherland,' suggesting that the moral values of the young Russian cadet Tolstoi are a model designed to help contemporary audiences value and love their fatherland. The film promulgates the standards of nineteenth-century Russia: honour and the readiness to stand by ideals irrespective of a potential risk to life. These were echoed in the launch of the vodka brand 'Russian Standard' and the competition initiated among the students of the Film Institute to make short films on the five components of the Russian character – creation, trust, perfection, experience, and patriotism. As the critic Lidia Maslova observed (*Kommersant*, 23 February 1999), the film is itself a commercial for the 'product Russia'. The campaign for Russian values on both commercial and cinematic levels also underscores the film's fusion of past and present, and film and reality.

The film pinpoints the divergence between the traditions of the east and the west. Russia has always sought to define its identity by reference to its allegiance to eastern or western cultures, or as having the unique mission to act as a bridge between the two. This is reflected in the long-standing debate between the 'westernisers', who considered Russia a backward part of European culture, and the 'slavophiles', who glorified Russia's native institutions and traditions. In this controversy, Mikhalkov's position is on the side of the slavophiles since he idealises Russia and portrays some western features, such as the business-oriented approach discussed above, in derogatory terms, even though the film is designed for western as well as Russian audiences.

Russian traditions are portrayed in great detail in the script. The rituals of 'Forgiveness Sunday' and the Shrovetide celebrations in the week before Lent take up a substantial, and costly, part of the film. Mikhalkov films, at length, scenes at the Shrovetide fair which show people drinking together and fighting each other, only to seek forgiveness the next day. The scenes also show us a theatre of Lilliputians re-enacting Napoleon's battles, factory workers engaging in fist fights on the ice, and a fireworks display. It is as if the world turns, temporarily, into a theatre in which social and class boundaries are broken in the true spirit of carnival, and 'man behaves like a beast while animals drink like people'. The spectator is presented with this image of Russia through the eyes of a foreigner, Jane, who is capable only of imitating Russian habits without ever comprehending the concepts behind them. In Russia, she remains a 'nobody', not allowed to see Tolstoi in prison, not taken seriously by Tolstoi's mother, and unable to travel within Russia. When she writes the letter to her son in 1905, she pretends to be a different Jane and claims the old Jane is just a 'friend'. Jane has played so many roles in her life that she just sheds one role and becomes a new person. Her roles and her history change so fast that one is never quite sure what to believe, and she appears to adapt her story to each changing situation very swiftly. She pretends, for example, to be McCracken's daughter, but then admits she is not. On another occasion she tells McCracken that her husband drowned in the Nile, while Radlov is told that he died in battle. Another 'fiction' emerges when we realise that in reality Jane was never married.

In breaking with her character Jane does nothing of substance to save Tolstoi. She explains her behaviour to him speaking through a closed door when he has already left the room. She is uninventive and cannot think of a role when asked at the prison gate what relation she has to Tolstoi; instead she offers herself to Radlov to try and save Tolstoi, prepared to soil their relationship by betraying Tolstoi's feelings. Dunia, on the other hand, is ready to strike Jane with a sickle when she comes into their house in Siberia to take Tolstoi away with her. Conversely, McCracken has an ideal he believes in, to such an extent that it dominates his life and he forgets everything else, takes no interest in the world around him, and is prepared to die for his ideal, trying to hang himself when funding is uncertain. The machine that embodies the meaning of his life, that conquers nature and makes him its master, is also a machine which destroys nature and causes long-term damage to the environment. Here the film-maker draws a parallel with Stalin, another dangerous, utopian dreamer in Soviet history, who attempted to conquer territory and master nature.

The values upheld in the film are typical of the nineteenth century, which Mikhalkov connects to the beauty, and the deep sense, of Russian folk traditions at a time before these were destroyed by the Soviet regime. The heroism displayed by Tolstoi is possible only in a setting of the previous century; contemporary Russia has no room for such heroism. *The Barber of Siberia* instils nostalgia in the spectator, not for the Stalinist and Soviet past as so many contemporary television programmes do, but for the Tsarist, pre-Revolutionary Russia, related to the present through the historical event that dominated 1998: the laying to rest of the remains of the last Tsar and his family, the Romanovs, in St Petersburg in July 1998.

Since the film's title plays upon the opera *The Barber of Seville* and includes a performance of Mozart's *The Marriage of Figaro*, we need to consider briefly the role of music. *The Marriage of Figaro*, the opera performed by the cadets, stands at the centre of the film. Tolstoi is singing Figaro's aria when he attacks Radlov, but Tolstoi is not as lucky as Figaro: Figaro wants to marry Susanna, but Count Almaviva tries to seduce the bride before the wedding. In reality, Tolstoi sees Jane 'seduced' by Almaviva–Radlov and takes fate into his own hands instead of leaving it in the hands of the fictional opera libretto, which would have secured a happy end: the Countess Almaviva discovers her husband in the garden trying to seduce Susanna – who is nobody else but the Countess herself in disguise. Though it has been suggested above that the only love acceptable was that for the Tsar, the film-maker allows one exception, which is the love of Mozart. In using the composer to represent the rejection of national (political) values in favour of artistic ones, Mikhalkov is making a political statement that politics does not matter when placed alongside a taste for great art or music.

Tolstoi first sings Figaro's aria 'Non piu andare' (from Act I) on the train; later he sings it instead of the cadets' March, that is to say, he betrays his love for the Tsar. On the train with all the convicts, in reply to the call from 'Susanna', the part the cadet Nazarov played in the production, he sings the aria again so that the cadets can find him among the convicts on the train. The portrait of Mozart – the visual, rather than musical representation of the composer – dominates Andrew's life as a recruit in the US Army. The typically Russian character is shown as stubborn, proud and ready to suffer. These qualities are also the outstanding characteristics of Andrew, and single him out from the other recruits who all, sooner or later, take off their gas masks and give up their defence of Mozart as a great composer.

Tolstoi plays the part of Figaro, and addresses the phrase 'Count, you seem to like my wife' to Radlov in the scene immediately preceding his attack. He snatches a bow from a violinist and hits the General, injuring his ear in a fashion which is not unlike that of a bad barber, as if he has 'shaved' the General's ear off. Tolstoi later works as a barber in Siberia where he has a place in the world and has found his path in life, which is humble but honest. While he cuts hair, the 'barber' wreaks destruction on a larger scale. Indeed, hair plays an important part throughout the film. Tolstoi has his head shaved before he is sent to Siberia, while Andrew's head is half shaven before the incident where the commander criticises the portrait of Mozart that hangs over Andrew's bed (mistaking the composer for a 'dame') and makes the recruits put on gas masks, which will be removed only if they agree that they 'don't give a shit about Mozart'. Radlov has problems with his thinning hair; he even consults a hair implant specialist, which is actually a trap set up by Jane to compromise him in case she cannot charm Radlov into supporting McCracken in front of the Grand Duke, but to no avail. His baldness is a sign of his vanity, though, and does not have the same implications as the shaving of heads. It is also, in his case, associated with impotence, which he tries to disguise through wearing a wig, and socially covers up by having Tolstoi read his proposal to Jane. The cutting of hair is an unnatural procedure, as is the cutting of trees by the 'barber'. In the context of one of the reforms in Peter the Great's programme of westernisation, which required the shaving of all civil servants' long beards, shaving may be seen as particularly 'unnatural' to Russians, who advocate instead the growth of hair, beards, and forests as a question of 'nationalist' pride.

The space of the city consists largely of the interiors of houses, while external views of streets normally show enclosed architectural spaces such as fences, courtyards and the Kremlin walls, which reveal the oppressive atmosphere of the city. This cityscape contrasts with the vast, open space of the Siberian forests, filmed from an aerial perspective and providing a visual frame for the film at the beginning and the end. The entire plot is set in Moscow, rather than in St Petersburg, the capital of the Russian Empire, with the exception of the final episode in Siberia and the interludes at the US base. It was in Moscow that foreigners like McCracken were developing new inventions for Russia. Life in the city offers distractions, and is characterised by social activity. It contrasts sharply with the wide forests of Siberia. In the end McCracken takes his invention to the provinces: to conquer Russian lands, to destroy Russian nature, just as Jane had destroyed Tolstoi's life. In the final analysis, Jane has destroyed the possibility of her own happiness as well as Tolstoi's life, and McCracken has 'wasted' ten years of his life on a machine that brings destruction and scares the inhabitants of the *taiga*. Characters are contrasted, though these contrasts are not simply black and white, but complicated and differentiated. The theme of the destruction of nature offers a larger dimension to the intrusion of Jane's values into Tolstoi's life. Destruction begins on the level of human values and ends with ecological disaster. Thus Mikhalkov moves from a concern with the individual to a larger scale, investigating the significance of human actions for the world at large and thereby creating a link between the individual and the global, the urban and the provincial, east and west, past and present.

The Barber of Siberia offers a moral statement in asserting the necessity of having principles, and it presents a positive hero with the potential to instil hope in contemporary Russian audiences. The film is also a commodity for export, designed to boost the image of Russia as a nation with high ideals, unwilling to compromise, and with a strong leadership. By using national and international stars, and by breaking the linear development of the plot through Jane's narrative voice, the film provides room for development and reflection, love intrigues and comedy, the portrayal of national rituals along with a foreign response to them. The film is simultaneously past and future, objective and subjective, national and international, a film that attempts to create a myth for audiences at home and abroad in a manner modelled on that of Hollywood. In a speech to the Fourth Congress of Film-makers in May 1998, Mikhalkov said:

> Have many of our fellow countrymen been in the USA? I imagine some five per cent; maybe even less, three per cent. Yet do many people know about the USA? Almost everybody does. But they know the America that the cinema has shown them. America has forced the world to perceive it through cinema.   (In *Iskusstvo kino*, 8, 1998)

In *The Barber of Siberia* he is clearly striving to offer an idealised view of Russia to foreign audiences and to create a 'myth' on similar lines.

As a political manifesto the film contains a strange nationalistic statement for the future of Russia, envisaging the resurrection of absolute rule and discipline which would reinstate a value system and thus benefit the Russian population. This has struck a chord with Russian audiences who love the film. As a commercial product this 'Russian *Titanic*' attempts to sell to western audiences the 'product Russia' as a country which may have strange traditions, but has sound principles of trust, honour and reliability. As an artistic product, it bears comparison with epics such as *Gone with the Wind* (1939) and it is filmed by Pavel Lebeshev, one of the most talented cameramen in Russia, in a brave attempt to market a Russian film in western style, and to show the world what a beautiful country Russia is.

References and Suggestions for Further Reading

Attwood, Lynne (ed.) 1993: *Red Women on the Silver Screen: Soviet Women and Cinema from the Beginning to the End of the Communist Era*. London: Pandora.

Berry, E. and Miller-Pogacar, A. (eds) 1995: *Re-Entering the Sign*. Ann Arbor, MI: University of Michigan Press.

Beumers, Birgit (ed.) 1999: *Russia on Reels: The Russian Idea in Post-Soviet Cinema*. London: I. B. Tauris.

Condee, Nancy (ed.) 1995: *Soviet Hieroglyphics: Visual Culture in Late Twentieth-Century Russia*. Bloomington, IN, and London: Indiana University Press.

Freidin, Gregory (ed.) 1993: *Russian Culture in Transition*. Palo Alto, CA: Stanford University Press.

Horton, Andrew and Brashinsky, Michael 1991: *The Zero-Hour: Glasnost and Soviet Cinema in Transition*. Princeton, NJ: Princeton University Press.

Kelly, C. and Shepherd D. (eds) 1998: *Russian Cultural Studies: An Introduction*. Oxford: Oxford University Press.

Lawton, Anna 1992: *Kinoglasnost*. Cambridge: Cambridge University Press.

Shalin, D. 1996: *Russian Culture at the Crossroads*. Oxford: Oxford University Press.

Credits

Director	Nikita Mikhalkov
Producer	Michel Seydoux
Production Company	TriTe (Russia) and Camera One (France)
Screenplay	Rustam Ibragimbekov, Nikita Mikhalkov
Editor	Enzo Meniconi
Director of Photography	Pavel Lebeshev
Art Director	Vladimir Murzin
Music	Eduard Artemiev

Cast

Julia Ormond	Jane Callaghan
Oleg Menshikov	Andrei Tolstoi
Richard Harris	Douglas McCracken
Alexei Petrenko	General Radlov
Vladimir Ilyin	Captain Mokin
Marat Basharov	Count Polievsky (cadet)
Nikita Tatarenkov	Prince Alibekov (cadet)
Georgi Dronov	Nazarov (cadet)
Artem Mikhalkov	Buturlin (cadet)
Daniel Olbrykhsky	Kopnovsky (McCracken's assistant)
Marina Neelova	Tolstoi's mother
Avangard Leontiev	Uncle Nikolai
Anna Mikhalkova	Dunia (maid)
Robert Hardy	Professor Forsten
Nikita Mikhalkov	Alexander III
Isabel Renault	Maria Fedorovna (Empress)
Filipp Dyachkov	Prince Mikhail (their son)
Evgeni Steblov	Grand Duke Alexei Alexandrovich

Filmography

Svoi sredi chuzhikh, chuzhoi sredi svoikh (*At Home among Strangers, a Stranger at Home* / *At Home among Strangers, Alone among Friends*, 1974)

Raba lubvi (*A Slave of Love*, 1975)

Neokonchennaya pyesa dlya mekhanicheskoovo pianino (*Unfinished Piece for a Mechanical Piano*, 1977)

Pyat' vecherov (*Five Evenings*, 1978)

Neskolko dnei iz zhizni I. I. Oblomov (*Oblomov* / *Several Days in the Life of I. I. Oblomov*, 1979)

Kinsfolk (1981)

Bez svidetelei (*A Private Conversation* / *Without Witnesses*, 1983)

Oci ciornie (*Dark Eyes*, 1987)

Autostop (1990)

Urga (*Urga: Territory of Love* / *Urga: Close to Eden*, 1991)

Anna 6–18 (1993)

Utomlennye solntsem (*Burnt by the Sun*, 1994)

Sibirskii tsiriul'nik (*The Barber of Siberia*, 1998)

Notes on the Contributors

Birgit Beumers is Lecturer in Russian at the University of Bristol. She is an authority on Russian cinema, theatre and culture post-1945, author of *Yury Lyubimov at the Taganka Theatre* (1997) and editor of *Russia on Reels: The Russian Idea in Post-Soviet Cinema* (1999).

Derek Duncan is Senior Lecturer in Italian at the University of Bristol. He has published widely on issues of gender in twentieth-century Italian fiction and is co-editing a book on European travel-writing. His book *Masculinity and National Identity in Italy* will be published soon.

Jill Forbes is Professor of French at Queen Mary and Westfield, University of London. She is an international authority on French cinema and author of many publications in the field including *The Cinema in France: After the New Wave* (1992) and *Les Enfants du paradis* (1997).

Annella McDermott is Lecturer in Hispanic Studies at the University of Bristol. She has wide-ranging interests in the fields of Spanish cinema and literature and has recently published, with Margaret Tull Costa, *The Dedalus Book of Spanish Fantasy* (1999).

Sarah Street is Senior Lecturer in Film and Television Studies at the University of Bristol. A distinguished authority on British cinema, her publications include *Cinema and State: The Film Industry and the Government, 1927–84* (1985, co-authored with Margaret Dickinson), *British National Cinema* (1997) and the forthcoming *British Cinema in Documents* (2000).

Stuart Taberner is Lecturer in German at the University of Leeds. He has published on Günter Grass, Uwe Johnson, Martin Walser, Monika Maron and Stefan Heym, as well as on German film, and is currently working on the writing of younger German authors in the years since unification in 1990.

Index of Film Titles

General Index